The Boundless Sea

The Boundless Sea

Self and History

沖廣

GARY Y. OKIHIRO

UNIVERSITY OF CALIFORNIA PRESS

University of California Press, one of the most
distinguished university presses in the United
States, enriches lives around the world by
advancing scholarship in the humanities, social
sciences, and natural sciences. Its activities are
supported by the UC Press Foundation and by
philanthropic contributions from individuals and
institutions. For more information, visit www
.ucpress.edu.

University of California Press
Oakland, California

Library of Congress Cataloging-in-Publication Data

Names: Okihiro, Gary Y., 1945– author.
Title: The boundless sea : self and history / Gary Y.
    Okihiro.
Description: Oakland, California : University of
    California Press, [2019] | Includes bibliographical
    references and index. |
Identifiers: LCCN 2019010296 (print) |
    LCCN 2019012913 (ebook) | ISBN 9780520973886
    (ebook) | ISBN 9780520309661 (cloth : alk. paper) |
    ISBN 9780520309654 (pbk. : alk. paper)
Subjects: LCSH: Asian Americans—Biography. |
    United States—History—Philosophy.
Classification: LCC E184.A75 (ebook) |
    LCC E184.A75 O379 2019 (print) |
    DDC 305.895/073—dc23
LC record available at https://lccn.loc
.gov/2019010296

Manufactured in the United States of America

28 27 26 25 24 23 22 21 20 19
10 9 8 7 6 5 4 3 2 1

To
Marina Amparo Henríquez

For
Gifting Me Life Anew

CONTENTS

ILLUSTRATIONS

Mere months before her tragic murder on August 17, 2006, Masumi Hayashi agreed to take my portrait for the cover of this book. Masumi and I were born in 1945; she was just over a month older. Like me, she was a Bruin, having attended UCLA. She was a professor at Cleveland State University, and that is where our resemblance ends. Masumi was an amazing, award-winning photographer.

Masumi Hayashi was born in the Gila River concentration camp in Arizona the day after Japan signed the surrender instrument that ended World War II. She grew up in the largely African American Watts area of Los Angeles, and graduated from the neighborhood's David Starr Jordan High School. She entered UCLA and then transferred to Florida State University, where she received her bachelor's degree in 1975 and a master's degree two years later. She was a teacher and an artist, whose works garnered prizes and awards. Public and private collections in the United States, Japan, Great Britain, and Germany include her creations.

From his studies in American studies at UC Santa Cruz, my son Colin called my attention to the extraordinary work of Masumi Hayashi. What drew me to Masumi's photographs were her panoramic montages, which, she wrote, reflected her "social and historical consciousness."[1] Masumi began at the horizon line, taking photographs in a horizontal circular motion until she completed 360 degrees. She then angled upward, continuing the same circular rotation until she captured the entire space around her. At her studio, Masumi and her assistants arranged the individual, printed photographs into a montage. The resulting photomontages range from 100 to 540 degree rotations, and they consist of as many as 140 individual photographs and as few as five.

Masumi's photomontages, accordingly, represent three-dimensional space on two-dimensional paper. They are hauntingly beautiful, the colors, composition, and changing light. No single photograph taken of a place in time can possibly capture the totality of complex, changing phenomena. Indeterminacy is a state of being. Masumi's photomontages represent discrete spaces at different moments in time pieced together in a grand summation of space / time. Her multiverse haunts, especially because of the horror of the places Masumi photographed—toxic waste dumps, abandoned prisons, postindustrial rubble, and the US concentration camps. Those sinister, human remains Masumi lovingly depicts as places of intense, aching beauty. "We see the surface," she observed, "but there is something beyond the surface."[2]

The shadow of her camera set on a tripod is a frequent feature of her photomontage landscapes. Masumi's presence, as shadow, occupies the space / time of her artwork, revealing a commitment and affiliation.

Masumi,
you move to the infinite multiverses of space / time.

The author, as shadow, on lava. Kalapana, Hawai'i, 2013. Photo by Gary Y. Okihiro, after Masumi Hayashi.

ACKNOWLEDGMENTS

In the uncanny realm of literature, Lisa Yun and Elda Tsou held my hand and led me toward memoir and poetry. Countless colleagues indulged my enthusiasm for breaking the narrative form with poetry and prosody, I recall, made mellow by fine wine. On translation, my Columbia graduate research assistant Adam Spry gathered and annotated the salient, theoretical scholarship, and my dear Marina A. Henríquez introduced me to the indefatigable Lydia Juliana Ama de Chile when she and a delegation from El Salvador visited Columbia University. My old friends from Botswana, Teresa Rantao Ogle and James Ogle, helped me with a 1975 recording of the rainmaker Timpa Mosarwa. Teresa transformed that oral text, not heard for nearly thirty years, into writing.

While the archives in England and Scotland supplied useful outsiders' views of Botswana and southern Africa, Batswana oral historians generously provided me with alternative perspectives and understandings of their finely textured social formation in motion. Especially helpful were Nkwane Gaealafshwe and Magatelo Mokgoko, both of Goo-Ra-Tshosa, and my translator, Selebatso G. Masimega, a local schoolteacher and politician.

I am grateful to Taira Tsugiko of the Haebaru Town Museum on Okinawa Island for organizing the student poster contest on Yonaguni Island; to my valued colleague and research companion Wesley Ueunten for our visits to Kudaka, Ishigaki, and Yonaguni islands; and to my wonderful colleagues at the University of the Ryūkyūs, Yamazato Katsunori and Akamine Masanobu. Akamine sensei, with his considerable knowledge, offered us historical lessons as we walked around Kudaka Island. Yamazato sensei translated my Yonaguni Island origin story from English into Japanese, and Yoneshiro Megumu edited his translation. Takai Shiho of Columbia University copied Yamazato sensei's edited text for inclusion in this book.

At San Francisco State University, I am grateful for the generous help of Special Collections reference specialist Meredith Eliassen, and colleagues Dan Gonzales, Jason Ferreira, and Wesley Ueunten. James Garrett and Jim Hirabayashi, the first dean of San Francisco State's School of Ethnic Studies, were helpful with their recollections of the 1968 strike.

John Cheng and I conversed and corresponded about space / time, and he proposed "Event Horizon" as the title for this book. The edge of a black hole—John, the historian of science fiction, observed—was evocative and appropriate for my interest in locating and warping history (space / time). There, at the edge, light cannot emerge beyond the horizon because of the intense, gravitational pull of the black hole. Sometimes referred to as the point of no return, the event horizon seems much too final and certain for my taste.

Michael Omi accompanied me on a field trip from the Bay Area to the college on the mountains. Although I knew the back roads of Napa Valley like the back of my hand, I got lost taking the old Howell Mountain Road but we eventually found our way. When we arrived on campus, to my great astonishment, Irwin Hall, the distinctive face of Pacific Union College for generations, was gone. I asked two passing students about the hall's disappearance, and they pointed us to what they knew as Irwin Hall, which turned out to be the mere back of the original structure. The history department, in which I majored, was still there, and on the wall of a staircase was a photograph of my graduating class. There I was, surveying the scurrying students who passed oblivious to my stares. Michael snapped a picture of the picture on the wall, and circulated it in amusement to show me as I appeared in 1967.

My wife, Marina, has been a constant companion on my travels for this book. We walked the beach on Kudaka Island and cursed the US fighter jets as they screamed across the Okinawan skies, drove to the magnificent stands of redwoods just north of Arcata, trod gently on the sacred lava fields and concentration camp at Tule Lake, visited with children in Izalco, and restored our health in Asochimi lands and hot springs. It was she who chose our home site on Pele's land, amidst amazing ōʻhia trees with their bright red, plump lehua blossoms, which embody the volcano's sister, Hiʻiaka, the gentle one. I intend to spend my final days in the embrace of that deity of healing and regeneration.

Introduction

The Boundless Sea 沖廣: *Self and History,* the final installment of my trilogy on space / time, follows in the wake of *Island World* (2008) and *Pineapple Culture* (2009), all published with my great gratitude by the University of California Press and editor Niels Hooper.[1] Unlike the expanding spaces of islands and continents of *Island World* and the tropical and temperate zones of *Pineapple Culture, The Boundless Sea* is a spatial collapse into the subject-self, but also about the writing of history and history's subjects, capacious quarters to be sure.

The trilogy, in its consideration of space / time, writes against normative, natural distinctions between space and time and assumptions such as the linear march of time from the past to the present and future orchestrated by periodization and the narrative form, and the management of discrete spaces, including nations, continents, and world regions. That ordering of space / time as a flexing of power is an imperial exercise and is foundational to the social sciences broadly and to history peculiarly. I explore that contention in the first two volumes, and continue that interrogation in this, the third.

At stake here is the power to name, classify, assign attributes, and rank, arising from the binary and hence hierarchical relations of the self as set against its other. Although mutually constituted and constituting, the immediate, manly continental self positions itself against its remote, feminine island other, while the civilized, manly, temperate race measures itself against its figured savage, feminine, tropical racialized others. Geographical and biological determinisms underwrite both the myth of continents and races, genders, and sexualities while imperialism and colonization, aspects of nationalism and capitalism, animate those discourses, materializing fictions of the mind.

HISTORICAL FORMATION

Historical formation and, in this volume, the memoir form are the methods by which I transgress the conventions and disciplines of history's time and space. I conceive of historical formations as space / time, indeterminate, simultaneous and expansive, in process and relational, as oral history or conversations between speaker and listener, author and reader, and as poetics and the spoken word, "talk story,"[2] rather than the penned narrative form.

Subject-position is critical in that mobile exchange, the distinction between voicing and hearing is blurred, authorship is suspect, and meanings not structures comprise the memorable and important. The formation is visually a montage, conversationally, an ensemble of discrete utterances particular to place and time, and discursively, a dialogical engagement and a moving conversation back and forth, side by side. It is important to note that this history, then, is a formation or a structure and a process, namely forms and relations in the making.

Historical formations, moreover, are like certain forms of women's self-writing, including testimonios, which are often told in relation to others and are introspective, nonlinear, and fragmented, a performance at odds with imperial dictations of authority and order from apparent lawless disorder.[3] At the same time, women's accounts as well as testimonies of silenced and marginalized individuals and groups are emphatic presences when seen against their spectral absences in the world of letters and the public sphere, and they can speak against subjection within the discursive sites of power.

In those senses, as a literary form and an intervention in power and its manifestations, I deploy memoir and the imagination to situate my subject-self and history.

Moreover, like new historicism that blurs the distinction between the literary and nonliterary, experience (discourse) and the archive (the material),[4] my use of memoir and the imagination arises from my belief that fiction and nonfiction, the subjective and objective, memoir and history are borderless and, in fact, history is memoir insofar as the historian's shadow lurks behind history's texts and memoir is history. Similarly, the body and mind, female and male, experience and theory binaries are false, because they are relational and mutually constituted, constituting. Phenomenology's experience is a way of knowing, an epistemology of the body as well as the mind.

The centrality of language and ideology—discourse—must not be missed in this, my consideration of my subject-self and my life's work. Although the subject cannot simply be a variant of discourse, as Michel Foucault suggests, subjectivities are interpellations of discourse. History's narrative form emerges from those strictures of language and ideology. In resistance, like Julia Kristeva's escape from Lacanian phallocentrism, I employ poetry and prosody, not as a prior, primordial condition but as a potential path to greater freedoms.[5] The semiotic is multivocal and disrupts the symbolic, as Kristeva points out, and rhythm, stress, pitch, intonation, and acoustic qualities defy encoding by vocabulary and grammar. As conversations, talk story and oral history can intervene in imperial history and restore a measure of dignity to the oppressed, "the wretched of the earth," my discursive communities.

Contradictions abound. Despite my claim to orality, this text appears in written form. My method of writing, nonetheless, involves multiple oral readings of my words. I write; then, I vocalize. I listen and rewrite. I must hear my words to feel their cadence and timbre, their song. I repeat the process, again and again, day after day. In that sense, this text, though a writing, is also a voicing not unlike my hearing of music, sounds produced and consumed by human bodies.[6] Before language, I felt the music's pulsating beats; before speech, I learned its meanings.

I realize that my use of tenses—past, present, and future—endorses a language of time. While writing against a linear construction of time, I deploy its language. I understand that those who subscribe to the reality of the past, present, and future might see them as temporal dimensions with nonrelational properties that change with the passage of time, which is essentially a spatial construct.[7] By contrast, I conceive of time as tenseless, despite my use of tenses, and conceive of space / time as relational and indeterminate, quantum approximations. In addition, while I write in the present, I agree with the feminist philosopher Elizabeth Grosz's critique of that privileging of the here and now, and aspire to direct temporality toward the unattainable, unknowable future.[8]

Watching Japanese television in Tokyo during the summer of 2008, my wife, Marina, and I witnessed the unfolding of time / space. In what the show's producers called a "simulcast," interviewers in Japan questioned Japanese residents in Brazil on the one-hundredth anniversary of Japanese migration to Brazil. Space was made manifest through presence, the materiality of Japan and Brazil, and time was evident in the understanding that the evening show in Japan featured Brazilians who were up early in the morning to appear on the program. Their bleary eyes and throaty voices testified to that time difference. Space was apprehended through time in that there were pregnant pauses between the questions asked in Japan and the answers given in Brazil. The microseconds required between question and answer told us there was distance involved. That commonsense, seamless connection between space and time in our everyday experience points to the mutually constituting and relational aspects of space / time.

THE HISTORIAN

I recognize voicing or writing oneself into history, whether as memoir or testimonio, can devolve into a whine or a boast. Moreover, self-writing can be of little moment to others. Herein, thus, I consider my subject-self in relation to my others and not as humanism's solitary, preeminent "I am." Additionally, my choice of stories and my telling of them reveal as much about those histories as about the historian. Despite denials to the contrary, histories bear the imprint of the historian located in space / time. In that sense, history is autobiography, and autobiography is history. To navigate your way through *The Boundless Sea*, thus, consider this intellectual autobiography of who I think I am at this writing.

Nearly forty years ago, I began to reflect on and direct my life of labor. Books were traces of presence, I believed. Ever since graduate school, I loved roaming the bookshelves of research libraries in search of titles that intrigued me. Drawn was I to old, dusty covers that were never checked out. For fifty or more years, I'd marvel, no human eyes danced across these pages. Eureka! I'd exclaim, I've discovered and revived this author and text. They came to life anew through my magical powers. The uncanny. Incantations.

In the quiet of the morning, I'd sit with my coffee contemplating my life's work. For years, it was a delicious daily observance. If we can assume a productive professional life of forty years, if lucky, and five to seven years for the completion of a single book, eight titles were the totality of that lifetime, a humbling figure and acknowledgment. To start, I settled on the subject of resistance as my unique contribution to scholarship. The theme of resistance came from African history wherein resistance signified both centering Africans and recognizing their agency, their ability of make history.

My graduate education was a product of my times—the late 1960s—that for me involved prominently Viet Nam and black power. I decided on my specialization, African history, before the founding of Asian American studies, and I left for a three-year sojourn in southern Africa during the formative years of

Introduction

ethnic studies, from 1968 to 1971. When I returned to resume my graduate studies, UCLA's Asian American Studies Center had just begun, and I joined the first cohort of graduate students in Asian American studies in the country. My graduate training was principally in African history, southern Africa in particular, but I also read in US labor and African American history, and my minor areas extended to historical linguistics and economic anthropology.

Although unclear to me at the time, my graduate education that appeared to be hopelessly disparate cohered through a particular logic. The received paradigm of Eurocentrism dominated both fields of study—African and US history. Deeds of European people, especially "great men," loomed large on those paradigmatic historical landscapes, and periodization and historical activity pivoted upon the articulation of Europeans with non-Europeans. In fact, before Europe, according to some ardent defenders of the faith, there was no history, only the "unrewarding gyrations of barbarous tribes in pic- turesque but irrelevant corners of the globe," in the choice words of British imperial historian Hugh Trevor-Roper.

Pivoting on the European, African history is periodized as precolonial, colonial, and independent (postcolonial) Africa, and Asian American his- tory as immigration, contact and interaction, competition and conflict, and inclusion. The first systematic studies of Africa were by anthropologists as specialists of primitive peoples and not sociologists or political scientists who studied advanced societies, and thus reflective of a racist division of intellectual labor. The science of primordial humanity was an imperial project by naming, classifying, describing, and ranking peoples and socie- ties as measured against their unnamed subject-selves. Likewise, US (Chi- cago) sociology viewed Asians as a nuisance to the majority group—styled "the Oriental problem"—insofar as the racialized markings of Asians (and Africans) resisted easy erasure and absorption through cultural assimilation. For those consensus scholars, homogeneity delimited the parameters of the national identity whereas diversity threatened its integrity.

The post–World War II anticolonial, antiracist struggles of the Third World paralleled and intersected with the domestic US aspirations for self-determination. Those, of course, were merely the modern phases of some four hundred years of contestations over imperialism and colonialism as discourse and material relations, but they informed my consciousness and identifications. Carter Woodson lamented the "mis-education of the Negro" in 1933, and Cheik Anta Diop in his *Nation negres et cultur* published in 1954 scored the "colonial mentality" of French assimilation and advanced an African history and culture. At the 1965 International Congress of African Historians held significantly in Dar es Salaam, Tanzanian president Julius Nyerere acknowledged the contributions of non-African scholars, but expressed the ardent desire of Africans to represent and understand themselves for their national development.

Three years later, Terence Ranger, historian of Africa and a leading figure in the "Dar es Salaam school," insisted on the primacy of African agency conceptualized as resistance and its links between proto-nationalist and nationalist movements. In that same year in the fall of 1968, students at San Francisco State and UC Berkeley formed the Third World Liberation Front and demanded, among other things, a curriculum and pedagogy for liberation. They conceived of themselves as members of the Third World insurgent masses enjoined in the historic global resistance struggles of anticolonialism and antiracism.

I am a child of that intellectual ferment and coupling. I emerge from that convergence of Afrocentrism (in the way I describe it above, not in its present US parlance) and Third World studies. I am a conflict, not a consensus, historian. I see consensus as a variety of functionalism and, as such, incapable of explaining change. I prefer analysis to description, and look for patterns that help to explain the social and historical formations. I foreground individuals, but simultaneously situate them within their wider social contexts, especially within the means and relations of production. But I am not a structuralist, and although I rely upon theory to frame and explain history, I insist upon evidence, including experience, to sustain the argument.

I harbor romantic notions about the masses and ordinary people, but I also recognize the limits of historical and social consciousness and their efficacy and am impressed with the power and ubiquity of oppression and the ingenuity of the ruling classes to change the forms and contents of control and exploitation. I am by sentiment and conviction a historical materialist insofar as I see the provisioning function and the means and relations of production as foundational, but I do not hold an overdetermined notion of class relations or see the formations of race, gender, and sexuality as false consciousness or mystification. I subscribe to the theory of social formation that is inclusive of material production that interpellates and is constituted by the social constructions and manifestations of race, gender, sexuality, class, and nation.

And finally, in terms of explanation, I employ the dialogical relations[9] of oppression and exploitation and resistance, or the curtailment of agency and the expropriation of land and labor against the ideas and deeds of subordinate classes directed at their liberation. The model is historical in that it accommodates movement and change and is not a closed or equilibrating system; it endows the oppressed and exploited agency while taking seriously structured relations of dependency; it distinguishes, in conflict terms, the histories of majorities from minorities (defined by power, not numbers) and connects the histories of the oppressed—African, Asian, and Native Americans, Latinxs, women, queers, workers, and aliens (documented and undocumented); and it is rooted in historical materialism and social formation.

In sum, I approach my life's work—African history and Asian American and Third World studies—in much the same way. I seek to recover pasts that have been neglected and distorted, articulate them from the perspectives of the oppressed for the purposes of accuracy but also for their empowerment. In turn, those theoretical and political positions have bearings upon my methodologies. To recuperate the consciousness and acts of people not inclined to leave written records, to give voice to voices unheard, I rely on oral history and the imagination and experience. Still, I agree with the historian Joan Scott's criticism of privileging experience over theory, and reject unproblematized, uncontested renderings of experience. And while I believe in self-representation, I endorse the argument by philosopher Linda Alcoff that we, scholars, can and must speak for others, our subjects.[10] Those influences, I surmise, you will find in my work.

The Boundless Sea is likely the last book on my list. After thirteen (not eight) titles, I have come to the end of my life's work. The prospect frightens and confuses. My discipline, which required four hours each day save Sunday for writing, was my life, my passion. My mother died mere weeks short of her 101st year, but to me she died years before her body expired. She existed, not lived, waiting, waiting for her final rest. Most of her hours she spent in bed, dreaming of the world to be. In death, she has been resurrected to her former self, her truer self, I know, and she lives in my writings and in your readings.

THE SUBJECTS

The Boundless Sea is a memoir and history and the writing of history. The subject-self and historiography, accordingly, are the subjects of this my final work. The book is divided into two parts: Part One, Subject-Self, represents the historian through his maternal grandmother, obāban, chapter 1; his mother, okāsan, chapter 2; and his father, otōsan, chapter 3. Part Two, Subjects, draws from the historian's lifetime of labor, including his first major project and a work begun but not completed: Tule Lake, chapter 4; Third World studies, chapter 5; Botswana, chapter 6; and History, chapter 7. A brief word about the subjects: Tule Lake began as a book-length study to build on my earlier work on religion and resistance at that concentration camp;[11] Third World studies was originally researched and written for this book but comprises instead a portion of a chapter in my *Third World Studies* (2016); and Botswana draws from my dissertation research and book, *A Social History of the Bakwena* (2000), the best researched and least known of my books.

Chapter 1, "Black Stream," a current of life, is obāban, my maternal grandmother and a central founding figure in my subjectivity. Okinawa Island is the site of my origins and thus ancestral devotions. The Ryūkyūs, reviled by some Japanese writers as "South Sea Islands" and its people as "Japan kanakas," instead insightfully offer scant comfort amidst shifting grounds, restless seas, and plentiful transplantations, in timeless constancy denying a permanent sense of place. That condition recalls the astute observation of the twelfth-century monk Hugo of St. Victor, cited in my *Island World:* "The person who finds his homeland sweet is still a tender beginner; he to whom every soil is as his native one is already strong; but he is perfect to whom the entire world is as a foreign place."

"Self," chapter 2, is my mother, okāsan, another mainstay of my subject-self. Herein I recount coming of age on a sugar plantation in Hawai'i, and trace the primary source of my education to plantation pedagogy. Cane fields foreshortened my range of vision, and the plantation's relations of production located my subject-position within their hierarchies of race and ethnicity, gender, sexuality, class, and nation. Escape from the mundane testified to the efficacy of historical agency, while mis-education cultivated a colonial mentality, which enervated and dulled a critical consciousness. Large-scale land expropriation from native people and migrant laborers, mainly people of color, enabled the imperial plantation, which was a prominent feature of global capitalism's career and spread. I am a member of that community of plantation laborers who once circled the earth's tropical band. Plantation pedagogy produces the subject I think I am, and interpellates, in resistance, my affiliations and identifications.

My father, otōsan, is the subject of chapter 3 in his various, changing forms, bodies (kino lau). "Naturalizations" name the processes by which migrating species become native, aliens become citizens. Some 30 million years ago, terrestrial biota traveled the currents of air and water from Asia and America to Pele's creation mid-Pacific. Having survived that immense crossing against incredible odds failed to ensure the naturalization of those life forms on islands where additional challenges awaited them. People of color, like my father's parents, found fields poisoned by white supremacy. From 1790 to 1952, naturalization in the United States was restricted to "free white persons," while in Hawai'i by contrast, Hi'iaka's gentle, healing touch moderated Pele's fires and nudged algae, mosses, ferns, and lichens to spread and thrive over the cooling lava.

"Extinctions," chapter 4, centers on the watered, fertile Tule Lake Basin, which was a place of life abundant and a terminus and killing ground, testing the wills of people for their right to exist. On the northeastern side of the life-giving waters rose a concentration camp for Japanese Americans, and on the lake's southwestern shore flowed the Lava Beds where Kintpuash and his Modoc band waged a war of survival against the depredations of white settlers and the US Army. There, in the abandoned and littered sites of cultural and physical extinction, I saw the ghosts of my ancestors consorting with the spirits of their forebears, American Indians, in the nearby lava fields, which comprise a segment of the "ring of fire" that connects America with Asia.

Chapter 5, "Third World," opens with "the problem of the twentieth century," the creation of the global color line as was first articulated by the African American scholar and activist W. E. B. Du Bois. Colonialism, or the exploitation of the lands and peoples of the "darker races" justified by the discourses of religion and science, produced European empires and their counter, Third World poverty and movements for self-determination and antiracism. Anticolonial intellectuals like Frantz Fanon and Albert Memmi denounced the erasure of the colonized from history, and they urged the restoration of "a whole and free man" and "a new humanity—a new humanism." Within that context, students of the Third World Liberation Front

(TWLF) at San Francisco State enjoined that Third World revolution. "Our goal is Third World Power," they declared. "Our essence is a New World Consciousness of oppressed peoples." The TWLF's demand for liberation comprises my generation's cause and directs my intellectual and political labors.

"Antipodes," chapter 6, reflects upon the geographical alignment of Hawaiʻi, the tropical islands of my physical birth, with Botswana, the landlocked, largely desert nation of my intellectual genesis. That apparent spatial opposition reflected the contrasting notions of history held by my Western-educated self and my African teachers who labored to free me from my imperious project, an economic history of the people who dance to the crocodile (ba bina kwena). Moving from island to continent, the northern to southern hemisphere required a radical recalibration of my space / time and a thorough unlearning of history and my assumptions of self and society. Only then was I afforded a fleeting glimpse of the time / space of my African other.

My world, my subject-self and subjects, begins along the imaginary color line marking the edges of the tropical and temperate zones, the Tropic of Cancer to the equator's north and the Tropic of Capricorn to its south. Cutting across the Ryūkyū chain and the Hawaiian archipelago, the Tropic of Cancer marks the sun's zenith north while its southern reach, the Tropic of Capricorn, meanders through Botswana. Those latitudes locate dividing lines and shared spaces that are relationally dependent, and they mark my subject-positions, liminally and multiply situated, emerging from islands and continents in the tropical and temperate zones.

"History," the final chapter, reflects upon the writing of the subject-self into history and, therewith, society and the choices made in that assignment and articulation. Moreover, I have chosen to posit and advance the idea of historical formation by deconstructing the polarities of space and time, islands and continents, tropical and temperate zones, historian and historical subjects, together with the binaries of race, gender, sexuality, class, and nation. Those projects, my life's work, arise from my antipathy toward a plantation and colonial education and mentality and their oppressive designs. More discretely, I refuse history's disciplining of its wonderfully perverse and intractable subjects, humans—"the oppressed"—with the power to liberate themselves through a poetics of time / space.[12]

Subject–Self

CHAPTER ONE

Black Stream

(Obāban)

Islands, like debris deposited along the curving bank of a vast river, the Kūrōshio or "black stream," trace the peaks named the Ryūkyūs. Their summits rise along the eastern fringes of the Eurasian tectonic plate in a gentle bending arc and, fastened to the earth's mantle, they press southward against the northward thrust of the Indian-Australian plate and eastward, contesting the westward probing of the Pacific plate.[1] Marine life—corals, seaweeds, mollusks, and fishes—percolating in the fecund Indo-West Pacific, navigate Oceania's surging courses to anchor, settle, and make homes in Ryūkyūan waters to become indigenous. Those spatial and temporal formations of land and sea and their biotic communities, both alien and native, and their activities distinguish the discursive and material contours of what we now call Okinawa.

Situated at the tip of that triangle of oceanic life, the Ryūkyūs form affiliations with Indonesia at one corner, the Philippines at the other, and all of the lands and waters hemmed therein. The islands' spread is even more capacious through mobilizations, which extend their reach beyond the Indo-West Pacific to the rest of Oceania and to the Eurasian continent and plate of which the islands form outposts along their easternmost frontier. Moreover, befitting its liminal location bordering two of earth's edges, the Eurasian and Pacific plates, and its geological ties with both Kyūshū to its north and Taiwan to its south, Okinawa, as a site of my origin, points in multiple directions and to mutable times. Thankfully, there is little comfort here, amidst shifting grounds, restless seas, and transplantations, in timeless constancy or a permanent sense of place.

My maternal grandmother, Chinen Kame, obāban, fled her bodily estate decades ago. Early last century, she left her mother on Okinawa Island, promising to return someday. She never saw her mother again, as far as I know, and her remains now rest between the sheer, green rise that is the Koʻolau mountain range, a former volcano, and the shimmering, teeming waters of Kaneohe Bay on the island of Oʻahu. Her views will take your breath away.

While lecturing at Nihon University in Mishima, Japan, during the summer of 2010, I was asked by a student if I was ever ashamed of my grandmother for having been a "picture bride" (shashin kekkon). The arrangement was common among the issei (first-generation Japanese in the United States) to circumvent US exclusion laws that made it difficult for Japanese women and workers to enter the US. Many white Americans, the student correctly noted, believed that picture and arranged marriages (matches made by parents) were immoral and uncivilized.

I told the class that my grandmother is the lehua blossom of the ʻōhiʻa tree that grows on the volcanic slopes of the cooler elevations. Sister of Pele, whose bodily form (kino lau) is the volcano and its manifestations, Hiʻiaka, a patron of the hula and a benevolent spirit, is the ʻōhiʻa tree, which hugs the contours of her sister's curving body. She is among the first plants to grow on the cooling rivers of lava. Her hot, bright-red lehua flowers bring joy, but upon their picking produce tears in the form of rain, which fall to the earth to inspire and nurture life anew. Hiʻiaka rides the black stream that flows deep and wide, bearing life abundant.

My grandmother is the lehua; her color is shamelessly red. Embarrassment is not an emotion resurrected by her memory. Only gratitude and

From her resting place, obāban's panorama, 2014. Photo by Gary Y. Okihiro.

The lehua, Hiʻiaka embodied, 2012. Photo by Gary Y. Okihiro.

admiration come to mind. I visit with obāban regularly on my hikes on the loop trail that begins at Keaīwa heiau,[2] a sacred site of healing, one of Hiʻiaka's arts, in the mountains above her ʻAiea home. On the trail along the mountain's spine grows a profusion of ʻōhiʻa trees, and at our home in Keaʻau on the Big Island, magnificent ʻōhiʻa stands with lehua blossoms soar above our acre of lava. My grandmother, like Hiʻiaka, is with me and comforts me still.

NATION / RACE[3]

I grew up believing I was Japanese. At least, that is what I was told. I was Japanese, my mother said, because my paternal grandparents were born in Japan before migrating to the islands of my birth, Hawaiʻi. Further, she continued, I was not Hawaiian like my friend Nelson nor was I Chinese like my neighbor Lionel; they looked different and ate weird food. You can visit their homes, she admonished, but don't eat the food. My father spoke mainly Japanese, when he spoke at all, while my maternal grandparents spoke Japanese with a distinctive Okinawan or Uchinanchu inflection sprinkled with salty Uchinaaguchi phrases, especially expletives. Secreted in their tonsu drawer and bedroom closet were dried sea snake, blackened by smoking, and a sanshin, a three-stringed instrument adorned with snake skin. The pungent scent and plaintive sound of Okinawa stayed within those sequestered quarters of the subject-self. Still, I was Japanese, they all taught me.

The modern nation-state, a European configuration of relatively recent vintage, was conceived of as coterminous with a people. That is, originally, conjured kinship or "blood" tracings delimited the members of a nation-community, and insofar as people constituted a nation, the nation defined the people who were commonly referred to as "races." In that way, we came to know the English race, the German race, and so forth; the very term "nation" derives from the Latin for "birth," indicating a common ancestry or descent and hence blood and thus race. Such mutual identity and identification is central to the idea of a nation / race, and as a creation of self (nation / race), it set and found itself against those the self was not, its others (other nations / races). Those ideas of nation / race assumed the natural order—timeless, universal, and absolute distinctions, which emerge from equally constant, certain, and peculiar others.

In reality, those inventions of nation / race are historical, arising in place and time—Europe and its Enlightenment—through human agency, and the borders of those inventions are fluid and under constant challenge and violation. Conquest and expansion altered those spatial and social margins, incorporating novel lands and diverse peoples not originally designated as community members. Migration likewise produced new subjects albeit not always equal or welcome. Indeed, those transgressions of place, together with the imperial expansion of the idea of the nation, expose the simplemindedness of the original formulation of an undivided, homogeneous nation and race.[4] Consider my identification with "Japan" and the "Japanese," along with their designations as a nation / race.

A founding history recounts that Japan was the homeland created for a race of people, the Japanese, who were descendants of Amaterasu Ōmikami, the sun goddess. As the fourteenth-century text *Jinnō Shōtōki* or *Records of the Legitimate Succession of the Divine Sovereigns* declared: "Japan is the divine country. The heavenly ancestor it was who first laid its foundations, and the Sun Goddess left her descendants to reign over it forever and ever." Japan was unique because it differed from "foreign" lands and peoples, its others. Japanese, another document explained, were originally "of one blood and one mind," forming the "Yamato race," and later, absorbed and subordinated others of alien "blood" became Japanese as subjects of the emperor.[5]

That version of its origin gained traction with the transformation of Japan into a modern, European nation-state—the kokutai (national polity). Earlier, following the Chinese worldview, kuni (country) referred to a local domain or region that was familiar and orderly in contrast with the foreign and disorderly outside that domestic sphere. But Western taxonomies and topographies enabled Japan to see a larger world, an array of competing nation-states and transnational races arranged in a hierarchy of merit, beauty, and worth—white Europeans, yellow Asians, black Africans, red Americans, and brown Pacific Islanders. Those European Enlightenment ideas were introduced to Japan by Westernizers such as Fukuzawa Yukichi in his *Sekai kunizukushi* (1869) or *Account of the Countries of the World.*[6]

Troubled by Russian expansion to its north in Kamchatka and the Kurile Islands and to its south by Europeans in China and Southeast Asia, Japan sought to delimit and consolidate its borders. Ezo or Ainu lands and the Ryūkyū Islands, formerly considered ikoku or "foreign countries" as listed in the *Wakan sansai zue* (1712) or *Japanese-Chinese Illustrated Encyclopaedia*, became parts of Japan as Hokkaido in 1869 and Okinawa prefecture ten years later. Further, assimilation or Japanization along with the suppression of Ainu and Uchinanchu languages and cultures became official policies of the Japanese state.[7]

Still, those of unrelated "blood" from the Ainu of Japan's northern frontier to the Uchinanchu of Japan's southern extremity stretched the physical area known as Japan and confounded the idea of its race, the (Yamato) Japanese. The former regime of discrimination based upon jinshu or physical type fell to the new order of Yamato minzoku or folk by the late Meiji period (1868–1912). Although different (and inferior), minzoku discourse held, Ainu and Okinawans were Japanese insofar as they shared a national (Yamato) history and culture. In the years leading to the reversion of Okinawa to Japan by the US occupiers, the myth of "Japonesia," as proposed by novelist Shimao Toshio in his *Japonesia no nekko* (1961), helped to suture those fractures at both ends of the reconstituted nation / race.[8] Japan, Shimao claimed, formed a unitary racial, linguistic, and cultural sphere from Hokkaido to Okinawa, giving rise to the Japanese who are distinctive from their kindred others in Indonesia, Melanesia, Micronesia, and Polynesia of the same, as some believe, Austronesian language family.[9]

Like the Meiji contexts of imperialism and national constitution, Shimao's Japonesia emerges from a contemporary condition of kokusaika or internationalization. Amidst an increasing traffic of labor, capital, and culture, including migration and language shifts, anxieties over loss of identity and distinctiveness can easily translate into political capital. Thus in a July 1985 speech, then prime minister Nakasone Yasuhiro claimed that Japan's eternal racial purity advanced an "intelligent society" whereas the mixed and colored populations of the United States could only produce a dull, superficial nation.[10] And the International Research Center for Japanese Culture or Nichibunken, established in 1987, bankrolled research projects devoted to the promotion and preservation of a singular Japanese culture. Accordingly, like the Kokugakusha or National Learning scholars of the eighteenth century who insisted upon Japan's pure essence undiluted by Chinese contaminants, twentieth-century intellectuals promoted state ideology to reach a popular consensus and commonsense.

Vexing, nonetheless, are the contradictions posed by those at the nation's fringes like the Ainu and their sustained movement for subjectivity, culture, and indigenous rights and the Okinawans and their resilient drive for self-determination, antimilitarism, and peace.[11] At the same time, subject peoples did not always resist their colonial condition, instead securing comfort and esteem in assimilation and mimicry. Thus, for instance, when the Fifth Industrial Exhibition in Osaka opened in 1903 with a display called "The House of Peoples" showing Koreans, Ainu, Taiwanese, and two Okinawan women being supervised by a Japanese man with a whip, some Okinawans expressed outrage because Okinawans, they insisted, were Japanese.[12]

Similarly, Ifa Fuyū (1876–1947), the "father of Okinawan studies" and a custodian of the Okinawa Prefectural Library, sought to redress the exclusion of Okinawan history and culture from Japanese discourses by grafting Ryūkyū's islands and peoples onto those of the Yamato trunk, contending that Okinawans were migrants from Kyūshū. That narrative can be traced to the Ryūkyūan historian Haneji Chōshū (1617–75), who cited language and race as indicative of a Japanese descent and a migration southward.[13] The discursive annexation and, in effect, subordination put forth by this brand of Okinawan studies sought to bestow redemption and esteem upon a conquered and subject kingdom and people.[14]

Both my maternal grandparents were reared in that Okinawa of the Meiji era, when the Japanese language was the sole medium of instruction in the schools to impart a "colonial mentality" to those subjects of imperial Japan. Implicit within that design, as was astutely dissected by anticolonial intellectuals such as Frantz Fanon and Albert Memmi,[15] were feelings of inferiority, shame, and even self-hatred among the colonized and of superiority, conceit, and prerogative among the colonizers. Those outcomes, they noted, were relentlessly created and related. Perhaps that was the root of my grandfather's distaste as a child for schooling, which was mandatory; he managed to escape that apparatus of the state because both he and his sister had the same names and she attended in his stead. Gender privilege, my grandfather enjoyed from an early age, but the debilities of race encumbered them both.

In the aftermath of World War I when it acquired some of Germany's holdings in the Marianas, including Palau and the Caroline and Marshall islands, Japan held them as strategic bases for its imperial ambitions. Those "South Sea Islands" gave rise in Japan to sciences of the tropics similar to European and US schools of tropical studies when their empires annexed the tropical band to their temperate homelands.[16] Anthropologists, biologists, medical researchers, and agricultural scientists visited the "South Seas" to study its lands and peoples and to see if Japanese bodies could adapt to the tropical sun, humidity, and heat. From 1914 to World War II, they studied societies and cultures, sexuality and pathology, and saw in their native, islander others measurable distinctions. Unlike the Japanese, they concluded, following the trail cut by

European discourses and sciences of the tropics, those kanakas were of inferior intelligence, sexually promiscuous, and lazy.[17] Still, even as those South Sea Islander others helped to constitute the Japanese subjectivity, Okinawans, as so-called "Japan kanaka," formed a link with those natives of the South Seas, revealing an unbroken line, a continuum along the spectrum of alleged difference between the contrived polarities of kanaka and Japanese.

Flight from one colonized island, Okinawa, to another, Hawai'i, failed to relax the bite of Japanese hegemony. In what became their adopted home, my maternal grandparents encountered and interacted with Japanese, called Naichi (insiders), by Uchinanchu. Their collective name, insiders, indicated their status in Meiji Japan's social hierarchy along with some of the attendant attitudes they widely held.[18] A Naichi student in post–World War II Hawai'i recited Japan's prewar imperial script: "Japanese was first made up of the mainland only, but later included the island of Okinawa. Here was found an aboriginal type of people entirely different from the Japanese . . . [who] regarded them as inferior since they were not pure Japanese and believed them to be uncivilized due to their queer and vulgar culture." Another Naichi student recalled that her mother learned that Okinawans were more primitive (yaban) than the Japanese: "Look at their facial features," she pointed out as evidence. "They look like Malayans or Filipinos. Some of their dances with all the waving around seem very primitive and look like the Filipino kind. Even their dress seems bright."[19] Little wonder that my maternal grandparents hid their Uchinanchu selves within their cloistered bedroom, and they, perhaps to protect me, said I was simply and genuinely Japanese. To uncover what was deliberately hidden from or spruced up for the colonial gaze in versions of my grandparents' and Okinawa's past would require some sleuthing.

Tou nu yu kara, yamatu nu yu, yamatu nu yu kara, amerika yu. (From the Chinese world to the Japanese world, from the Japanese world to the American world.)[20] The Uchinaaguchi yu conjures both space and time in its meanings of world or society and era or historical period.

LOCATING OKINAWA

Mystification by outsiders might have begun with a history of China's Sui dynasty (589–618), the *Sui Shu*, which referrred to Liu-ch'iu (Ryūkyū) and Liu-ch'iu-kuo or Ryūkyū country. Apparently, the designation embraced both Okinawa and Taiwan, two islands off continental China peopled by non-Chinese or barbarians. In a probable attribution to Ryūkyūan women, the account described them as natives who "tattoo their hands with black ink, in insect and snake designs." Greater differentiation is offered by Japanese documents, which refer to islands now considered part of the Ryūkyūs as early as 616, and a record of a Japanese diplomat to China in 779 mentions Okinawa Island, so-named by its inhabitants.[21] On that island, by the middle of the fourteenth century after warfare and acquisition, arose three contending principalities: Hokuzan to the north, Chūzan in the middle, and Nanzan to the south.

King Satto (1349–95) flexed Chūzan's powers by extending his control beyond Okinawa to Miyako and Yaeyama islands and by building Shuri castle as the center of his domain. In 1372, Chūzan seized advantage over its rivals by submitting to Ming China (1368–1644) as a tributary state, thereby receiving diplomatic recognition from the most powerful polity in the region along with profitable trade relations across the China Sea. Although Okinawan traders at least since the mid-fourteenth century frequented ports in East and Southeast Asia, Ming China facilitated that traffic.[22] Following Chūzan's lead, Hokuzan and Nanzan became Chinese tributaries, and toward the end of the fourteenth century Chinese diplomats, merchants, and craftsmen settled in Kumemura near Naha. Beginning in 1392 and for nearly five hundred years, Okinawa sent students to the Chinese Imperial Academy.[23] In 1416, Chūzan annexed Hokuzan and in 1429, Nanzan.

The Satto dynasty ended in 1422 with the rise of Shō Hashi, who expanded trade with Japan, Korea, China, and Southeast Asia. Okinawa's commerce was considerable, starting with warehouses at Quanzhou and Fuzhou on the Fujian coast for tribute for China's rulers.[24] On Okinawa Island, Chinese diplomats and merchants in Kumemura recorded that traffic, indicating the reach of China into Okinawan affairs. Between 1425 and 1570, 104 ships left the island laden with sulfur and horses from Okinawa, silk, satin, iron and copperware, ceramics, and medicine from China, and swords, bows, armor, screens, fans, lacquerware, and gold from Japan; 58 sailed to Siam (Thailand), and the rest to places like Palembang (southeastern Sumatra), Sunda Kalapa (Jakarta), Samudra (northern Sumatra), Patani (a Siamese port in eastern Malaya), and Luzon (the Philippines).[25] They returned carrying pepper, wood, cloth, perfumes, and wines, which they resold in China, Japan, and Korea for enormous profits. Pepper, for instance, sold in China for 750 to 1,500 times its cost in Southeast Asia. Much of those gains went to the royal treasury, strengthening the hold of the Shuri or central government over regional lords and subjects.[26]

Indicative of the extent and nature of that commerce, the great temple bell at Shuri castle was inscribed in 1458 with the boast:

> Ryukyu kingdom is a superior land in the South Seas
> Gathering the cream of the three Korean states,
> Maintaining close relations with China and Japan.
> She is the Land of the Immortals,
> Gushing forth between these two states.
> Ships are a means of communication with all nations.
> The Kingdom is full of rare products and precious treasures.[27]

The trade declined after the sixteenth century when Portuguese ships from Macao and Chinese vessels supplanted Okinawa in the Indo-West Pacific (South Seas) carrying trade.

In the spring of 1609, Japan's Tokugawa Ieyasu authorized the Satsuma invasion and conquest of Okinawa. The kingdom fell, and King Shō Nei was taken to the Satsuma capital, Kagoshima. The Satsuma were the ruling family of the southernmost province of an emerging Japan. After an exile of two years, the king was allowed to return to Okinawa, having pledged his submission to Satsuma and his promise to send tribute to Edo, the Japanese capital. At the same time and to complicate matters, Japan found it profitable to allow Okinawa to continue in its status as a dependency of China because of its importance brokering the Indo-West Pacific traffic. In that way, Ryūkyūan commerce allowed the Satsuma to engage in foreign trade indirectly despite the Tokugawa policy of isolation, and Ming China was able to acquire goods from Japan despite its prohibition of trade with the Japanese. Okinawa thrived in this ambiguous position as a foreign, dependent nation of contending masters, Japan and China, while maintaining its principal means of production and its political sovereignty.[28]

Regular tribute to China and Japan allowed the contradiction[29] to continue mainly because the relations benefitted all involved. Both Japan and China likely knew of and winked at Okinawa's tributary status to them both. Okinawans, at the same time, were required to develop sensibilities and practices that would conceal or not call attention to their divergent loyalties. The performance was what mattered. Accordingly, Satsuma officials prohibited Okinawan traders from speaking Japanese, having a Japanese hairdo, or wearing Japanese dress, and an eighteenth-century guidebook, the *Ryokōnin kokoroe*, instructed them on how to conduct themselves as Okinawans and not Japanese with the Chinese. Further, the Satsuma urged the Ryūkyū kingdom to take every opportunity to ingratitiate itself with the Chinese and to express openly their indebtedness to China's emperor.[30]

Pragmatists, Okinawans used the Japanese calendar when dealing with Japan and the Chinese calendar, with China. State histories, like the *Chūzan seikan* (1650), Okinawa's first offical history, were written in Japanese and emphasized close ties with Japan, while the *Chūzan seifu* (1701) omitted reference to the Satsuma or the kingdom's position as its tributary state and instead emphasized its connections with China.[31] Those chronicles were clearly concocted for their respective readerships in China and Japan. Amidst a cultural resurgence in the arts and literature, Chinese and Japanese language existed side by side and intermingled in Ryūkyūan writings. And yet, perhaps because some might have considered those linguistic innovations as hybrid and hence impure and inferior, Okinawan intellectuals debated Japanese versus Chinese assimilation even as (Chinese) Confucianism, including patriarchy, class distinctions, and the state bureaucracy, grew in influence in the kingdom. As a result, a scholar claimed, the Ryūkyūan worldview came to resemble the Confucian world order, and Okinawans saw China as "the center of the East Asian world and the source of cultural values."[32]

That attraction toward one pole reveals the tension and price exacted by service to two masters and the magnetism of assumptions and valuations of purity. Tribute, particularly when trade declined, was twice as onerous, and dependency outweighed sovereignty in that balance. Similarly, separate calendars, records, diplomatic missions, and behaviors were both encumbering and necessary for a degree of independence. Moreover, performances of Ryūkyūan subjectivity and nationhood for outsiders concealed as well as exposed the nation / people, while contingent subject-positions were simultaneously exhilarating and precarious. Those temporal and spatial complexities afforded opportunities for those empowered to invent traditions and histories to advance their interests.

NORTH WIND

Despite the pervasive Confucianism of the period and official denials of Satsuma dependency, Japan exerted increasing authority over Ryūkyūan affairs. As a result, there emerged a counternarrative to the Chinese versions, which hitched the kingdom to Japan. That reorientation might be found in Ryūkyūan Queen Shō Nei's poem, the last entry in the *Omoro-sōshi* (1610), one of the earliest texts of the kingdom and a collection of divine songs completed a year after the Satsuma invasion, which refers to "when the northerly wind blows."[33] The wind, as deployed in contemporary works,[34] possesses generative powers, and its workings, those of the north wind, likely gave form to one of Okinawa's origin stories, at least as told by the Ryūkyūan ruling class.

The myth of Amamikyu, possibly of Japanese derivation, traces the Ryūkyūan people to divine origins and legitimizes the Shō rulers (1422–39, 1470–1879), who, in their later years, turned the kingdom from a southerly direction toward Japan, especially during the Tokugawa (1600–1868). The Amamikyu creation story, according to Ifa Fuyū, comes from the Amabe clan of Japan's Inland Sea who, in the third century, were in service to the Yamato. The Amabe, with their migration to the northern Ryūkyū islands, became associated with the creator diety, "Amami person," who visited the Ryūkyūs from over the eastern sea. That eastern homeland, the nirai kanai, was a great island of abundance and happiness and the source of all knowledge, including agricultural arts.[35]

A version of that creation story as recorded in the *Omoro-sōshi* narrates:

At first, in the old time, in the beginning
   The Great Sun God
   Beautifully shone
And long, long ago, in the beginning
   The Great Sun God
   Beautifully shone
And the Great Sun God
   The Grand Sun God
And looked far down
And bent down, looked down, far away
   (There was something floating)
And decreed to Amamikyo

directed Shinerikyo
And said, let there by islands
And said, let there be countries
   (Amamikyo came down from heaven)
And many islands
And numerous countries
   (she has made)[36]

Through the Amamikyo creation account, which appears after the 1609 Satsuma invasion and resembles Japan's Amaterasu Ōmikami (sun goddess) beginnings,[37] Japanese culture seeped into the Ryūkyūan fountainhead, the *Omoro-sōshi*, with the complicity of Okinawan intellectuals and leaders, thereby legitimizing Yamato (Japanese) and Shō political and cultural dominance. The magnitude of that theft is better apprehended when considering that the *Omoro-sōshi*, whose first volume was compiled in 1531, is the earliest documentation of Ryūkyūan memories, aspirations, worldviews, and subjectivities.[38]

Additionally, the several consequential versions of the creation story endorse an increasingly more stratified, hierarchical social order together with more insular ideas of the nation and its people and their proper place within the social formation. According to the *Omoro-sōshi*, the sun god directed Amamikyo to create islands and countries and to populate them with humans. Greater differentiation appears in an account of the Shinto religion by the priest, Taichū, the *Ryūkyū shintōki* (1605), which divides the people into a hierarchy of lords, priestesses, and commoners, reflecting the social transformations underway. Still, all humans descend from Amamikyu. A mere forty-five years later, in the *Chūzan seikan* the Tentei (heavenly emperor), upon the request of Amamikyu, sends to earth his son and daughter who then have three sons and two daughters. The Ryūkyū king descends from the first son, the local lords from the second, and commoners from the third; the high priestess descends from the first daughter and the noro (local) priestesses from the second. The 1650 Amamikyu or creation myth recounting, thus, traces the separate genealogies of the monarchy, lords, and peasants, together with the high priestess who was generally the ruler's sister and the noro, often the sisters of district lords.[39] Those distinctions of birth and rank mirrored the evolving and more rigidly layered social order, and validated its structured privileges for the few and their counterpart, poverty for the masses.

The Amamikyu story appears to originate from Amami-Ōshima and the islands closest to Japan's Kyūshū coast where Japanese crossings, including people, ideas, and material objects, were frequent. According to a version from those islands, Amamikyu first descended on Amami-dake hill and governed Amami-Ōshima before migrating southward. Acknowledgment of the Amamikyu tale appears to end at Okinawa Island, failing to make inroads farther south. It is instructive to note that the ruling Shō dynasties originate from those zones of Yamato (Japanese) predominance, from Iheya Island, to Okinawa Island's northwest. Not surprising, therefore, is the frequency of the word "amami" for place names, gods, and priestesses in the northern Ryūkyūs, and its decline when moving southward. As a study and close reading of the account concludes, the Amamikyu creation myth belongs to "the Japanese cultural sphere."[40]

OCEANIA

By contrast, among Uchinanchu outside the Japanese cultural sphere, including Kouri, Miyako, and Ishigaki islanders, the origin story is less grand. Their founders, a brother and sister, as in other Oceanic creation stories, are human, not divine. They form horizontal relations, not vertical, and are equals though not the same; the sister presides in the sacred realm, while the brother, in the secular. The sister-brother ancestors who escape a flood to become the progenitors of the people is a narrative common to Southeast Asia and Oceania.[41]

"A long time ago, a long, long time ago," a Miyako Island deluge account begins, "there were the Bunazee siblings.[42] One fine day, the brother and sister went out to the fields to work. Suddenly from far off in the ocean, they saw a mountain-like wave . . . . The brother, concerned for his sister, [carried her] with great difficulty up a high hill . . . . The tsunami swept away all life from the land. Resigned, brother and sister built a grass hut and pledged to be husband and wife." The sister gave birth to the ajikai mollusk at first, and then to a human child. Gradually the island became filled with people who descended from the sister and brother and honored them as the kami (deities) who regenerated the island.[43]

Also on Miyako Island, sixteen sacred women sing a fusa (trance song)[44] during the winter festival held in honor of the founding mothers of their village.[45] The fusa, in trance time, conjures the "timeless time" of the island's beginnings and affirms women's prerogatives over their homes, including their hearths and songs. Those song's subjects are, at once and remarkably capacious, singular and plural, human and divine. Accompanied and not possessed by the kami, the older women transmit the song to the younger women together with its powers, as they sing:

> The gods peaceful
> the householders gentle
> descending from the original village
> descending from divine Shiraji
> the great gods want our song
> they desire the god-shamans' trance song
> pushing, pushing, coming down
> descending to this earth
> descending to Myāku Island
> since they all have come down
> since all the gods have gathered
> Machimi of the true house
> master of a hundred trance songs

thanks to the mother gods
thanks to the awesome gods
blessed by their permission
blessed by being filled
let us dance a hundred trance songs
let us dance to countless songs
let us dance a hundred dances
let us dance countless dances
let us step to trance songs and then return
let us step to the dances and then return
we householders and mothers
we god-strong and mothers
because we are child gods
because we are born into a line of gods
thanks to the mother gods
thanks to the awesome gods . . . .[46]

Ryūkyūan cosmology involving women's leadership in spiritual matters connects with the Oceanic world such as in the Trobriand Islands and Tongan kingdom, where women, because of their reproductive powers and cycles, are endowed from birth with rare and wondrous abilities.[47] In addition, the sacred fire in Ryūkyūan hearths, which women oversee and which is central to ancestor worship, resemble Polynesian beliefs. Sacred women conduct ancestor and funeral rites, and pray for the health and well-being of their families, and they lead in ceremonies at the village sacred grove (utaki) to honor the kami-founders, male and female.[48] The idea of kami itself in its various manifestations in Shinto Japan and Ryūkyūan religions situates it within the mana complex of Oceania. Both kami and mana refer to awe-inspiring powers, which electrify humans and other life forms, inanimate objects, and events.[49]

Moreover, sisters are spiritual patrons of their brothers, and on Yaeyama Island sisters bless the fields and harvests and are entitled to first-fruit gifts from their brothers. Sister-kami or sister-deity is not necessarily supernatural or transcendental but is human, immanent, and yet mysterious insofar as sisters possess an efficacious spirit. Finally, although the sister-brother dyad was at times displaced by a husband-wife binary with the rise of Confucian status ethics, patriarchy, and state and religious hierarchies, this belief in sister-kami persisted throughout the Ryūkyū chain, including the northern islands of the Japanese cultural zone, drawing them all southward toward Taiwan and the Philippines and parts of Melanesia and western Polynesia where its counterparts can be found.[50]

On July 5, 2009, my research companion, Wesley Iwao Ueunten, and I decided to rise early to see the sun appear over the ocean to the east. My wife, Marina Henríquez, Wesley, and I had toured Kudaka Island the day before with the expert guide and teacher Akamine Masanobu, a professor of anthropology at the University of the Ryūkyūs. The island, minutes off Okinawa Island's southeastern shore, is a sacred place headed by holy women or noro. As we approached Ishikibama, a beach and the site of a ceremony held annually, Wesley found a coconut deposited on the shore by the receding tide. There are no coconut trees on Kudaka, and very few on Okinawa Island; the black stream, we knew, came from the south, bearing gifts.

Kudaka Islanders, Akamine sensei told us, assembled at Ishikibama facing the ocean. There, praying to the rising sun for strength, the supplicants looked toward nirai kanai, the source of all life and prosperity. Grains, our gentle mentor told us, came to the islanders in a pot from over the eastern sea. The first couple, a story of Shuri derivation goes, lived on the island without grains. One day, the man saw a white pot floating in the breaking waves, and tried unsuccessfully to retrieve it. His wife told him to wash himself and wear a white robe; having performed those rituals of purification, the man was able to snare the bobbing pot. Inside, the couple found seeds of barley, millet, and other plants, which was the start of grains culture in Okinawa.[51]

But that July morning facing the sea, Wesley and I discovered that the sun rose to the northeast of Ishikibama, and worshippers assembled there must have faced southeast, the direction of the shoreline and incoming tide, we came to understand. Their backs would be turned on Shuri, the kingdom's center, and nirai kanai would be over their shoulders to their left toward rows of jagged rocks worn by the wind and waves. Each year, families took three stones, imbued with the powers of their ancestral homeland, from the beach to keep in their homes for protection from harm. The Shuri version of the proceedings at Ishikibama indicates a first couple, a man and wife, but Kudaka Islanders say, Akamine sensei quietly noted, that the first couple were, like the Oceanic accounts, a brother and sister.[52]

On Taketomi Island, a brother, Shidubuji, and his sister, Afareshi, are credited with the invention of boats and the art of navigation. Watching a floating leaf gave the pair the idea of a buoyant craft, which they built and sailed to Kuroshima, an island to the south. There, observing an eel swim, they contrived a long oar, the wa-sen, which they mounted on the stern and deployed, steering the boat back to Taketomi. The brother and sister, sailors and navigators, are the founding figures of Taketomi Island.[53]

Farther south and closest of the Ryūkyūs to Taiwan on Yonaguni Island, a man on a boat from the south, possibly Luzon in the Philippines, arrived to find the land barren and devoid of life. From sea, he shot an arrow, which penetrated the earth and, he discovered upon his return, made it bloom with grasses and trees in profusion.[54] The man later returned with his family to populate the island. One day, dark clouds gathered blocking the sun, and prodigious rains fell, flooding the land but also carving out hills, valleys, and rivers, making it beautiful for the survivors. After about four months, the sun broke through the clouds, and where its ray first kissed the earth the people built a shrine called Tidan Dukuru or "place of the sun."

The survivors were happy, and they ate wild berries, fruits, roots, fishes, and shell fishes. Those days ended when the sky turned yellow, then orange, and red, and the ensuing heat seared the land, consuming all the plants, animals, and people. A family managed to hide in a cave near the island's center, and thereby survived the intense fires. Their members emerged when the land cooled, and they erected a village at Dunada Abu, learned to cultivate the land and store surpluses, and became the people of Yonaguni.

Yet another disaster and another period of regeneration awaited those islanders when an enormous tidal wave swept over the land, taking everyone with it except a woman who held two babies in her arms. One, a boy, was the child of her brother, while the other, a girl, was hers. She faced a painful choice of sacrificing one child to save herself and the other child. She chose to abandon her own child, favoring her brother's son to preserve the male line. The moment her daughter was engulfed by the raging waters, the flood receded. Yonaguni Islanders, accordingly, all descend from the pair, a sister and her brother's son.[55]

The Kūrōshio current figures in all those founding, drift voyages, bringing not only coconuts to the southern Ryūkyūs but also peoples and other organisms to populate their waters and lands. And although situated within the temperate zone, the Ryūkyūs are tropical in climate and plant life because the black stream carries heat and moisture from the tropics. The islands' southeastern coasts, like Ishikibama beach, receptive to the Kūrōshio, comprise contact zones and sacred places of remembrance and identification.[56]

An Aragusuku story celebrates a young man's feat of paddling to the Philippines every night and returning the next morning with the kuba palm.[57] The plant is associated with sacred groves, utaki, especially on Miyako and Yaeyama islands, and on Hatoma, the island's principal deity alights on the kuba leaves, which rustle, and descends to earth along the palm's curved trunk. Those sacred groves of kuba, in the words of a researcher, convey "an impressive sense of peace and quiet [and] communion with Nature."[58] At the same time, the kuba imparts an apprehension of activity and intercourse beyond local, tranquil places; the sacred palm connects Okinawa with the Philippines, which is a Ryūkyūan homeland to the south called Pae-Patera or Hae-Hateru(ma).[59] Whether a gift or a theft from abroad, the kuba palm was transplanted in Ryūkyūan soil and made indigenous and central to Ryūkyūan subjectivities.

RELOCATING OKINAWA

The Ryūkyū kingdom's central role in brokering exchanges among East Asian states and between East and Southeast Asia for nearly three hundred years suggested to some a reversal of the Japan-Okinawa relationship of dominance and subordination.[60] Yanagita Kunio (1875-1962), a contemporary of Ifa Fuyū and the "father of Japanese folklore studies," proposed that the Japanese were migrants from the south through Okinawa from China as indicated by language, rice culture, and the cowrie shell monetary system. Like Murayama Shichirō and the archaeologist Kanaseki Takeo, Yanagita believed that the early Ryūkyūan language belonged to the Austronesian family of Taiwan and Oceania, and Kanaseki hypothesized two waves of Melanesian migrations to Okinawa and Japan. Both note the close cultural ties until the seventh century between Okinawa and Taiwan, from whence some believe spread Austronesian languages,[61] and Yanagita, in his *Kaijo no michi* (1961), traces Japanese people and language back to Okinawa and from there to Micronesia.

Yanagita's intention might have been to decouple Japan from postcolonial Korea and continental Asia, and he, like others involved in the "noble savage" discourse of the first half of the twentieth century called minzokugaku, might have seen Okinawans as native peoples unpolluted by the

Black Stream (Obāban)

contaminants of modernization and linguistic changes that were sweeping Japan.[62] Still, his claim provided an opening for Okinawa's escape from Japanese assimilation, and pointed to the possibility of the islands' coterminous orientations northward and southward. As is now indicated from excavations on Miyako and Yaeyama islands, early populations shared a lifestyle with other islands to their north but also possessed a material culture similar to the Philippines and Micronesia.[63]

Other recent evidence affirms Okinawa's (and Japan's) southern roots.[64] The Jōmon, central figures in the Yamato (Japanese) tradition, suggest descent not from Northeast Asian migrants as is stipulated by state ideology but from southern China or even possibly Southeast Asia. The hunter / gatherer Jōmon, physical anthropology shows, bear Micronesian and Polynesian traits, and they all ultimately derive from Malaysian stock. Okinawans, Japanese, and Ainu were a Jōmon people who inhabited those islands for about ten thousand years to 2300 BC. Beginning around 400 BC, they were absorbed by the Yayoi, agriculturalists from northeast China who spread into Kyūshū and moved south and north except Hokkaido where the Ainu predominated.[65]

That Jōmon foundation, an archaeologist surmises, was common not only to Hokkaido, Japan, and Okinawa but also Taiwan, East Asia, and the Philippines, and it spread into the Pacific with the migrations of Oceania's peoples, the Micronesians, Melanesians,[66] and Polynesians from their Southeast Asian homeland.[67] "Therefore," he concludes, "in both the geographical and biological senses, Japan is an outpost of the Asian continent and, at the same time, an island group in the Oceanic world."[68] That view of Japan's multiple origins reconstituted by successive migrations from diverse sources and peoples is affirmed by linguistic evidence, which shows how shifts in the Japanese language mirror those population changes.[69]

Those historical ties suggest the provisional and situational nature of modern metageographies of world regions, which place Okinawa and Japan within the orbit of East Asia, along with Korea and China. The Ryūkyū

Islands' physical, cultural, and economic histories place them in both East and Southeast Asia, along with the Philippines and Indonesia, encompassed by the Indo-West Pacific triangle of oceanic life.[70] Women's spiritual powers, the sister-brother dyad, and the Ryūkyūan ideas of kami carry the scent of Oceania, and even if not a member of the Austronesian language family as most linguists now believe,[71] Uchinanchu are Pacific Islanders, inhabitants of Oceania, like the so-called "kanakas" of Japan's South Seas and Filipinos of Naichi taunts. Okinawa's multiple plantings astride and in violation of spatial divides underscore the discursive and material qualities and interests of essentializing notions such as nation / race, and they suggest alternative ways to conceive of our world and its peoples.

Moreover, it is important to acknowledge in this deconstruction of Japan that Okinawa likewise is a social construction and a moving object. King Satto's fourteenth-century expansion of Chūzan to Miyako and Yaeyama islands, and the middle kingdom's annexation of Hokuzan and Nanzan the following century, indicated the spatial spread and expansion of Okinawa, which was never a static, singular entity. In fact, it appears, based on Miyako and Yaeyama accounts, that the islanders posed a serious threat to Chūzan's trade monopoly, dispatching their own ships to China and Southeast Asia. Seeing its wealth siphoned off by those southern islanders, Shuri invaded, conquered, and depopulated Miyako and Yaeyama and peopled them with loyal subjects, islanders from Kuroshima, who sent tribute to Shuri.[72]

Ryūkyū's islands, as revealed in their stories of regeneration, are not always sedentary but also in motion. A case in point is the Shiraho, Ishigaki Island creation account of humans who emerge from the amankani (hermit crab) hole. The story appears to validate the settled land claims of Shiraho's people, but tracing its possible derivations complicates and extends the account's spatial reach. Shiraho's origin story might in fact be an import from Hateruma Island, whose migrants repopulated the town following the devastating 1771 tsunami that killed about a third of Ishigaki Island's population and nearly all of Shiraho's people.[73] Hateruma Islanders, like others in the Yaeyama and Miyako group, narrate recurrent engagements with the Philippines, signifying a more distant site of origin and composition. Additionally, Ishigaki's people might have come from Taketomi Island, which some Ishigaki Islanders regard as their ancestral home, and in turn Taketomi Islanders tell a brother-sister, drift voyage origin story,[74] a creation chronicle of Oceania. Shiraho, as a people and place, thus, makes manifest the kinship of the self with other life forms and peoples across imagined and imposed divides, including species, islands, world regions, and nation / race.

My subject-position is similarly multifaceted and fluid though not free, like the black stream governed by the physical properties of variable wind directions, temperatures, and densities. I emerge from the amankani of discourses involving language and ideology whose powers are authorized by apparatuses of the state and its social formation.[75] Those agencies produce subjects as distinguished from their objects by placing them within society's regulatory regimes.[76] Okinawa and Uchinanchu, Japan and Japanese, East Asia and East Asians exemplify those geographies, discourses, and subjectivities. Only when in transit and perched precariously between and among those imperial estates while holding on to multiple affiliations can we expose and contest them, as I have come to realize in my search for origins.

Weary after a week of meetings and lectures at the University of the Ryūkyūs on Okinawa Island in the fall of 2009, I boarded the monorail that takes passengers from Shuri station to the Naha airport. At one of the stops, a family boarded the car and there sitting directly across from me was my grandmother. Her performance was impeccable, pretending not to know or recognize me. But sure as life, there she was, my grandmother. I followed her act, trying not to stare but I could not help a broad smile. My grandmother had finally, assuredly returned to her mother and island home in Okinawa.

CHAPTER TWO

Self

(Okāsan)

My mother, okāsan, Kakazu Shizue, is the soul of my being. In August 2018, during my last visit with okāsan, I cooked for her miso soup, fried butterfish, and warm rice with pickles. She said they reminded her of the times when food tasted deliciously Japanese and home-cooked. My son and her nurse, Colin, and I marveled at how much she ate. I left her that Friday at the senior center, and flew to our Big Island home and then to New Haven never to see her again. Just over a week later, she tired of life.

GENESIS[1]

I can only marvel at the possibility of systematic thought and acts of creation among plantation workers after a day's labor. Rising before the crack of dawn to the smell of boiling rice and fried spam, I sensed my aching arms and legs refuse the stiff jeans and khaki, long-sleeved shirt I wore without fail. For two summers, I labored for the multinational Del Monte on the island of Molokaʻi, picking pineapples in fields baked by the tropical sun and choked with clouds of suffocating white powder that lined the undersides of the plant's silvery spikes.

Walking between two rows of pineapples behind a mechanical boom, a dozen of us, Frantz Fanon's "the wretched of the earth,"[2] plodded to the steady, relentless register of the harvesting machine. We twisted the ripening fruit off its plant stalk, snapped off its crown with one motion, and heaved the shorn body onto the boom's conveyer belt, which carried it to a waiting truck, all under the watchful eye of the luna or field boss, an imperious figure who stood at one end of the boom.

Our protective gear compounded our misery. Heavy chaps hung over our jeans and extra sleeves pinned to our shirts warded off the plant's needles, wire-mesh goggles protected our eyes when reaching down into the thorny undergrowth, straw hats shielded our head and face from the piercing sun, and heavy work boots trampled the uneven ground and poisonous scorpions and centipedes. Some drew bandanas across their nose and mouth to filter the thick dust.

The sociologist C. Wright Mills, in an essay on "intellectual craftsmanship," suggested that intellectuals should keep a daily journal of their activities and ideas. Those, he proposed, comprise files to spark the "sociological imagination," which enables comprehension of "the larger historical scene in terms of its meaning for the inner life."[3] After picking twenty truckloads of pineapples on a good day, the only thought and energy I had was to get to bed. Even dinner seemed too large an obstacle on the way to the heavenly sack. I could not imagine how my fellow workers could pause to reflect upon their day's experiences, much less write poetry, paint landscapes, arrange flowers, or stitch exquisite patterns onto cloth. I have seen seasoned men faint in the field from the heat and exhaustion.

Had I the agency to apprehend my condition in its wholeness of the subject-self and society, autobiography and history as prescribed by Mills in a book published about the time of my pineapple days, I might have railed against foreign, multinational corporations that occupied native, Hawaiian lands and exploited men and women, young and old alike, whose rough hands plucked fleshy, tropical fruit for gentle, civilized palates in the temperate core.

It was not unremitting, fortunately, my life of plantation labor, picking pine. Daydreaming about possibilities also occupied my youthful days.

My mother's family in front of their ʻAiea plantation home,
ca. 1938. Courtesy of Kakazu Shizue.

I would die before my thirty-second year, I was sure, and thus I had to achieve my fame quickly. My parents were not quite so lucky. My father worked at the ʻAiea sugar mill and my mother cleaned the homes of rich, white people near Leʻahi (Diamond Head) well before they could complete their primary schooling. Their earnings gifted me the luxury to contemplate my condition and "project," as some scholars are fond of saying.

I recall lazy Sunday mornings and afternoons lying on my bed staring at the ceiling, discerning patterns formed by water and rust stains from the leaky tin roof above. Most disturbing was the shape of a human body outlined on the sagging, cardboard ceiling. One day the victim would fall through, I was convinced, and smother me. Our house, distinguished only by its paint color, stood in a line of little boxes on the hillside built by the Honolulu Plantation to specifications and materials attentive to the needs of the tropics and, above all, economy.

Self (Okāsan)

I was ignorant of and hence ungrateful for the four-month great strike of 1909 in which some seven thousand sugar workers from all the major Oʻahu plantations, including the one at ʻAiea, struck for higher wages and better work and living conditions. Instead of "pigstylike homes," a strike leader insisted, workers deserved family cottages for their children.[4] Although the strikers returned to work without the slightest evidence of success, having endured mass evictions, harassment and intimidation, and the arrest and imprisonment of strike leaders and sympathizers under emergency measures, the following year the Bureau of Labor and Statistics urged and the planters adopted a program of paternalism designed to derail worker unrest by providing them with "recreation amusement" and "more comfortable and attractive quarters."[5]

Our regulation, three-bedroom house, with an interior kitchen, toilet, and shower and a yard large enough for vegetable plots and fruit trees, was a handiwork of that strike. I should have been appreciative but by the 1950s, the decade of my small kid time, I resented the roof that dripped, the termite-infested walls and floors that were peppered with holes and grooves, and the windows, which were too small to admit the cooling breezes that descended the Koʻolau slopes.

My lack of gratitude under the regime of planter paternalism was heightened by my growing realization that plantation bosses lived a distance from the workers' quarters and their houses and yards were palatial and indulgent by comparison. I remember being awestruck when my maternal grandfather, Kakazu Kame, took me to the manager's white house, which stood at the end of a long, winding driveway lined with stately palms and rose two stories above well-manicured lawns and gardens. I flashed on stumbling upon the set of *Gone with the Wind*. My grandfather was a "yard boy" on that estate, and I am afraid I was less attentive to helping him with his tasks than with collecting and eating the fallen mangoes on the great lawn.

Part 1. Subject-Self

I discovered, much to my delight, in the course of my many expeditions into forbidden territory, that workers commonly planted vegetables in the cane fields alongside the water ditches, making use of the plantation's resources for their own needs. Although petty in the big picture, those instances of trespass, as members of the coarser class, were our delicious secret pleasure.

Doubtless, growing up on the 'Aiea plantation was the primal and paramount source of my education. The plantation shrouded my world behind a curtain of cane, which surrounded our camp, and it produced and located my subjectivity within its social formation and hierarchy. The planters, I subsequently learned, deliberately drew those limited horizons because they feared losing their workforce, the children of plantation workers, to upward and outward mobility.

Public schools and the "back-to-the-soil" movement promoted agriculture for boys and domestic "sciences" for girls in an effort to keep them on the plantations by dampening their aspirations for full equality. Plantation education, *American* education, was designed for useful labor. In that regard, the University of Hawai'i president counseled young people in 1930: "Do not count on education to do too much for you, do not take it too seriously. Do not expect a college degree, an A. B. or a Ph. D., to get you ahead unduly in this world."[6] That advice, Hawai'i's ruling class directed us, was in keeping with our "Americanization," which required us to stay in our place, as workers, gratefully.

The field of study called "race relations," in force during that interwar period, explained the "problem" we, the dispossessed masses, posed to the ruling class and race. Our agency, race relations held, our demands for self-determination, equality, and human dignity, constituted "the problem of the twentieth century," as I will later explain in greater detail. We, plantation laborers of the tropical band, the oppressed masses of the Third World, must content ourselves with remaining in our assigned place in the modern world-system. Global order and tranquility, the desired ends of empire, race relations scholars held, result from white supremacy and nonwhite subservience.[7] In that way, race relations, as discourse, consorted with colonialism, as practice.

Hawaiʻi's sugar plantations, begun in 1835 by William Hooper of Boston, grew to dominate the life of the kingdom by usurping some of the best agricultural land and consuming enormous amounts of freshwater, employing the largest share of the workforce, and controlling capital and its exchanges through an interlocking network of blood and business alliances. The core of that oligarchy descended from New England missionaries who undermined the religious bases of Hawaiian society, language, and culture and from merchant capitalists who systematically exploited the islands' natural and human resources, including Hawaiian labor, sandalwood, and whales.[8]

Certain of Hawaiʻi's rulers joined in that pursuit of god and mammon to their immediate but not long-term advantage, even as many of the kingdom's subjects protested that dispossession in petitions, mass movements, armed uprisings, and retreats to isolated enclaves where they continued their devotion to the ancestral land, waters, and skies.[9] The political theft of the kingdom was completed in 1893 by the force of arms, and the US annexed Hawaiʻi five years later.

The plantation system, which predominated from the 1860s to World War II, lured to the islands Europeans, Africans, Latinxs, Pacific Islanders, and Asians, like my grandparents, to work in the fields of cane and pineapple. Fundamental to that settler society was its social hierarchy that named and ranked individuals as groups and allocated them privileges on the basis of class but also race, ethnicity, and gender. Whites or "Americans," we were told, occupied the structure's penthouse because of their self-evident abilities, while those who were not white remained in the outhouse due to their manifest incapacities. During my coming of age, I had Portuguese neighbors in our Japanese camp, but they were exceptions to the rule that segregated Hawaiians from Chinese and so forth to pit one group against the other, and thereby depress wages and reduce the potential for class unity and action across color and culture lines. Women and children in all groups fell below men as their dependents.

Japanese had their social hierarchies. My mother was Okinawan; my father was Japanese. They were a mixed-race couple. Japanese in Hawaiʻi, Tamashiro Baishiro recalled, believed that "Okinawans were of a different race. They thought that the Okinawans had tails . . . . They looked down on Okinawans, therefore we had much hostility. Yeah, then when we wanted to marry with *wahines* [women] from Japan they would not allow that. I had difficulty getting married to my Japanese *Naichi* wife, too. They would say Okinawans are just nothing."[10] The Naichi, having conquered and colonized Okinawa since 1609 as we saw, might have taken comfort in their belief of superiority over allegedly inferior people (Japan kanakas), but that false consciousness masked the material reality of stratification in the plantation social structure that failed to differentiate between Japanese and Okinawans while serving the masters' strategy of divide-and-rule.

Our predicament, C. Wright Mills points out, arises from the trap of daily life that can easily occupy the totality of our attention and activity and our need to rely upon that very experience to plot our escape from the personal and immediate. Reason, "the advance guard in any field of learning," he contends, will allow us the possibility of progressing past that befuddlement by installing discipline and systematic thinking to give direction to our search for meaning, "to make a difference in the quality of human life in our time." Further, "scholarship is a choice of how to live as well as a choice of career."[11] The personal is political.

Consciousness, the Brazilian educator Paulo Freire explained, is learning to apprehend social, political, and economic contradictions and to resist

Self (Okāsan)

oppression. A critical consciousness, he proposed, creates subjects or knowing, acting agents as opposed to objects. Moreover, because colonization
dehumanizes, the oppressed, Freire urged, must become agents of history to
change and transform the social order and in that struggle become "truly
human."[12]

I was not precocious, alas, in deploying reason or critical consciousness to
direct my thoughts and actions because, in part, colonialism and plantation
schooling encumbered any extravagant ambition I might have harbored
with the inertia of the mundane. Yet, in retrospect, that brand of "mis-
education"[13] in the service of planter paternalism gave shape to the content
of my character—a contrariety and contempt for a "colonial mentality."[14]

In addition to shaping the person who I think I am through processes of
affiliation and disidentification, plantation pedagogy structures and sus-
tains my life's narrative and work. Some of those teachings impressed indelibly upon my consciousness include a profound regard for hard, manual
labor, a deep distrust of the ruling class and caste and institutions of their
creation, an imperative to infringe upon bounded estates, and an unalloyed
and unapologetic identification with the oppressed and those relegated to
the margins.

FRAGMENTS

The imagination, C. Wright Mills maintains in his commentary on intellectual
work, sets the scientist apart from the technician, and requires systematic
reflection and thinking beyond the collection and marshaling of empirical
evidence, a research procedure "thin and uninteresting."[15] That imagination,
I have come to learn, while susceptible to a deliberate crafting—the tireless
and exhaustive search for evidence and, as Mills outlines, a comparing of
extremes, inversions, and relationships—can also involve the quantum
mechanics of chance and fleeting opportunities seized. Above all, imagina-

Part 1. Subject-Self

tion, I hold, begins with a centered self, located in space / time, and the ability to vacate that self for the place, time, and circumstance of the other.

That retreat and advance, that choice of position, the Marxist philosopher and literary critic Raymond Williams points out, involves a commitment and affiliation, an identity of one with the other. Authors and their texts are not autonomous; they exist within particular places and times as individual entities and their articulations with others. Authors, everyone insofar as we perform and script our lives in dialogue with social spaces, and their texts, their lives, take on social forms and meanings. In that sense, all writing and lives make claims and express implicitly or explicitly points of view. They bear the mark of affiliation.

Genuinely committed writing and living arise from the author's "whole being" and hence "necessarily, his real social existence," Williams maintains. As such, writing is self-composition and a creation that can offer a new dispensation, a new formation insofar as writers—historical agents— and their scripts interact.[16] Although Williams is concerned with literal authors and their writings, conventions, forms, and languages, I extend his analysis to humans all of whom write and read their lives in conversation with society. Moreover, I subscribe to his thesis of political commitment and writing, Mills's scholarship as life and career, which wells from one's whole being and social consciousness.

"I come from the city of Haifa, but I remember little of my birthplace," begins the self-writing of revolutionary Leila Khaled as told by George Hajjar.[17] Often told in relation to others, including men, women's autobiographies, unlike men's, are generally introspective, understated, oblique, nonlinear, and fragmented, according to a foundational, critical study of women's self-writing.[18] Women's autobiographies also resist erasure in the dominant discourses, and can engage the discursive sites of power, including colonialism and patriarchy.[19]

Self (Okāsan)

The American writer Annie Dillard once described her memoir as moving "from the interior landscape—one brain's own idiosyncratic topography—to the American landscape, the vast setting of our common history." Toni Morrison's imagination allows her to fill the absences within documents and archives that void the "interior life" of her African American narrators. Her creative voicing of her subjects offers a more compelling and, yes, truer account of an otherwise dead, vacant past.[20]

In fashioning this version of my subject-self, I acknowledge that I am exposing, performing, and validating my craft and formation as a subject and historian. Such are the barren and fecund natures of the memoir form. In addition, experience, insofar as it constitutes consciousness and history, is a discourse and subject-position and is accordingly a construction within the disciplines of language and ideology. As explained by Joan Scott in her important critique: "Experience is a subject's history. Language is the site of history's enactment. Historical explanation cannot, therefore, separate the two."[21] But there is agency, also, in this discourse of the subject-self, which involves struggle, contestation, and resistance in an unfolding act of creation.

If her mother is the lehua blossom, my mother is the sacred woman who sings fusa (trance songs), "Machimi of the true house" and "master of a hundred trance songs." Her fusa animate and impart prosody to my consciousness and constitution. What can you say about a solitary life—a lifetime filled with commitments and good deeds?[22]

Okāsan was born to migrant laborers from Okinawa. On a personal level, her father might have fled Okinawa, seeking refuge from Japan's colonial rule, and her mother, escape from the grinding poverty of peasant life in Ozato village on Okinawa Island. From another standpoint, from a world-system perspective, my mother's parents were among the tens of thousands

My mother with her mother and father, ca. 1938. Courtesy of Kakazu Shizue.

of migrant workers from Okinawa and Japan recruited by Hawai'i's sugar planters. They moved from the periphery to the core, supplying cheap, efficient labor to produce fruits of empire to profit masters of industrial and finance capital.

Kakazu Shizue, as her parents named my mother upon her arrival, had the mixed fortune of being the eldest, following her older brother's early death, in an unforgiving line of six girls and four boys. That birth order assured her inability to attend her beloved school and guaranteed, like her parents, a lifetime of hard labor. While still a teenager, her father took her to serve an apprenticeship with a barber in Honolulu, wrenching her from her family and country home.

As a young woman, Shizue, in the company of her equally beautiful and talented sisters, found time for fun, relaxation, and the latest in dress, fashion, and makeup. As the "Shizue Supremes," or was it the "Kakazu Kool Kittens," they belted pop tunes on the Japanese radio. They were the talk of the town, and boys flocked to them like bees to nectar.

One of them was my father, Okihiro Tetsuo, who was a distant admirer of my mother. Shizue, to the contrary, hung out with the "in" crowd, and Tetsuo, a kibei or a Japanese born in the US and educated in Japan, was definitely a square, too Japanese. We would call him a "Japan-tōsō" or "definitely Japanese." Okāsan ignored him.

My father, however, knew Japanese culture, and accordingly ingratiated himself not with the object of his affection but with my mother's parents. He helped my grandmother bottle her homemade beer, and brought presents, notably milk and custard pie, which were family favorites. When he was ready to marry, he deployed a "go-between" or baishakunin, his friend Norman Suzuki, to approach my mother's parents with his proposal of marriage. Of course, my grandparents thought Tetsuo a great match for their daughter, so they urged my mother to accept his grand offer. Although difficult, largely out of respect for her parents, my mother said, she agreed to marry my father.

The Hawai'i National Guard discouraged Japanese from service, because they were "not much wanted."[23] Despite that racism, forty Japanese were in the National Guard in October 1940 when it was federalized and divided into two regiments—the 298th and 299th Infantry. My father was among those units when Japan attacked Pearl Harbor on December 7, 1941. In April 1942, while stationed at Schofield Barracks in Wahiawā, he married my mother. In June, the Army shipped my father and his unit to the continent for basic training. Okāsan, worried over her husband's war service, consulted a kahuna or Hawaiian priest when she learned he had been ordered to the front to fight Fascism in the European theatre.

The kahuna told her to place freshly cooked rice before the family altar, or butsudan, to ensure my father's safety. As long as the rice bowl cover was moist, the kahuna said, her husband was protected. Okāsan performed that devotion faithfully, except for one day when she forgot, and upon remembering, found the rice bowl cover nearly dry. She was horrified. Later, my mother received a message informing her that my father had been injured. He received a leg wound from the shrapnel of a German grenade. In the end, my father survived, unlike many of his comrades-in-arms, fled North Africa and Italy, and returned in January 1944 to my mother in the islands of his birth.

Necessity exacted many more years of work from okāsan. She served as a maid to rich, haole families, trimmed and packed pineapples at the cannery, and sweated in 'Aiea's Navy laundry, pressing sailors' uniforms for the occupying US Navy. The heat along the line of pressers was intense because of the ample steam required to coax the cotton fibers to align. Even the humid, motionless air outside the plant seemed cool by contrast. Countless of my mother's ambitions and dreams must have shriveled and died in that pressing room. But she succeeded in retiring from the laundry that was, years later, razed and transformed into an empty, fenced-off lot. Only its concrete foundations remain, mute evidence except of those who remember the noise and bustle of the place, where hundreds of Asian and Pacific Islander women sweated and toiled, making a living.

So what can I say about that solitary life, a quiet life of dignity and worth? That she relished her days with the keenness of anticipation; that she always had a ready smile and a hand to lend to those in need; that she found god and religion to comfort her during many a dark night; that she reared two children—her greatest achievement, she said—who went on to live lives she could only dream of and sometimes fail to comprehend, but she was happy for them, nonetheless; that she walked this good earth for nearly 101 years, a good and upright woman, decent and generous beyond words.

I came into language making sense of my world in Japanese, Uchinaaguchi (Okinawan), and what most locals know as pidgin. The first language of both my parents was Japanese; in fact, my father, unlike my mother, grew up in Japan and went to primary school there. His Japanese, thus, was an updated version of the language, not the Meiji Japanese my mother learned from her parents. Both also spoke plantation pidgin English. My grandparents spoke mainly Meiji Japanese, frozen in time, isolated from the dynamics of language change in Japan since their departure in the early twentieth century. While colonization required them to learn, read, and speak that version of Japanese in school, they spoke Uchinaaguchi as their first language with their parents at home.

While my parents were at work, I stayed with my grandparents, mainly my grandmother who lived next door. Hearing versions of Japanese and Uchinaaguchi was common in my childhood experience along with plantation pidgin English. Uchinaaguchi words like hai sai or "good day, good evening," gachi maya or "greedy," and chaa bira or "excuse me" masqueraded as Japanese in my mind, along with pidgin such as bon dance, Japanese and English for o-bon or "festival of the dead," and buta kaukau, Japanese and Chinese pidgin for "pig food" or "slop." Buta or "pig" is Japanese, and

Part 1. Subject-Self

kaukau, from Chinese pidgin chow chow for "food." I learned my Japanese from my grandmother. No pilikia, eh? or "no worry," obāban would soothe me in her best Japanese or so I thought. Pilikia is Hawaiian for "trouble" or "bother."

Whenever it pleased her, my grandmother made andagi or Okinawan doughnuts. She was peerless in their production. She deftly squeezed lumps of gooey dough in one hand, and plopped them into a pan of sizzling oil to form perfectly shaped balls, as plump as a lehua. The trick was in the roundness of the doughnut, which danced on the oil, oozing happiness. (Happiness is the meaning of my first-born son's Japanese name, Sachio, and mine, Yukio.) Its crisp, golden brown skin and sweet, white flesh are best eaten hot. When you crunched on obāban's andagi, your cares vanished in an act of wizardry, like the pile of andagi on the table. My grandmother made swell doughnuts.[24]

The Hawaiian language developed for over a thousand years before its speakers heard foreign tongues. Refined largely in isolation, the language embraced periodic infusions from Polynesian immigrants who spoke related languages. It was mainly English speakers, in the act of empire and colonization, who affected most profoundly the Hawaiian language. Hawaiians encountered British Captain James Cook and his men in 1778, and British and American traders followed, introducing their versions of English. Hawaiians interacted with those haoles (foreigners), and many Hawaiians served on their ships, resulting in "makeshift" languages of Hawaiian and English under conditions of social and economic intercourse.

Beginning in 1820, Protestant missionaries from New England taught English to Hawaiians and two years later reduced spoken Hawaiian to a written language to translate the Bible and spread the gospel. Thousands, including children and adults, flocked to the mission schools, which by 1832 enrolled an estimated one-third of all Hawaiians. Literacy in the Hawaiian vernacular soon became nearly universal, and the written language became a primary instrument for transmitting European ideas and values (and their resistances).

Written Hawaiian was not the living, spoken Hawaiian. The written language depended upon a standardized alphabet devised by English speakers, it borrowed Hawaiianized words from the English, Greek, and Hebrew, and through translations it assimilated English idioms. Those changes to the Hawaiian language, observed the sociolinguist John Reinecke, had "a destructive influence upon the preservation of, and further composition in, the elevated, extraordinarily allusive, and obscure poetic and religious special language."[25]

Conversely, Hawaiians "broke" English in their makeshift, trade language, which was called hapa haole (half foreign). Hapa haole pidgin formed a basis for plantation pidgin English as the language of command deployed by bosses to direct their Hawaiian, Asian, and Latinx workers and as the language of laborers to communicate with each other. The complexity of plantation pidgin English arises from its mobility and differences among speakers of Hawaiian, Chinese, Japanese, Korean, Filipino, Portuguese, and Puerto Rican. Each group added their traces to the language. Plantation pidgin English thus was unstable, not unified, obstreperous and defiant of classification, and gloriously diverse, depending upon the speakers, their grammar, vocabulary, idioms, and their accents that gave it its rhythm.[26]

Mainly because of their demographic dominance during the formative period of plantation pidgin English, the Chinese and Portuguese probably had the greatest influence on the evolution of that language. During the second half of the nineteenth century, they built upon Hawaiian pidgin or hapa haole and English, and added their vocabulary, pronunciation, and sentence structure. By the early twentieth century, with the birth of a second generation of plantation pidgin English speakers, the language was formalized into Hawai'i Creole with distinctive rules, vocabulary, and grammar. Called simply pidgin, Hawai'i Creole was the first language of the home, workplace, and street, and policed only by its practitioners.[27]

Portuguese men were particularly influential because many of them became lunas or overseers of sugar workers. Their languaging was the instrument of command, exerting power over laborers and their speech. Japanese speakers, like my grandparents, then adapted those influences. Bōbora head is an example of a common pidgin English blend taken from the Portuguese, abóbora or "gourd," by the Japanese in Hawai'i who used bōbora to mean "pumpkin" and bōbora head to mean "very Japanese" or "pumpkin head." A round, pumpkin-like head for a "very Japanese" man was evidenced in his haircut, which was called chawan cut or "bowl" cut in Japanese and English. A chawan cut was achieved by a barber placing a bowl over the customer's head, and trimming his hair following the bowl's lip.

Such was the interpenetration of languages that I long thought hoe hana or "working with a hoe" was a Japanese term. Hanahana, which I believed was Japanese for "work," is plantation pidgin English from the Hawaiian hana for "labor" or "activity." Pau hana, then, means "finish work" or the end of the workday from the Hawaiian pau or "end." When my grandmother cautioned me, No huhū! or "No get angry!" in English and Hawaiian, I heard her speaking to me in Japanese.

Pidgin was my first language. It separated the locals from the haoles. It nurtured a sense of community among the oppressed. As the African writer Ngūgī wa Thiong'o explained of the colonized and their agency: "It is an ever-continuing struggle to seize back their creative initiative in history through a real control of all the means of communal self-definition in time and space. The choice of language and the use to which language is put is central to a people's definition of themselves in relation to their natural and social environments, indeed in relation to the entire universe."[28] Pidgin formed a dividing line between whites and nonwhites, between the owners of the means of production and the workers.

I was shocked into discipline when my auntie, a grown woman of over fifty at the time, admitted to me that she and my mother, silver and gold (kinjin) according to Japanese reckoning, were ashamed to speak and interact with haoles because "we jus mokes, eh" (mokes, possibly from the Hawaiian moka or "waste matter, refuse, filth"), uneducated, brutish barbarians. Although adults to my eyes, my mother and auntie felt like mere children in the presence of haoles, those who held the power of speech. My teachers at the plantation and then Christian mission school instilled in me that same hard lesson by punishing us for speaking pidgin, scolding and at times spanking us into submission to "standard" English. Educated people, the civilized, our teachers recited, spoke proper English.

The state instituted racial segregation in the public schools on the bases of "standard" and "nonstandard" English. During the great sugar strike of 1920, which involved 8,300 Filipinos, Japanese, Puerto Rican, and other workers, 400 concerned, mainly white parents petitioned public school superintendent Vaughn MacCaughey for segregated schools for English-speaking children to protect them from the corrupting influences of plantation pidgin English. MacCaughey agreed and wrote to Hawai'i's governor: "Such children *have a right to such an education* under conditions that will insure them and their parents that it can be had without endangering those standards and character quality which are distinctly *American* and which must be preserved and kept inviolate."[29]

As a result, Central Grammar School opened its doors in the fall of 1920 as the first "English standard school." Five years later, the school had a student body of 546 white children, 135 Hawaiians, 78 Portuguese, and only 27 Chinese and 16 Japanese at a time when the Chinese and Japanese constituted about 60 percent of the total number of students enrolled in Hawai'i's public schools. Three other elementary schools in Honolulu were designated

"English standard schools," and a junior and senior high school completed the twelve-year system. English thereby upheld racial segregation, which *Brown v. Board of Education* (1954) ruled violated the Constitution's equal protection clause and was thus unequal.

Tests administered in 1941 comparing students in "standard" and "nonstandard" English schools showed sixth graders in "standard" schools achieving a 6.2 grade level, while their counterparts in "nonstandard" schools scored at a 5.4 grade level. The gap widened as students continued their education. Ninth graders in standard schools reached a 9.4 grade level, while their peers in "nonstandard" schools fell to a 7.6 grade level, and twelfth graders in "standard" schools scored two full grade levels above the "nonstandard" students. Those who spoke "standard" English were destined to become leaders, while the masses, "nonstandard" English speakers, were groomed for lifetimes of labor.

I remember in elementary school consuming voraciously texts set in New England. In that world staged by "standard" English, I went to grandma's house in a horse-drawn coach, harvested corn and pumpkins in the late summer, watched the leaves turn golden and fiery red in the fall, and in winter skated on a frozen pond. It never occurred to me that outside that gilded cage of language, cane, not corn fields, covered the land as far as the eye could see, the only seasons were wet and dry, and I, alas, was not a Pilgrim.

The last class of "standard" English students graduated from Roosevelt High School in 1960. In that year, I attended a mission high school just down the street from Roosevelt High, named for Teddy, which rose majestically on the hillside. Like their namesake, the imperialist TR, those "standard" English speakers were called "Rough Riders." By contrast, I spoke plantation pidgin, despite my years of "mis-education," which tried to wean me away from my childish, broken tongue.[30] I was addicted to the free style of the language, its beats and cadences, its relevance and immediacy, its contrariness, its creativity, and above all, its poetry, its rhythms. I was hopelessly "wan moke," like my auntie and mother, and would never amount to much.

THE DANCE

The poet and pan-Africanist Aimé Césaire, in his impassioned discourse on colonialism, contrasted colonialism's achievements—diseases cured, standards of living raised, miles of roads, canals, and railroad tracks laid, acres planted, and tonnages of cotton and cocoa exported—with "societies drained of their essence, cultures trampled underfoot, institutions undermined, lands confiscated, religions smashed, magnificent artistic creations destroyed, extraordinary *possibilities* wiped out." Moreover, Césaire soared, "I am talking about millions of men torn from their gods, their land, their habits, their life—from life, from the dance, from wisdom."[31]

Subjects torn from "the dance," from movement, from agency, from history are features of colonialism. Hula, American missionaries preached, debauched and lured women and men into promiscuity, idleness, and sin. "Heathen song and dance," Hiram Bingham of the first company sent in 1819 by the American Board of Commissioners for Foreign Missions sternly warned, promoted lasciviousness, and he pressured Hawaiian rulers to ban the practice. As early as 1823, some aliʻi halted hula performances, the queen regent Kaʻahumanu issued an edict forbidding public hula performances in 1830, and the Hawaiian legislature passed civil codes in the mid-nineteenth century to regulate and discourage the dance.[32]

Foundational to Hawaiian song and dance is the Pele and Hiʻiaka cycle. Most hula hālau (schools) recite that history, and its chants form a part of the training of dancers. Perhaps the best-known complete version of the cycle was published by Nathaniel B. Emerson, and dedicated to the last Hawaiian ruler, Queen Liliʻuokalani, and "her beloved Hawaiian people."[33] The history recalls the journey of sisters, Pele and Hiʻiaka, from Polynesia, making landfall in Hawaiʻi and traveling the length of the archipelago in search of a home. The chant details the changing weather and landscape, and expresses an abiding love for the islands that became a haven for the sister voyagers. Those allusions to the natural environment hold deeper meanings than a mere travelogue in that they express a worldview, mirror the changing moods of the characters, and convey personal messages in omens and signs known only to the songs' composers.

Pele, the older sister and volcano deity, and Hiʻiaka found a suitable home on the Big Island of Hawaiʻi in the place called ka lua o Pele or Pele's pit, Kīlauea crater. During a deep sleep, Pele's spirit wandered back to Kauaʻi, where she met Lohiʻau at a dance, and with her beauty and mystical chants entranced him. After three nights, Pele left Lohiʻau and returned home, promising to send for him. Distraught, Lohiʻau committed suicide by hanging himself.

Unaware of Lohiʻau's death, Pele summoned her sisters and asked them to travel to Kauaʻi to escort Lohiʻau back to her. All of them refused, except Hiʻiaka, who agreed to go out of love and respect for her older sister. Before leaving, Hiʻiaka asked for and received from Pele a promise not to destroy her beloved ʻōhia groves in Puna and her friend and hula teacher, Hōpoe.

Pele assigned Hiʻiaka a traveling companion, and together they set off for Kauaʻi. The journey was long and dangerous, and many times Hiʻiaka had to rely on her powerful skirt to summon aid from the family of Pele divinities. Her songs that greeted people and personified the natural environment along the way became kau or sacred chants. During a stop, a chief and kahuna, Malaehaʻakoa, divined that Hiʻiaka was of the Pele family so he ordered a feast in her honor and led in the performance of a dance accompanied by a long chant or poem, chronicling the deeds and events that marked Pele's presence in Hawaiʻi. The song and dance recalled Hawaiian history, and legitimized the Pele family's ties to the islands.

When Hiʻiaka learned that Lohiʻau was dead, she went to the cave where his body lay. Hovering over the cliff at the cave's entrance was Lohiʻau's spirit, which Hi'iaka captured and forced back into Lohi'au's body. Summoning all of her powers of healing, Hi'iaka restored Lohi'au's strength through songs, which kahuna learn to cure diseases. As she had promised, Hi'iaka took Lohi'au to Pele, but found that Pele had broken her pledge and destroyed her beloved 'ōhia groves and had turned her teacher, Hōpoe, into a stone that to this day dances in the sea of Nānāhuki.

Hula traces the movements of the sun, moon, stars, and other heavenly bodies that mark the seasons and steer voyaging canoes. Hula is the whisper of the wind, moving through tall grass and sifting through the leaves of trees. Hula is the surf rushing to the beach, the swaying of seaweeds in the ocean's currents, the bamboo bending in a breeze. Hula personifies nature. "Like nature," observes kumu hula (master hula teacher) Pualani Kanaka'ole Kanahele, "hula is rhythmic, inclusive, transformative, physical, spiritual, healing, and above all, it is Hawaiian."[34]

The Pele and Hi'iaka cycle contains chants that are foundational for the hula and for the healing arts. Hi'iaka is thereby associated with both the dance and regeneration, and because countless poets, artists, and priests have called upon her name, she is, according to Hawaiian folklorist Katharine Luomala, "the greatest of all artists known in Polynesian oral literature."[35]

The hula is poetry in motion. It is Hi'iaka's gift and masterwork. Moreover, beyond its haunting beauty, syncopating rhythms, and stimulating complexity of poetic expression, hula recorded a people's voyaging through space/time, their kinship and social relations, and their deep learning and rich culture. That literature is history, constituting a people in place through time and in relation to their ever-changing society and environment, in motion.

When the dancing stopped, the people's culture and history died, as Césaire insightfully, poetically noted. The anticolonialist Albert Memmi observed that the colonizer attempts to remove the colonized from history and therewith community,[36] and that erasure, the revolutionary Frantz Fanon added, is accompanied by the insertion of the colonizer into history. "The settler makes history," he wrote, "his life is an epoch, an Odyssey. He is the absolute beginning." Colonialism strives to deny the people their past, Fanon explained, because national culture depends upon that grounding to enable a consciousness of peoplehood. The contest over national culture, he concluded, is the struggle for liberation, involving "the whole body of efforts made by a people in the sphere of thought to describe, justify, and praise the action through which that people has created itself and keeps itself in existence."[37]

Despite colonialism's edict, the hula, the dance continued, in secret schools and far-off, hidden places past the precincts of policing and surveillance. Hawaiians kept alive the dance, their history and culture. Hawaiian dance prevailed, returned to its place of prominence at the coronation of King Kalākaua in 1883, flourished under Queen Liliʻuokalani, and experienced a revival in the movement for Hawaiian language, culture, and sovereignty in the twentieth century. The dance refused to die.

Self (Okāsan)

CHAPTER THREE

Naturalizations

(Otōsan)

My wife, Marina, sensed it immediately. On a rise facing east, she felt the restoring breeze on her face. Her wild hair billowed behind her, and she pronounced that this was the place, our Kea'au home in the district of Puna.

Hi'iaka sang to Pele before her departure to fetch Lohi'au:

Puna dances in the wind
Moving through the hala grove at Kea'au
Hā'ena and Hōpoe dance
The female sways
Revolving at the sea of Nanahuki
Perfectly pleasing, the dancing
At the sea of Nanahuki
Puna's sea resounds in the hala
The voice of the sea is carried
The lehua blossoms are scattered
Look toward the sea of Hōpoe
The dancing woman at the sea of Nanahuki
Perfectly pleasing, the dancing
At the sea of Nanahuki.[1]

The hala or pandanus was brought to Puna by Ka-moho-ali'i, Pele's revered older brother who accompanied, indeed, led his sisters, Pele and

Puna's hala, 2014. Photo by Gary Y. Okihiro.

Hi'iaka, as a shark and navigator from Polynesia to Hawai'i. Ka-moho-ali'i planted the seed that grew into the sacred hala tree, and with Pele he ate blossoms from the tree with salt and sugar cane.[2] Ka-moho-ali'i is the spiritual leader of the Pele fire clan, and he is the foundation upon which Pele builds land.[3] The hala's fruit with its bright reddish-orange color, a reference to Hi'iaka, is famous in mele or song, and sections of the fruit are used to make leis. On her mission to Kaua'i, Hi'iaka wore a hala lei. The hala's dried leaves are especially valuable for thatching mats and house building, and women weave its strips into intricate pillows, baskets, and fans.[4]

The wind, in Hi'iaka's chant, filtered through Kea'au's pregnant hala groves, is captured by the saying:

Puna, paia ʻala i ka hala.
Puna is fragrant with hala.[5]

Puna is the place where hula was born as recorded in Hiʻiaka's chant, on the beach at Nānāhuki, in the ʻili of Hāʻena, the ahupuaʻa of Keaʻau, in the Puna district. Hōpoe, Hiʻiaka's teacher and friend, dances in the wind. The word hōpoe also means fully developed, as round as a lehua blossom, and like the sun's encompassing dome as it arcs across the sky. The easternmost land of the Hawaiian archipelago, Puna is where the day begins with the rising sun, and it is the direction from whence the Moaʻe Lehua or trade winds blow, stimulating movement and scattering the slender lehua petals. Accordingly, "Puna is the source of regenerative energy," notes kumu hula Kanahele, the site of creation and healing.[6]

My wife chose our landing well. Life flows from life's terminus. Our Keaʻau home on hallowed, borrowed ground began as Pele's fire that consumed all before her. Rains followed, and upon contact with the fiery, explosive lava, rose to form mist and clouds. From the heavens rain fell, cooling and moderating Pele's heat, softening and healing with Hiʻiaka's gentle touch. Algae, mosses, ferns, and lichens blanket the lava, and flowering plants, led by the ʻōhiʻa ʻa lehua, rise from the black basalt that rain and roots without fail crumble into soil. Hiʻiaka works her powers in the abundance that is the Puna rain forest.

Clarence Edward Dutton, a graduate of Yale College, described the Puna area in his 1882 geological travel account. Descending Kīlauea's summit, Dutton wrote, the expedition left the ʻōhiʻa forests to "find ourselves among the beautiful kukui or candle-nut trees with their bright green foliage and dense shade. Again the trail descends obliquely a long, steep hillside, which sweeps downward quickly to a broad, smooth platform near the level of the sea, which is now only two or three miles distant. On every hand are fields

Sisters, Hiʻiaka and Pele, ʻōhiʻa ʻa lehua on lava, 2012. Photo by Gary Y. Okihiro.

of pahoehoe [a type of lava] half covered, or even less than half covered, with a hardy prickly grass growing in the merest film of soil." Microclimates, Dutton observed, produce changing vegetation. "Trees of many varieties with strongly contrasted habits and foliage, blended in ever-varying tints, betoken the splendor and languor of tropical vegetation. The sea-coast is margined in many places with abundant groves of cocoanut palms and dense thickets of pandanus." In places, Dutton found, Puna's exuberant hala groves formed "an impenetrable jungle with their strange aerial roots."[7]

Hawaiians must have known, and geologists confirm, that Pele's Kīlauea home is the vent from which lava flowed to form the land that is Puna. Pele, Hiʻiaka, and Ka-moho-aliʻi comprise thus a single family and ecosystem. Although appearing as a small bump on the much larger slope of Mauna Loa, Kīlauea is a separate volcano fed by different pockets of magma in the earth's

Naturalizations (Otōsan)

crust. The massive Mauna Loa and Mauna Kea, however, affect Puna's rainfall and thus vegetation, which is Hiʻiaka's regeneration, by trapping the Moaʻe Lehua (trade winds) and forcing them to rise and yield their abundant precipitation. Little wonder, Hiʻiaka chanted, "Puna dances in the wind," the dance of life.

The night my father died, he came to me in a dream. Uncharacteristically, he asked me my permission to give up on life; he was weary, he said, of struggling for every breath. I told him to go to the light. In a blinding flash he was gone, embraced by the light. Since that day, otōsan has visited with me. In his house the night of his passing, we sat with our mother to comfort her. From the darkness outside, a huge katydid landed on the screen door, its big, unblinking eyes looking in as if to survey our grief. The morning of his funeral, he came to me in a full, brilliantly colored rainbow. Years later, in the dead of winter in New York City's Morningside Park, my father flew past us in the form of a mejiro,[8] a tiny brown bird flecked with yellow and green. (Otōsan, in his retirement, fed and fixed injured and helpless sparrows, and mourned them when they failed to recover.) Yet again, I found a dead mejiro on our air conditioning unit. Otōsan tried to fly into our Columbia apartment, but bumped into and broke his neck on the glass window. I took his body, and buried him under birch trees in neighboring Riverside Park. Each morning I chant otōsan's name in fond remembrance and in celebration of his changing states, his kino lau (forms).

NATURALIZATIONS

Over 30 million years ago, the ocean's organisms and land's biotic communities island-hopped across the Pacific to colonize the Hawaiian chain of islands. Those lineages of terrestrial biota began as migrating, foreign species from Asia and America, and through a process of naturalization, made themselves endemic and native to Pele's creation. Hawaiian flowering plants reveal, moreover, remarkable adaptive abilities, radiating and branching from a single ancestor, area, and microclimate to other worlds.

Favorable ocean and wind currents and bird migrations that brought plant spores and seeds to Hawai'i fail to ensure their survival. Establishment requires conditions suitable for the foreign ferns and flowering plants such as pollination agents like a specific insect or bird. Only then can they reproduce, cross-pollinate, and endure. Countless varieties, most originating in Asia, failed to survive because of their chance misfortune, their quantum mechanics. Fern spores, for instance, will not thrive if deposited on exposed, dry lava fields. Naturalization was a severe challenge for migrants broadly.

My father's parents, like fern spores on the leeward or dry side of the island, failed to establish themselves in Hawai'i. Okihiro Sanguemon was born in 1889 on a farm just outside of Hiroshima city. His parents, Okihiro Yosaku and Nakamoto Asano, were rice farmers who had six children, two boys and four girls. Sanguemon was the younger son. Both sons left Japan for the US, the first-born to California to study and work, and the younger, to Hawai'i's sugar plantations to labor. Those forms of migrant labor typified the first-generation Japanese experience on the continent and in the islands.

Sanguemon arrived on O'ahu in 1906 as a contract laborer, working at the Waipi'o sugar experiment station and then for the Honolulu Plantation at Waimalu. After several years, Sanguemon sent for a "picture bride." He married Nogami Taka from an adjacent village, and in September 1915 she arrived in Hawai'i. My father, Tetsuo, was their first-born in 1916, and when he was less than a year old, his mother, feeling ill, took him with her to Japan. After recovering, Taka left otōsan in the care of his aunt, Okazu, Sanguemon's younger sister, and returned to Hawai'i.

Back in Waimalu, Sanguemon and Taka had two sons, Shogo and Takeo, in 1919 and 1921, but news of his older brother's death in California probably in a train or mine accident compelled Sanguemon to return to Hiroshima in

1922. As the sole surviving son, my grandfather was responsible for the Oki-hiro family farm. In Japan, Taka and Sanguemon had two daughters, Fusai and Kayoko, and two more sons, Hango and Hiroshi, for a total of seven children.

Even if the Okihiro family had decided to stay in Hawaiʻi, my paternal grandparents, like all Asian migrants, could not have undergone naturalization to become US citizens. The state directed that process, which it deemed as "natural," when it is instead a profoundly social construct. The first Naturalization Act (1790) disqualified Asians from citizenship by restricting national membership to "free white persons." Freedom and race were the requirements for US citizenship even as expropriation (Indian land) and bondage (African labor) enabled property and freedom for whites. The 1790 act rendered Asians "aliens ineligible to citizenship."

Of sixteenth-century derivation, "naturalization" or "to be born" originally referred to the admission of foreigners into the rights of citizens. That entry into civil rights contrasted with the alien whose condition was deemed to be unnatural and often illegal. Naturalization was later applied to the process by which alien species of plants and then animals adapted to new environments. Within the US, in contrast to foreigner, the alien or "persons of color" figured both bondage unlike the normative "free white person" and incapacity in law and citizenship.[9]

Roger B. Taney, chief justice of the US Supreme Court, made clear those prerequisites of freedom and race in his majority ruling in the matter of *Dred Scott v. Sandford* (1857). Indians, wrote Taney, were from the start considered aliens and foreign nations, albeit "under subjection to the white race." Another race under subjection, Africans, like Indians, were "not included, and were not intended to be included, under the word 'citizens' in the Constitution, and can therefore claim none of the rights and privileges which that instrument provides for and secures to citizens of the United States."

Part 1. Subject-Self

The 1790 Naturalization Act, the chief justice pointed out, distinguished between "free white persons" or the "citizen race" and "persons of color" or those "not included in the word citizens, and they are described as another and different class of persons."[10]

Although "free white persons" included white women and children, nineteenth-century law affirmed their dependency under white men. Like people of color, white women belonged to "another and different class of persons." White women, except for the single and widowed, had few incentives to naturalize, which required payment of a fee. Most women did not hold property, and white women could not vote until 1920. As a result, US citizenship was of little consequence to them. In 1855, Congress granted citizenship to women married to men who were or became US citizens, and after 1907, all women acquired their husband's nationality. Thereby women, as dependents and "property," held derivative citizenships. To wit, general practice held that a white woman married to an alien could not naturalize, women's naturalization being a consequence of her husband's status.[11] In 1922, the Cable Act or Married Women's Act granted white women the right to naturalization regardless of their husband's status, while taking away the citizenship of all women married to Asians or "aliens ineligible to citizenship" based on the Naturalization Act (1790). Although repealed in 1931, the Cable Act made marriage to an Asian comparable to treason.[12]

While Mexicans revolutionized the nation's peoples when they became US citizens in 1848 (Treaty of Guadalupe Hidalgo), they achieved that status through the artifice of whiteness as conferred by the treaty. Race was a fiction of treaty making. The American Revolution really occurred when Africans after the Civil War and Indians in the early twentieth century, as persons not of the "citizen race," became US citizens with supposed rights. Asians, specifically Japanese and Koreans, were the last to acquire the ability to naturalize in 1952. Aliens they remained until the nation could no longer sustain the rhetoric of equality amidst the practice of racial segregation and inequality before the judgment of the Cold War world, especially of the Third World.

My paternal grandparents, having returned to Japan in 1922, missed the season for naturalization. Their sons, Tetsuo, Shogo, and Takeo, however, chose to exercise their rights of citizenship as the Constitution's Fourteenth Amendment (1868) guaranteed. Having been born in a US territory, Hawai'i, they were US citizens by birth. In 1932, as a sixteen-year-old, my father, Tetsuo, returned to the islands, staying with his aunt, Kanesue, his father's older sister who worked on the Honolulu Plantation at Waimalu. Otōsan joined her in field labor, but soon transferred to the islands' sole sugar refinery in 'Aiea, where he lived in the bachelors' quarters. He started on the mill's ground floor in the sugar packing room, and moved up to the second floor, working as a machine operator.

In 1938, my father's younger brothers, Shogo and Takeo, joined him, barely escaping Japan's draft for its Imperial Army. The brothers sent remittances to Japan to repay their father who had borrowed money to pay for their passage to Hawai'i. When the war came in December 1941, a member of the Office of Naval Intelligence placed my uncle Shogo on his list of "subversives" destined for confinement, but an officer in the Military Intelligence Division put a note next to uncle Shogo's name, stating that his brother, Tetsuo, was serving in the US Army. That asterisk likely saved uncle Shogo from internment's sweep.[13]

On December 7, 1941, martial law was declared in Hawai'i, and in the days and weeks following that "day of infamy," the military governor dismissed the 317 Japanese who served in the Territorial Guard, and officers disarmed all nisei soldiers in the 298th and 299th Infantry, my father's regiments. A soldier described how on December 10, "our rifles, ammo, and bayonets were taken from all us AJAs [Americans of Japanese Ancestry] with orders to stay in quarters—not even to go for a 'shi-shi' [piss] break!" Two days later, the military returned their rifles, but the nisei soldiers knew they were not fully trusted by their commanding officers.

Those dismissed from the Territorial Guard formed a "volunteer" labor battalion to string barbed wire, complete roads, remove rocks, dig ditches, and build warehouses. The Japanese had to prove what whites assumed as normative and an inheritance, the rights and responsibilities of citizenship. Presumed guilty by reason of race, the Varsity Victory Volunteers (VVV), as they called themselves, "set out to fight a twofold fight for tolerance and justice," in the words of a prominent member.[14]

In May 1942, the military governor recommended that Hawai'i's Japanese American soldiers, at the time serving in racially integrated units, be mustered into a segregated unit, and the following month, 1,432 men of the newly created Provisional Battalion set sail for the continent, otōsan among them. They were hastily assembled and were not told about the army's plans for them. "Before we had any chance to bid goodbye to our loved ones," recalled Spark M. Matsunaga, "we found ourselves on board a troopship sailing for God-knew-where. Speculation was rife that we were headed for a concentration camp."[15]

In Oakland, the men were hustled onto trains that transported them into the American interior. A soldier described how on the last day, the train slowed and stopped. Looking across the tracks, the men could see a concentration camp with barbed-wire fences and guard towers. "For half an hour we sat silently in our seats," he remembered, "thinking only of the worst; many were pensive with grim and hollow faces. Then, suddenly, as if to alleviate our pained thoughts, the train backed slowly out of the yard, switched to another track, and continued on."[16] The nisei soldiers filed out at Camp McCoy, Wisconsin, where they trained to defend democracy and where, in a corner of the base, was a concentration camp that confined leaders of the US Japanese community.

The men of the renamed 100th Infantry Battalion encountered additional indignities. They marched and trained with wooden guns before the army

Naturalizations (Otōsan)

trusted them with real firearms, and twenty-six from Company B, my father's unit, were assigned to a secret project in Mississippi where on Cat Island they played the enemy for attack dogs. "Most of us were transferred to Cat Island to pollute the island where the dogs were with the smell of 'Jap' blood," said Takata Yasuo. "Later results showed that this did not make any difference . . . . Each dog trainer sent his dog out to find us. When the dog spotted us, the trainer would fire a shot and we would drop dead with a piece of meat . . . in front of our necks. The dogs would eat the meat and lick our faces. We didn't smell Japanese. We were Americans. Even a dog knew that!"[17]

"I will never go back to the mainland," my father told me emphatically. I knew that otōsan had trained, as a member of the 100th, at Camp McCoy and somewhere in the South, perhaps Mississippi, but I never fully understood why he disliked the US continent so much. I had gone to college in California, and had secured a teaching position at Santa Clara University in the Bay Area. I wanted him to come and visit—to see my family, stay at our new home, visit my workplace. I wanted him to feel good about his years of toil, his taking two jobs working by day as a garbage collector and by night as a janitor to put me through college. Those efforts were not wasted, I wanted him to know, and his years of sacrifice and hard labor had made possible my sufficiency. For years, he refused to leave Hawai'i until a few months before his death. He made the journey to California with my mother in tow the winter before his final illness.

I remember it well, that visit. We took pains to make it comfortable, hoping he would enjoy the stay and perhaps return. We showed him San Jose's Japantown with its famed tofu and manju shops, Buddhist temple, and restaurants, and took him to the lovely Japanese garden at San Francisco's Golden Gate Park. One day, we drove down the Monterey coast, and his eyes lit up when Fort Ord came into view. He had passed this way, he said, during the war.

Only after completing the research for my book *Cane Fires* did I understand my father's opinion about the continent and his almost obsessive interest in the war. Having served in the 100th, he often said, was his life's proudest achievement, and as if to publish that belief, he carefully mounted and prominently displayed his army pictures, insignias, unit citations, and prized Purple Heart on the walls of his 'Aiea plantation home. My father failed to see the publication of *Cane Fires;* I could only show him the type-script as he labored to breathe with an oxygen tank by his bedside. Years of spraying poison in the cane fields, otōsan whispered, must have damaged his lungs. As he lay dying, I tried to tell my father I finally understood the reasons for his avoidance and fascination.

The "good war" for otōsan was not a matter of masculinity, love of coun-try, or democracy. He did not set out with the cheers and gratitude of the nation ringing in his ears; he did not have that comfort. He left Hawai'i's shore knowing that his parents were in a village outside Hiroshima, that his brothers, Hango and Hiroshi, were probably in Japan's military, and that his own country distrusted him and his kind. He left behind his newly married bride who had rushed out to Schofield Barracks to spend a few minutes with him, and set sail for the continent where white soldiers taunted the nisei, calling them "Japs," where segregation and Jim Crow ruled the South, and where bus seats, benches, and drinking fountains bore the labels "Colored" and "White." My father must have gotten his fill.

So when he stepped on Africa's shore facing Italy and the landing to engage the enemy, my father must have known that the bloody battles ahead would help determine the future of Japanese America. He did not last long. Like too many of his comrades, enemy fire wounded my father so severely he never saw the front again. Others who escaped serious injury pressed on, up the boot of Italy, into France and Germany, where a unit of nisei soldiers were among the first Allied troops to open the gates of Dachau death camp in April 1945.

My father must have had his fill of racism, hypocrisy, and blood sacrifice. He must have known that when President Franklin D. Roosevelt announced the draft for nisei and piously declared, "Americanism is not, and never was, a matter of race or ancestry," he lied. Roosevelt had earlier signed Executive Order 9066 (1942) that authorized concentration camps for Japanese in the US.

I would like to think that what prompted my father's final visit to the US continent was his realization that his service secured his claims, together with those of his children and grandchildren, to that nation-state, the United States. In 1944, George Aki, a chaplain, described the fighting in Bruyères, France. The men of the 100th, he wrote, "are obedient and brave; they charge right into machine gun fire and are mowed down, but those who can get up, charge again and again in waves, like the waves beating on the shores. Our losses are heavy . . . . My spiritual life is at its lowest ebb," he confessed, "for I see so many of the men, close friends, who are giving their all; too many. The sacrifice is too great."[18]

I can understand my father's feelings about the war. As he wished, he earned his final rest in Puowaina's or "hill of sacrifice" (Punchbowl Crater) National Memorial Cemetery of the Pacific, where we visit with him each year to bring him fragrant flowers, trim the grass, and wash his tombstone. The scrolled photographs of his army units that extend across the wall and his carefully framed citations still hang in the living room of his home decades after his death.

As far as I know and probably as my father feared, my grandfather, Okihiro Sanguemon, was a casualty of the world's first atomic bomb that incinerated Hiroshima on August 6, 1945, killing instantly an estimated 80,000 to 100,000 people. A Red Cross volunteer, my father's father rushed into the city to tend to the living. One of the nearly 100,000 who died from the effects of radiation within five years, my grandfather died four years after the nuclear holocaust.

A mere twenty-two miles off Kīlauea's coastline, Pele works her fiery object. Called Lōʻihi, a mountain rises from the ocean floor through Pele's vents,

My father and his bride, ca. 1942. Courtesy of Alice Okihiro.

renamed Pele's pit after a series of earthquakes in 1996 collapsed the seamount's summit. Like Kīlauea, Lōʻihi nestles along the side of the sloping, massive Mauna Loa, and is the youngest of the mountains that comprise the Emperor Seamount Chain, which extends from Alaska to the Big Island of Hawaiʻi. A mere 400,000 years old, Lōʻihi is over 10,000 feet high, and will emerge above the Pacific's waters some 10,000 to 100,000 years in the future.

The deity Lono was particularly active around Lōʻihi that summer of 1996. "Great Lono dwelling in the waters" is associated with clouds, storms, lightning, thunder, rain, wind, and rainbows, but he is also of the earth and its fruits, crops that depend upon his rain for abundance. Lono is fertility, thus, and of the regenerative powers. His heavenly displays of lightning and thunder have an earthly counterpart, the earthquake. A chant praises:

Lono the rolling thunder,
The heaven that rumbles,
The disturbed sea.

Lono arrives, heralded by clouds, and he makes fruitful the earth:

Clouds bow down over the sea,
The earthquake sounds
Within the earth,
Tumbling down there
Below Malama.[19]

A swarm of over four thousand earthquakes engulfed the Lōʻihi seamount, shaking its summit and causing debris to tumble down its sides. Lono's jolts, between July and August 1996, were the largest in number and intensity recorded for any Hawaiian volcano and caused an enormous discharge of clouds of hydrothermal material that boiled and billowed in temperatures that exceeded 200 degrees Celsius. On Lōʻihi's crater floor, north slope, and summit, hydrothermal vents supply ideal environments for microorganisms. Rich in carbon dioxide and iron, the vent fluids fortify oxidizing bacteria, and varieties of shrimp, tubeworm, and fishes inhabit the ecosystem, which some scientists believe to be the incubator for the first life on our planet. The flux of energy and dissolved minerals provide a rich oasis for microorganisms. Together, Pele and Lono generate intense heat and first life on this submerged island over 3,000 feet beneath the ocean's surface.

The Moa'e Lehua or trade winds blow from off Puna's shores, fluttering the hala leaves and scattering the lehua petals. Anchorages are temporary and insufficient to check nature's ceaseless movements and flows. Even the earth moves on liquid currents. The hot spot that produced the seamounts and islands of the Hawaiian chain is a mobile fissure that migrates southward. After creating the kupuna or "ancestor" islands of the Emperor Seamount Chain and Ni'ihau and Kaua'i, Pele moved to O'ahu, Maui, Hawai'i, and Lō'ihi. Naturalization is unnatural. Citizenship and, with it, rootedness are not of nature; restlessness, border crossings are the order of things. We humans all share "a tradition of migration," observed the Chicana poet Gloria Anzaldúa, "a tradition of long walks."[20]

Travel, the twentieth-century sociologist Robert E. Park notes, is the human norm from ancient Rome to the modern era. Contrary to the indigenous tradition of long walks, European expansion, conquest, and colonization, he writes, have secured the entire world for throngs of travelers and installed familiar conventions. Writes Park: "Everywhere along the main routes of travel one encounters, with slight local diversities, the same mixed populations and the same cosmopolitan cultures. Everywhere one pays tribute at a European bank, patronizes European shops, and lives in European hotels, where he eats European food and pays European prices." That, however, is the tourist's first impression, Park cautions. Behind that European façade is "a seething mass of native life that is quite alien."[21]

Robert Park, a major figure in the study of race relations as we will later see, introduced the book written by one of his former students, Andrew W. Lind. Based on his doctoral dissertation, Lind's *Island Community* (1938) recounts Hawai'i's history as the impact of humans upon the land likening it to naturalization and ecological succession. Those processes for Park parallel the rise and fall of empires, which he analogizes to human birth, growth, and death and the ecological succession of one species over another.[22] In fact, Park's race relations cycle applies natural history to the social world, from contact to competition, conflict, accommodation, and finally, assimilation.

Absorption, though, and "a new equilibrium" are not the endpoints of those natural processes. "For society is, like a plant or any other living thing," Park points out, "a moving rather than a stable equilibrium. Always it is involved in a process of becoming; always it exhibits something that corresponds to what is here called 'succession,' and 'succession,' as the ecologists have used the term, seems to include at once the processes of development and evolution."[23]

SUCCESSION

Like my father before me, I made landfall on the continent in California's Bay Area. High school friends from Pacific Union College met me at the San Francisco airport to take me to Angwin and "the college on the mountain, among the fir clad hills."[24] It was good to see them, my former classmates. High school graduation in Hawai'i can be hectic. Mounds of leis piled so high that you could barely see over them, taxing your senses of touch, smell, and sight. Flash bulbs crackled, some exploded, blinding you like Lono's flashy exhibitions on a dark night. In the islands, graduating from high school was a great achievement because few continued on to college. Your high school branded you, marking an end and a beginning. People in Hawai'i know you by identifying your high school. "Wat school you wen graduate?" is a common first greeting. Most of us then went on to jobs. In 1963, I was queer because I left to continue my studies on the continent.

On landing, my first impression of California was its chill; there was an unfamiliar bite to the air. The sun had set, and the road seemed unending. Dozing, I recall waking to hulking shadows of eucalyptus trees outlined along the highway's edge as we threaded our way along the narrow Silverado Trail through Napa Valley's fabled vineyards, up the winding Howell Mountain Road, and entering, at last, the gates of the Seventh-Day Adventist college on the mountain.

Set in a crater I discovered the next morning, the college squatted on Indian land. During my frequent hikes through the surrounding hills, I found proof of their presence—meticulously flecked obsidian arrowheads everywhere. The Ashochimi were still there, despite having vanished from the scene for nearly a century. As far as I know, the Ashochimi peopled what whites called Howell Mountain. "Their settlements lay in the valleys," the anthropologist A. L. Kroeber wrote, "but their territory was one of mountains, mostly low, indeed, but much broken."[25] Important Ashochimi towns in the valleys included Caymus (Yountville), Anakota-noma (near St. Helena), and Mayacama (Calistoga). Generally, California's Indians were mobile, following fish and game and seasonal harvests of acorns, berries, and roots. Migration for most was a way of life even though their niches, consisting of valleys and hills, conspired to separate one group from another.

Their relative isolation gave rise to many languages, and to multilingualism encouraged by trade, marriages, and exchanges. A nineteenth-century observation that the Ashochimi "display great readiness in learning their neighbors' tongues" must have applied to most all of California's indigenous peoples. A great Ashochimi leader, a report noted, spoke fourteen languages and dialects.[26] Similarly, when the Mexicans and Spaniards arrived, Spanish

Naturalizations (Otōsan)

loanwords entered Ashochimi speech through trade relations, like the Hawaiian makeshift trade language, hapa haole.

My circuits through Ashochimi country were to escape the alien, cold world that was the college. The rules on Howell Mountain required that I unlearn my pidgin language, and my "moke" behavior and dress. I practiced speaking like "wan haole" in earnest, although years later sharp ears could still detect my pidgin intonation. In English when asking a question, the pitch rises and finishes on a high note, whereas in pidgin, the sentence begins high and falls to a low pitch at the end. I could not escape (or resist) that fine corruption, discerning ears informed me.

While a history professor at Cornell University, I delivered a brief talk in Los Angeles in my native pidgin. I thought it hilarious for my audience to witness the spectacle of an Ivy League professor speaking in the language of my auntie, mother, and mokes. A newspaper reporter in the audience missed the humor in his story the following day. The Cornell professor, he wrote, could not sustain speech in proper English, but "reverted" to his native pidgin. A thin veneer was my acquisition of English and civilization; beneath that cover was my genuine, uncivil self, which was irrepressible.

In addition to speaking standard English, Howell Mountain civility required proper table manners. I watched, much to my surprise, students in the college cafeteria line routinely place a knife, spoon, and fork on their trays. Eating with chopsticks and certainly without a dinner knife was the best behavior I could muster. I imagined unblinking eyes, stern and unforgiving, policing my every move. Under that surveillance and discipline, I became adept at placing a napkin on my lap, and deploying my knife, fork, and spoon as the occasion and food required. A friend from Hawai'i studied, indeed, memorized Emily Post's book of etiquette to ensure his cultural competence to deflect ridicule. In a San Francisco diner, a white couple conversed loudly over my use of knife and fork to eat a sandwich with a scoop of mashed potato on top draped with brown gravy. "Look, Henry," the woman seemed to exclaim, "a native."[27]

Ashochimi trails were irresistible. I loved those long walks and countless hours clambering over immense, ancient boulders, smelling the pine trees and manzanita blooms, and watching turkey vultures soar and circle on updrafts while sniffing and spying the valley far below. Walking carried me away from the white barber who remarked my thick, black hair dulled his scissors, and from the college rules that stated God was not pleased with interracial dating.[28] The college required a high school classmate of mine from Hawai'i and a white student from the continent to seek prayerful counsel when they began dating. It was as if crossing the color line was not only a sin but a mental illness as well.

God's will regarding interracial coupling was expressed in the Biblical passage, "be ye not unequally yoked."[29] I swear, in a book written by the church's founding prophet, Ellen G. White, I happened upon a photograph (doctored?) of a black man with spots on his back. Miscegenation's sorry child, the illustration depicted, "the tragic mulatto." It stunned me, the photograph. It mattered little to the social engineers on Howell Mountain that in 1948 the California high court had found the state's miscegenation law to be unconstitutional. In *Perez v. Sharp*, by a slender 4-3 margin, the court declared marriage to be "a fundamental right of free men" and thus protected under the Fourteenth Amendment.[30]

It was twelve years after the US Supreme Court ruling on *Brown v. Board of Education* (1954) and segregation's legal end, when the chairman of the department of religion, a holy man and a trustee of the prophet's estate, told me I could not pastor a white church. Upon that hearing, I quit the major and faith. At the time, I was studying theology and in my third year of koine

Greek, hoping to follow in the footsteps of existential philosophers and liberation theologians. Racism killed that youthful dream.

From Inspiration Point overlooking Pope Valley, you can see the California sky, pellucid blue like the waters of Waimea Bay on Oʻahu. From the ocean, I knew the lighter blue at the sky's shores rimming the earth signaled shallow waters, and its dark, azure zenith showed its great depth. I swam miles across the sky, crawling or was it backstroking on the currents of warm air called thermals, analogs of the hydrothermal vents on Lōʻihi's rise beneath the sea, lifting to the ether of the heavens. Far away from the putridness of inhumanity, I ascended in straight lines to the vanishing point.

Marooned on the continent, I cried for my island home in Pacific waters to the far west. I should have bathed in the hot springs of Mayacama (Calistoga) in the valley at the foot of Howell Mountain. There in the volcanic pools Ashochimi brought their sick, wounded, and infirm to cure their maladies by immersing their bodies in the healing waters and warming mud. They built scaffolds of willows and brush, and reclined their sick on those beds suspended above the restoring steam. The rich, mineral vapors encircled, caressed, and rejuvenated them. Well-worn trails to the hot springs testified to their powers.[31] I should have joined the pilgrimage to sweat the evil of Howell Mountain from my pores because those poisons still course through my veins. I can feel the sting of their venom some fifty years later.

Ashochimi numbered an estimated 1,000 to 1,650 in 1770. The Spaniards and Mexicans arrived with their herds of cattle, driving off game and taxing the freshwater and streams. Spanish missions absorbed and dispersed the Ashochimi, and settlers occupied their land, like Edwin Angwin, a Cornish immigrant who named the town of Angwin in 1874. My college, established in Healdsburg, California, in 1882, moved to nearby Angwin in 1909. The following year, the US Census counted a mere seventy-three Ashochimi.

According to an ethnography, the Ashochimi cremated their dead, and threw their ashes into the air to transport their spirits to a cave on the shores of the Pacific Ocean. After spending some time there, the spirits took flight over the ocean farther westward toward the setting sun.[32] Riding the trade winds like plant spores from the continent, they might have cohered with the regenerative Moaʻe Lehua, rustling Puna's hala leaves and scattering lehua petals.

Laura Fish Somersal, daughter of Mary John Eli of Geyserville, California, was born in 1892 and was the last fluent speaker of Ashochimi or Wappo (from the Spanish name, Guapo or "brave"). Somersal was able to learn the language because her mother was blind so she was excused from attending the local Bureau of Indian Affairs school where she would have been forced to learn English to the exclusion of her native tongue. Somersal escaped that fate, and worked all her life as a cook, hop-picker, and housekeeper. During the 1970s, she became a language consultant and teacher. Somersal was a master basket weaver, like the creator, and possessed a wide range of basketry skills.

When Somersal died in 1990, the Ashochimi language apparently died with her.[33] "Although a few elderly individuals retain some knowledge of the language," a study published in 2011 found that "none has a speaking knowledge, and Wappo is near extinction." The report ended on a note of finality: "Since there is no modern group for which Wappo is the heritage language, no retention effort is underway."[34]

After graduating in 1967, I fled the college on the mountain for graduate studies in history at UCLA. There, under the tutorship of the US labor historian Alexander Saxton, I read Whitney R. Cross's remarkable *The Burned-over District: The Social and Intellectual History of Enthusiastic Religion in Western*

New York, 1800–1850 (1950). The book freed me from the bonds of the church and grief that was Howell Mountain. The religion, Cross showed, was a distinctively western New York affair but also rooted in New England's Second Great Awakening and the birth of enthusiastic religion, and, as I learned, it sparked the cause of imperialism and foreign missions.

The Hawaiian castaway ʻŌpūkahaʻia inspired Christian missions to Hawaiʻi, I describe in my *Island World* (2008). He died in Cornwall, Connecticut, but fellow Hawaiians Hopu and Kaumualiʻi departed Boston's Long Wharf on October 23, 1819, with the first missionary company bound for the islands dispatched by the American Board of Commissioners for Foreign Missions (ABCFM).[35] How could my mother and her brothers and sisters convert to a faith uniquely western New York and New England? I mused. My family's experiences in Hawaiʻi were as distant from New England as my grade-school readers that had so captivated my imagination as a child.

I attended a Hawaiian mission school in Honolulu, not unlike the Foreign Mission School established in Cornwall in 1816 by the ABCFM for "the education of heathen youth."[36] As I describe in *Island World*, among the school's students in 1818 were six Hawaiians, two Society Islanders, two Malays, and eleven American Indians. Christianity and civilization were the twin pillars of the school's curriculum wherein uncultivated natives received instruction in cultivation—home care, agriculture, commerce, and mechanics.

In Hawaiʻi, manual labor, missionary David Belden Lyman believed, held the power to lift a people from barbarism to civilization. With that conviction, Lyman established the Hilo Boarding School for boys in 1836. His intention was to mold heathen youth into "useful, Christian citizens" by taking, in the words of the school's commemorative pamphlet, "Hawaiian youth in their natural uncultured state and by dint of unsparing painstaking [effort] to impart to them such mental and moral furnishing as they were able to receive and appropriate, in combination with a wholesome physical training in the ways of social and civilized life."[37]

A principal feature of my mission education, it seems to me, both in Hawai'i and California, was the extraction of the heathen in me and insertion of the useful, Christian citizen. My speech, table manners, dress, and comportment were surface reclamation projects. Deeper were transformations of language and ideology, the discourses of Christianity and civilization. Like baptism by immersion, the old died and the new witnessed a resurrection. As the founder of the first American Indian boarding school declared: "Kill the Indian in him, and save the man."[38]

Whether out of a desire to pluck forbidden fruit, a contrariness bred by plantation education, or a colonial mentality, I aspired to cross the color line. Out-of-the-blue and in the quiet of Irwin Hall chapel, which no longer exists, at the college on the mountain I asked a white classmate if she would marry me. She said she feared pregnancy and childbirth. At the time, she was a brilliant student and an aspiring nurse and, later, physician. The question remained unanswered, and we both graduated. She went on to medical school, and I went on to study African history at UCLA.

In 1971, I married in Botswana, at the time a black-ruled nation in the heart of white supremacist southern Africa, returned to resume my graduate education at UCLA, and four years later, revisited Botswana to conduct fieldwork for my doctoral dissertation. After a year of research on the day of our departure from Botswana, there at the Gaborone airport was my intended from our college days. There she was a physician with her physician husband, equally yoked, nearly halfway around the world from our last encounter and some eight years later. Immaterial was space / time, because there she stood as round as a lehua blossom, pregnant with her first child.

Otōsan, you were a man of few words, but you were a presence. Communion was through the complex, labor-intensive dishes you carefully prepared: (Hawaiian) lau lau, (Chinese) mango seed, and (Japanese) makizushi. Their tastes, salty, sweet and sour, salty and sweet, and their smells of the earth, the trees, the sea, remain with us, your gifts embodied. Your autopsy report described you as "a thin Oriental male." That clinical description utterly fails to capture your essence. A pinned butterfly in a museum case is not a butterfly.

It was my friend Ronald Takaki of UC Berkeley who returned me to the Napa Valley nearly three decades after having taken my leave from the college on Howell Mountain. A day of restoration, Ron promised, in Calistoga's hot springs and a massage followed by a fine dinner paired with the valley's ungodly wines. Ron, I remember fondly, liked white linen tablecloths. It was splendid, the day, and entirely memorable.

My wife, Marina, and I have been regular, if infrequent visitors to Ashochimi country ever since. We roam the valleys, and avoid the mountaintops. Gnarly oaks heavy with acorn and beneath, grapevines, their leaves glistening like hot lava, yellow, orange, red—Hiʻiaka's colors—in the low October sun are achingly sublime. The people who once walked that earth beckon us. We follow them to their mud and mineral baths to coax from our bodies the toxins of centuries.

Subjects

CHAPTER FOUR

Extinctions

A peerless coastline bursting with islands, towering redwoods, and mountain ranges cut by fecund valleys and prodigious though threatened
rivers, the land and its waters are saturated with the blood and power of
their native peoples—Chilula, Hupa, Karuk, Whilkut, Wiyot, and Yurok.
Many of them still tread softly in those cool, damp forests, gathering
the bounties of the earth, and fewer fish the waters for the diminishing
salmon that was once their staff of life. Like the ever-present fog that
with the ocean's tide breaks and foams toward the land and then retreats
back to sea, the American Indian presence permeates that sacred place
named irreverently since 1850 by Europeans, Humboldt Bay and, later,
county.

Alexander von Humboldt, the German naturalist and the county's namesake, breezed through Spain's America from 1799 to 1804 and my *Pineapple
Culture* (2009).[1] His monumental *Personal Narrative of Travels to the Equinoctial
Regions of America* (1814–25) helped fix the tropical band as a field for scientific
and economic exploitation and as a narrative and landscape for aesthetic,
imperious representations. Like his kind, Humboldt failed to apprehend the
presence of indigenous peoples, except as "savages of America . . . in whose
character we find a striking mixture of perversity and meekness," lending "a
peculiar charm" to an otherwise exuberant theatre of vegetation bursting
from the "eternal spring of organic life."[2] By contrast, Indian country bears

the inscriptions and agencies of plants, animals, and peoples in equal measure.

In 1976, Humboldt State University in Arcata, California, tendered my first academic appointment to teach in its fledgling Ethnic Studies Program housed in a former dwelling at the edge of campus. From our offices below, we trudged up a long flight of stairs to get to the classrooms on the campus proper. Marginality was a designed, arduous state. My colleagues and I team-taught Introduction to Ethnic Studies, and I taught all of the courses in Asian American studies. Teaching was our overriding preoccupation— heavy class loads, large numbers of demanding students, course preparations and office hours, and extracurricular student needs both academic and personal.

I recall with great fondness an unbound, free-spirited Chicanx student, Juan Rivera, who without fail carried his large, aluminum-framed backpack filled with his sole earthly possessions, lived in a hollowed-out redwood tree, and visited me each morning to wash in our toilet before trudging off to class. Juan was an exemplary human being.

Besides the centrality of Indians to the region, Chinese and Japanese worked the land. In the nineteenth century, Chinese gold miners panned the inland rivers, planted trees for their pharmacopoeia, and in Weaverville built a Daoist "Temple Among the Trees Beneath the Clouds." Along the Pacific Coast, Chinese worked for whites as field hands, cooks, and domestic servants, and in Eureka, the county seat, a small, crowded Chinatown of hotels and boardinghouses, laundries, restaurants, and shops took precarious root. As in the interior mining areas, whites in coastal towns like Eureka, Arcata, Crescent City, and Ferndale routinely accused the Chinese of depriving them of jobs and assaulted them with impunity. During the 1870s, several companies fired their Chinese workers, and on Chinese New Year's Day, 1875, whites rioted in Eureka's Chinatown. In 1882, aware of the Chinese Exclusion Act being debated in the Congress, whites in Eureka met, formed a standing committee, and passed a resolution banning the Chinese from California. Three years later, Humboldt's citizens expelled all of the Chinese, some 1,500 men and 50 women, from the county.[3]

In violation of the region's slogan, "The Chinese Must Never Return," I settled in Arcata and then Eureka during my three years at Humboldt State. I was aware of the 1885 expulsion, and learned of the October 1909 bombing of the Tsuchiya Bros. store in Eureka. Japanese, too (not that it made any difference to racists for whom all Asians were alike), were unwelcome. In the early morning hours of Memorial Day 1978, I heard what sounded like a shotgun blast through the front door of our Eureka house. Making my way gingerly from our bedroom to the living room, recalling my time in South Carolina a decade earlier, I could see the moonlight shining through a gaping hole in the door. On the floor, I found a heavy rock, the object that hit with such force that it shattered the sturdy, wood door. No burning cross on the front lawn, but a granite boulder in our home. Thereafter, I found our garbage can upturned with refuse scattered on the grass, and discovered broken trees and shrubs. Our neighbors saw and heard nothing, they said, and I acquired a German shepherd dog to ward off the cowardly terrors of the night. At least one citizen of the county remained determined to rid Humboldt of the Asian stain.

As a UCLA graduate student in the mid-1970s and like many of my peers, I undertook a pilgrimage to Manzanar concentration camp for Japanese during World War II in the Owens Valley of southern California. From my post at the northern end of the state, I planned with my Humboldt State students a pilgrimage to Tule Lake concentration camp, Manzanar's counterpoint, toward the interior near the Oregon border. Driving past majestic Mount Shasta, we descended to the tule (a water reed) lowlands filled with immense flocks of geese, ducks, and water birds of every color. Their conversation was sustained and loud, unencumbered by (Emily Post) rules of etiquette. Extending for miles in every direction, the basin supported huge, fertile fields of agricultural production made possible by the rivers and silt deposits. But this place of life abundance was also a terminus, a ground of extinction, confounding the peoples' will to exist.

Along the northeastern side of Tule Lake emerged a concentration camp for Japanese, and toward its southwestern flank flowed the Lava Beds where Kintpuash ("Captain Jack") and his Modoc band waged a war of survival against the depredations of white settlers and the US Army. For five months in 1873, as the Chinese were being expelled from Humboldt County, the Modocs defied extinction on their native soil. The Tule Lake basin, home to the Modocs, attracted white trappers and traders in the 1820s for its fur-bearing animals and markets for goods, horses, and slaves, especially native girls. Modocs participated in those exchanges and raids for human chattel, but they also suffered infringements upon their domain by whites, particularly after the discovery of gold in 1851. Settlers followed the miners, and their insatiable appetite for agricultural land led to the imposition of reservations for the Klamaths and Modocs in 1864. Modoc refusal to acquiesce to that federal program of removal, confinement, and assimilation precipitated the war of extermination conducted against them.

Similarly, Tule Lake concentration camp, designated a "segregation center" by the government in 1943, exemplified its war against the Japanese and its attempt to extinguish their culture and hence their existence as a people. That policy of the War Relocation Authority (WRA), headed by Dillon S. Myer, was "Americanization" allegedly for the benefit and uplift of the subject, dependent people through cultural assimilation and a scattering of them throughout the US continent. The Japanese as a people were to vanish, like the Indian, and cease to exist. Myer later carried "Americanization" with him to the Bureau of Indian Affairs, which he led from 1950 to 1953, and fittingly the program for American Indians was called "termination."[4]

WEAVERS[5]

Modoc country was blessed and given to them by the creator, Kumookumts, a man / woman who traveled as an old woman who made baskets, women's work, but never completed them. The earth, then, was a flat disc, the center of which was a small hill of original earth matter on the east side of Tule Lake. Kumookumts, as if weaving a basket, expanded the world outward from that nucleus. In one version, the woman / man created people by scattering seeds that grew into Indians, and in another, Kumookumts plucked his / her armpit hairs to produce humans.

Allies of the creator were Weasel who had the ability to move through water, on land, and from treetop to treetop, Spider who could leap into the air and fly as swiftly as a bird, and Eagle who perched on mountaintops to see everything below and into the distance as far as the ocean. Kumookumts, in addition to giving life to humans, imparted to them knowledge of edible and poisonous plants, methods of healing, and a heartfelt spirituality. Then the creator ceased to exist but left tracks upon the earth, tracings that bear names.[6]

Physical manifestations, such as the sun, earth, moon, stars, mountains, and bodies of water, bore powers that humans could summon by addressing them as persons. "You, rocks! You, mountains! Give me my deer. I am hungry. I don't want to starve," a woman declared. "You are going to help me. This is my country; it is here for me. I don't want to be naked or hungry. You're not generous. [But you should be.] Help me. Give me food, venison, clothing."[7] In fact, the physical world operated as known in the realm of humans. At a council meeting, which lasted for five years, Moon agreed to shine at night, and all decided on the length of the day and the seasons. Coyote wanted the winter to last for twelve months, but most preferred that winter and summer be limited to three months each. The majority agreed that all living things, including humans, should be mortal because, as Mole reasoned, "I want them to grow old, and get cold when they sit down and shake and die. Flowers, trees, and everything living must die or the world would get too full."[8]

Modocs, meaning "people to the south" as designated by the Klamath Indians to their north, organized themselves into small bands that moved with the seasons and the menu of available foods procured by gathering and hunting. They migrated along the eastern littoral of the Cascade Range of mountains north past the bend of the Lost River, east to Goose Lake, and south to the foothills of Mount Shasta. Within that territory, Modocs divided themselves by places of primary settlement, calling those who lived to the west of Tule Lake, the center, the Gumbatwas or "people to the west," those occupying the eastern reaches along the Lost River they named the Kokiwas or "people of the far out country," and those at the center along lower Lost River and Tule Lake, the Paskanwas or simply "river people." They were all Modocs and those designations simply located their primary affiliations, which were neither ethnic nor political units. Modocs moved freely among those three locations but were identified with their main site of settlement, testifying to the power of place.

Small Modoc villages consisted of two to three houses each accommodating one to three families that averaged five members, while large ones held six to eight houses and very large ones, over eight houses. Those lined the rivers and lakes of Modoc country, and they included permanent and temporary summer and winter settlements and fishing, hunting, and gathering villages. Winter homes were more substantial constructions while summer homes consisted of bushes and shrubs, befitting the weather and nomadic life of hunters and gatherers.

The waterways were generous in supplying food, including ducks, geese, and other game birds, the wocus or water lily whose seeds were ground into a fine meal for bread, and the epos, a nutritious root that was a staple of the Modoc diet. In June and July, the bittersweet camas, a rare and highly valued bulb, was ready for harvest, and in August the huckleberries ripened in the cooler elevations. In a gendered division of labor, women gathered and processed plant foods, and men hunted rabbits, deer, antelope, and bighorn sheep. Together they provided for the people's sustenance. Women wove baskets from tule reeds and men tanned animal skins for clothing. Baskets were functional and their designs, creative works of art.

As indicated by their founder, Modocs were principally weavers. Their use of tule reed was a distinctive attribute of their weaving, and their tule carrying baskets were designed for utility as well as comprising aesthetic expressions with spiritual and social significance. The baby basket lashed to the mother's back, for instance, marked the entry of the infant into the world both physical and spiritual. In the basket, additionally, the mother secured the baby's head, causing a flattening of the skull which identified the child as a Modoc. The practice would change in the nineteenth century when the use of baby baskets decreased, but the tradition of weaving continued undiminished and remained central to the subjectivity and constitution of the Modocs as a people.

Neighboring peoples, including the Pit River nations, the Paiute, the Shasta, and the Klamath, respected Modoc country. Modocs were closest to the Klamaths with a common language, marriage ties, and kinship obligations. All had relations of exchanges and occasional conflicts and wars. The Klamath were trade partners to the north, the Paiutes challenged the Modocs to the east, the Pit River Atsugewi and Achomawi contended with Modoc sorties in the south, and the Shastas troubled the Modocs because they lived to the west where the dead dwelled in the spirit world.

Humans occupied Modoc country some 12,000 to 15,000 years ago, and people who became Modocs exploited and in turn were shaped by their natural world. "Their harsh environment created not only a theological base," explained Patricia James Easterla, a Modoc, "but a whole ethical and economic system that is difficult to comprehend when viewed without an understanding of the Modoc's age-old interaction with that environment."[9] Each mountain and rock formation, every river and lake, all the plants and animals that inhabited that world had names, told stories, and shaped the Modoc social formation in its wholeness.

Foreigners, mainly women and children, entered Modoc society through warfare and the slave trade. By capturing women, Modoc men undermined the masculinity and patriarchal systems of their rivals, primarily the Pit River Indians and Paiutes, and women's labor and reproductive abilities added value to the Modoc social formation and reduced the wealth of their enemies. Modoc men married captured women, thereby rendering them members of Modoc society, and enslaved captives, including children, and traded them with their neighbors.

The immense, near-solitary sacred mountain, called Shasta by whites, rising above the vast lava plain was the creator's home, according to the Karuk. As proof, you can see smoke curling through the smoke hole of his dwelling, they observed. Depending upon one's location in relation to it, the once-active volcano held different meanings. For those to its west, the mountain marked the day's start and life's beginnings; for those to its east, like the Modocs, the mountain was where the sun set, the place of life's end. The Karuk said that when the whites arrived, the "Old Man Above" abandoned his mountain home and went away.

TRANSACTIONS

Fur traders were among the first whites to trespass upon Modoc country. They introduced goods and diseases that threatened to destroy the people and damage their relations of production. Soon thereafter, white settlers followed in their wake together with the Indian policy of their nation-state. The Modoc traffic with whites began as extensions of exchanges with their

Indian neighbors in woven baskets, obsidian for arrowheads and tools, foods, and slaves.

The Northwest Company's 1817 expedition along the Columbia River in what became Washington State, and its Fort Walla Walla erected in 1818 with a significant number of Hawaiian laborers, was the entering wedge that opened Modoc country to the Pacific world and European commerce. As I write in my *Island World*, at its start, Fort Walla Walla consisted of twenty-five Canadians, thirty-eight Iroquois, and thirty-two Hawaiians, and in 1821 the Northwest Company merged with its rival, the Hudson's Bay Company, to become the dominant firm in the Northwest. That was the ambition of George Simpson, chief factor of the Hudson's Bay Company and governor of the territory, when he declared in 1824 his intention to double the profit of the fur trade. Simpson's reach extended to the north into British Canada and south to the Klamath.

Initially, not having the desired beaver, the Modocs came only indirectly into contact with white traders through their goods, including beads, metal implements, weapons, and horses. Even those indirect introductions were dramatic. Horses shortened distances and increased contacts, altering time / space, and warfare and hunting were by far more lethal with metal knives and rifles. Enemy raids required the Modocs to join the European trade networks to keep pace with their neighbors. Along the Columbia River, the Klamath and lesser numbers of Modocs exchanged furs and labor for iron goods, weapons, and alcohol. White fur traders ventured into Modoc country for the first time in 1824 in their quest for animal pelts.

Although European goods boosted productivity especially in hunting and raiding, they also led to a decline in other aspects of the Modoc economy. Metal containers replaced woven baskets, thereby affecting the weavers, and labor turned from a subsistence to exchange economy to acquire trade goods such as furs, skins, and slaves. Diseases decimated and crippled native bodies, making contacts more consequential. During the 1830s, epidemics swept through the region, and caused the Modoc population to decrease from about a thousand to 500 people, and by 1860, their numbers dwindled to approximately 300.

Those material transactions were devastating, and they were amplified by the ideological transformations in the Christianizing and "civilizing" mission of certain white colonizers. In 1836, Presbyterian missionaries arrived among the Cayuse in Oregon to assimilate the conquered people. But the Cayuse rebelled in 1847, attacked the mission, and killed thirteen of the invaders. Precipitating factors might have included the introduced diseases that killed scores of indigenous peoples, and the conviction that missionaries violated and directed the Cayuse to neglect native spiritual beliefs and practices, which had kept their world whole and healthy. Those transgressions accelerated with the arrival of increasing numbers of white settlers crossing the Overland Trail to settle in Oregon Territory claimed by the US in 1846, and California's Gold Rush of 1849, which led to the spread of gold miners who scoured rivers and staked claims throughout California and the Northwest. Against that inundating flood, the Cayuse and other Indians of the region rose up in defense of their land and people.

Whites passing through Modoc country with their wagons, horses, and herds of cattle trampled valuable digging grounds for roots and bulbs, destroyed berry patches, and drove off game. Modocs, in turn, attacked wagon trains and killed stray cattle. Through the seduction of trade and the rapid destruction of their resources and livelihood, Modocs were gradually drawn into the compass of capitalism to sell their labor for goods and cash. Two years after Mexico's 1848 treaty with the US, California was admitted into the union. Native peoples thereby became aliens in their own land, and the state required them to carry passports or papers giving them permission to work in white towns and businesses. Modoc men worked on white farms, women served as domestics and some, as prostitutes, and children were easily indentured. Indians, like other people of color, could not testify against citizens or whites, and their mobility and freedoms were restricted.

The federal government rejected treaties negotiated by California's Indian Affairs commissioners, leaving Indian country open to white miners and settlers. To compound the problem, the Modocs straddled California and Oregon, and each had different administrators and regulations governing their lives. In Oregon Territory, the federal government appointed a superintendent and district agents to oversee Indian affairs. The winter of 1851–52 was especially tough on the Modocs, resulting in food shortages and starvation, which encouraged raids on white settlers and wagon trains. By 1852, officials in Oregon Territory and Washington, DC, agreed on the need for reservations to segregate Indians from whites and to give the citizen race greater access to and rights over Indian land.

In that same year in California, a group of whites from Yreka found and buried eighteen to twenty bodies of white men, women, and children of a settler train who had been killed by Indians, they charged. In retaliation, whites circled a Modoc village and killed some forty-two men, women, and children. They marched through Modoc country, destroying villages and food stores in their path. Known as the "Ben Wright's Massacre" for the raiders' leader, the deed solidified Modoc opposition to all whites in and passing through their lands. Ben Wright later suffered the same fate he had visited on Modoc country at the hands of Indians in Oregon.

One of those whose family members perished in the massacre was a young Modoc, Kintpuash, who two days after Ben Wright's depredations called a council meeting. Kintpuash was born around 1840, and grew up along the Lost River where he witnessed the devastating changes forced upon his people by foreign invaders. A leader's son, Kintpuash advised the people to make peace, not war, with the whites to survive. Earlier, as a child during a council meeting where his father urged his people to stand and fight against the invading settlers, Kintpuash stood up in opposition. "I see that the white people are many," Kintpuash told the council. "If we value our lives or love our country we must not fight the white man."[10]

In 1863, a California official negotiated a treaty with the Modocs, Klamaths, Shastas, and Scott Valley and Hamburg Indians. The state guaranteed to protect Indians from whites encroaching into their country if they promised to refrain from war among themselves and against whites and ensured the safe passage of whites through their lands. By contrast, Oregon signed a treaty in 1864 with its Klamath and Modoc populations that carved out a Klamath reservation to which Modocs and Paiutes agreed to move. Kintpuash was one of the twenty-seven Indian leaders who signed the treaty, possibly because he believed removal was the only way to keep Modoc families and communities relatively intact and secure. The federal government erroneously held that by signing the 1864 Oregon treaty the entire Modoc people had given up their ancestral rights to the Tule Lake and Lost River country, which lay in California. Instead, the California branch of Modocs believed they were entitled by the 1863 California treaty to remain on those lands that were theirs from the beginning. That confusion illustrates how the Modocs struggled on multiple fronts to retain their sovereignty from lawless whites and vigilantes, and the competing claims of the federal government, Oregon Territory, and California and their district agents.

The white flood and violence led to a split among the Modocs, and alienated them from the land that constituted them as a people and society. Moreover, on Klamath land in Oregon, Modocs were at a disadvantage. Old Schonchin's Modoc band lived in Oregon Territory, and they were the first to remove to the Klamath reservation in 1864. The following year, Kintpuash's band, which lived along the Lost River and Tule Lake in Oregon and California, joined them despite their belief that Klamath country was "not a safe place for Modoc Indians."[11] Indeed, gathering and hunting suffered in the new environment, and government efforts to convert Modocs to Christianity and capitalism disturbed their worldviews and material relations. In addition, as they had feared, the Klamaths discriminated against them as strangers to the land. Gradually, Kintpuash's people fled the Klamath reservation to return home.

There they remained until 1869 when Congress ratified the treaty signed by some Modocs five years earlier, and the government allocated new lands for Modocs on the Klamath reservation and gave them blankets, flour, and beef to induce them to return. When a group of about forty-five refused, a detail of soldiers rounded them up and forcibly marched them back to the reservation. Government rations ceased in 1870, Klamath harassment of Modocs and white assimilation continued, and production through gathering and hunting proved insufficient for subsistence.

In the midst of dislocations both physical and ideological came the "Ghost Dance" that resisted the white invasion, and quickly spread throughout Nevada, California, and Oregon in the 1870s.[12] A social movement premised upon Indian cultural revival and renewal to counter the dispossession and forced assimilation, the "Ghost Dance" was disseminated by charismatic prophets like Wovoka, the Paiute spiritual leader, who foresaw the resurrection of Indian dead and expulsion of whites with prayer, fasting, and dance. Many Modocs embraced those beliefs, which provided an ideological base for armed rebellion and movements for self-determination and cultural regeneration.

GENOCIDE

From the beginning and throughout the course of the nation's imperial march from the Atlantic to the Pacific, the US and its citizens pursued the extermination and physical removal of Indian peoples.[13] As foreign nations, American Indians warred against and signed treaties with the US, and they visited its territories as aliens. The US Supreme Court in *Worcester v. Georgia* (1832) held that the Cherokees were a "foreign state," albeit under US rule, a status affirmed by Chief Justice Roger Taney in the court's *Dred Scott* (1857).

The US and some of its peoples, especially missionaries and educators, also practiced assimilation or the cultural extinction of American Indians. Absorption of Indian nations by the US nation-state was the intention of the Dawes Act (1887), which proposed to break up Indian lands into individual allotments, enabling the federal government to consider Indians as individuals and not nations. Following that policy and after the 1890 US Census declared that there were no more frontiers because whites had filled the continent, the US Supreme Court ruled in *Lone Wolf v. Hitchcock* (1903) that Congress held plenary powers over American Indians who comprised "domestic dependent nations" in affirmation of *Cherokee v. Georgia* (1831). That absorption of American Indians into a state of domesticity and dependence as wards was extermination of another sort but extinction just the same.

While some Modocs chose to remain on the Klamath reservation, Kintpuash and a group of about 370 Modocs returned to their homeland in April 1870 to free themselves from the stifling controls of the settler nation-state and from Klamath prejudice. Their homecoming, however, was not to a former, pristine state. Since the 1864 treaty and their removal, Modoc country had changed rapidly. According to a contemporary observer: "Nearly every foot of it fit for cultivation has been taken up by settlers whose thousands of cattle, horses and sheep are ranging over it."[14] As a consequence, Modocs had to work for white settlers to supplement their subsistence activities as the price of relative freedom. Their independent conduct, nonetheless, offered a poor example to other subject peoples so, as was put by an Indian agent for the Klamaths, Kintpuash had to be "brought into subjection or exterminated."[15] Federal Indian Commissioner Francis A. Walker expressed his government's position clearly in a letter dated July 6, 1872, to his agent in the field: "You are directed to remove them [the Modocs] to the Klamath reservation peaceably, if you possibly can, but forcefully if you must."[16]

The US military carried out that order in November 1872. Still the Modocs refused to leave their homes. At a meeting on November 28, Captain James Jackson tried to arrest several leaders, including Kintpuash. The soldiers ordered the Modocs to surrender their arms, which they did except Na-lu-is (aka "Scarfaced Charley") who kept his revolver at his side. One of the soldiers stepped forward to forcibly remove his pistol while swearing at him and threatening him with his pointed gun when Na-lu-is drew his pistol and he and the soldier fired at the same time, both missing their targets. The Modocs fled to the Lava Beds in three groups. Meanwhile, other Modocs along the Lost River exchanged fire with the US troops and settlers who had attacked and burned "Hooker Jim's" camp, and in retaliation a band under "Hooker Jim" killed about a dozen white settlers, men and boys, before retreating to the Lava Beds to join the first groups there. Thus began the "Modoc War" when in fact the conflict was precipitated by the US and was, properly, the US War on the Modocs.

News of the conflict reached the San Francisco and, later, the national press. President Ulysses S. Grant sought a speedy end to the hostilities by appointing a "peace commission" to the Modocs to cease their resistance, return to the Klamath reservation, and surrender those responsible for the settlers' deaths. Among those selected for the commission were Indian agent Alfred Meacham, General Edward Canby, Winema, a Modoc and Kintpuash's cousin, and her husband, Frank Riddle, who served as intermediaries with the Modoc patriots. Meanwhile, Indian agents in California and Oregon debated and blamed each other for the war, and in March 1873 various whites tried to negotiate a settlement with the Modocs who were holed up by the US Army on the Lava Beds. The assembled soldiers reached a force of over 600, against an estimated 74 men and 85 women and children among the Modoc defenders.

The leaders were divided between "Hooker Jim" and others who favored war and Kintpuash who advised negotiations. The majority like "Black Jim" preferred fighting over being "decoyed and shot like a dog," and when Kint-puash persisted in his position, the others dressed him with a basket cap and shawl, women's dress, and taunted him, saying he was a coward and a "fish-hearted woman" and "nothing more than an old squaw."[17] As Kintpuash tes-tified at his trial, "I wanted to make peace and live right; but my men would not listen to me. The men that were in the cave with me never listened to what I said."[18] Kintpuash eventually joined the others in a plan to kill the peace commissioners, perhaps because virtuous leaders followed the wishes of their people or to recoup his manhood and standing as a Modoc man and patriot.

Winema learned of the plot and warned Meacham and Canby but the general insisted that they proceed with the meetings, which were held in April 1873. From past experience, the Modocs distrusted the commissioners and their promise of peace. After all, the offspring of Kumookumts were at war with forces intent on destroying them and their way of life. A mere month before the peace talks, Canby had proposed to send the Modocs to Angel Island, which since 1850 was a military base, to be imprisoned there before their removal to Indian Territory, Oklahoma, so they could never again rise to challenge the US. Angel Island, located in San Francisco Bay, would later serve as a detention center for Asian, Latinx, and European migrants while the US government deliberated their fitness for admission within the nation.[19]

During the fateful meeting of April 11, 1873, Kintpuash asked for a troop withdrawal, a return to Modoc lands along the Lost River, and peace with the white settlers. Canby refused to listen and demanded instead an uncon-ditional surrender and the complete removal of Modocs from their country. Canby's uncompromising posture prompted Kintpuash to declare, "Now we stop," and he pulled out his pistol and shot the seated general at point-blank range.[20] Kintpuash and others finished off the wounded but still alive Canby before turning on the other commissioners, killing one and seriously wounding Meacham.

The Modocs retreated to their stronghold in the lava fields to await the expected retaliation from the US Army. Formed hundreds of thousands of years ago by volcanoes at the junction of the Sierra and Cascade range of mountains that ringed the Tule Lake basin, the Lava Beds was a Modoc home given to them by the creator. They had names for its lava tubes and caves, outcrops and passageways, and they called the area accurately "the land of burnt-out fires." There they chose to make their last stand in defense of their home and maker's gift. To the soldiers, by contrast and like early white foreigners to Hawai'i in my *Island World*,[21] the Lava Beds was a "hell with the fires gone out," and one described it as a "black ocean tumbled into a thousand fantastic shapes, a wild chaos of ruin, desolation and barrenness—a wilderness of billowy upheavals, of furious whirlpools, of miniature mountains rent asunder, of gnarled and knotted, wrinkled and twisted masses of blackness."[22]

After shelling the Modoc position with artillery, the US troops advanced on two fronts from the east and west in single file, each soldier carrying a carbine and sixty rounds of ammunition. The defenders used the cover to their advantage, sniping and firing and moving, punishing the invaders. It took the soldiers six hours to cover half a mile. The second day, the officer in charge of the western flank sent a message to his counterpart on the eastern front: "We will endeavor to end the Modoc War today . . . . Let us exterminate the tribe."[23] The troops moved to within fifty yards of the Modoc stronghold before settling in for the night. The Americans suffered twenty-three casualties, including six dead.

Determining that their position was untenable, under the cover of night, the Modocs retreated to another position, leaving behind an old man and woman too feeble to travel. When the soldiers found them the next morning, they killed them and scalped the old man to display as their trophy. The triumphant US commander reported to his superiors that he had succeeded in dislodging the Modocs from the Lava Beds. They were moving south, he wrote, and "no effort will be spared to exterminate them."[24]

In fact, the Modocs were nearby, still in their lava home. They taunted the troops, ambushed their patrols, and kept moving a step ahead of the soldiers. They embarrassed the US Army, which dispatched a new commander, Jefferson C. Davis, to take charge of the war. When he arrived, Davis found the morale of his forces at a low ebb. They were frustrated and beaten. But the Modocs too wearied of war and their life on the run. They were low on supplies, food, and water. Cut off from Tule Lake, they relied on ice formed in caves for their meager water supply. Some gave up, and with their families left Kintpuash in the Lava Beds. On May 22, 1873, sixty-three Modocs, including twelve fighting men, went over to the US lines to surrender. They appeared gaunt, disheveled, and defeated. An astonished observer described them as "half-naked children, aged squaws who could scarcely hobble, blind, lame, halt, bony."[25] This was the enemy.

Shortly thereafter, on June 1, 1873, Kintpuash and his greatly diminished band surrendered. His people were exhausted and hungry, he said, and his legs had simply given out.[26] As US soldiers shackled Kintpuash and his companions, a newspaperman noted perceptively, "they made no complaint or resistance, though they felt keenly the indignity, but stood silently to let the rivets tighten to bind them in chains."[27] The war was over, but the killing had just begun. Along the way north to Fort Klamath, settlers intercepted a wagonload of Modoc prisoners near Lost River. They murdered four men on the spot in the wagon, splattering their brains on their families, according to an account.

William Tecumseh Sherman, the Civil War general and scourge of Georgia, was the army head in Washington, DC. He, perhaps more than any other, felt keenly the Modoc military successes against US troops, having lost sixty-five killed and sixty-seven wounded.[28] Sherman assured his commander in the field: "You will be fully justified in their [Modoc] utter extermination." After their defeat, Sherman told the *New York Times*: "Treachery is inherent in the Indian character"; and he wrote to the

Part 2. Subjects

Quakers: "if all [Modocs] be swept from the earth, they themselves have invited it." To a friend Sherman confided he was "sorry" that Kintpuash and "most of the Modocs were not killed in the taking." Finally, to his officers in charge, Sherman directed the court martial and execution of the Modoc leaders, the trial and hanging of those responsible for settler casualties, and the dispersal of the rest of the Modocs "so that the name of Modoc should cease."[29]

The US attorney general intervened, ruling that Modocs were a separate nation at war with the US. They were, he wrote correctly but belatedly, "a distinct people" and "in no sense citizens of the United States, and owe it no allegiance; they are governed by their own laws . . . they occupy and possess the lands they dwell on by a quasi absolute right, and cannot be legally dispossessed of them by any power." The US could only deal with the Modoc nation through the instrument of treaties, and thus the captives had to be tried as war criminals by a military tribunal.[30] The Fort Klamath stockade held 155 of those "war criminals," 44 men, 49 women, and 62 children. Whites like the influential abolitionist and suffragist Lucretia Mott, church groups notably the Quakers, and organizations such as the Universal Peace Union, Cooper Institute, and American Indian Aid Association denounced the proceedings and urged clemency.

The trial of Kintpuash, Schonchin "John," "Black Jim," "Boston Charley," and two youth, Slolux and Barncho, began at 10 a.m. on July 5, 1873. They were charged with "murder in violation of the laws of war" and "assault with an intent to kill in violation of the laws of war," both charges arising from the attack on the peace commissioners. Within three days the trial was over, and all were sentenced to death.[31] Execution was set for October 3, 1873. That day, the four men ascended the scaffold. The two youth were spared for imprisonment on Alcatraz Island. Barncho died there, but Slolux was released in 1878 to Indian Territory, Oklahoma. As an object lesson and a prize of conquest, the severed head of Kintpuash and the three other leaders made their way east destined for the Surgeon General's Office and eventually to the Smithsonian Institution, the nation's historical memory.[32]

The remnant, some 153 Modocs, considered enemies of the US, including 54 women and 60 children, became "prisoners of war" after their defeat. As Canby had planned, they were chained and herded onto cattle cars for the long journey to Indian Territory, Oklahoma. Children and mostly old men and women, according to a teenager who spotted them near Seneca, Missouri, the exiles, worn and weary, reached their destination in late November 1873.

On this alien land and like "civilized" people, the Modocs farmed grains, raised cattle, sent their children to mission boarding school, and worked for wages in nearby towns and on white farms. In the process, their health deteriorated, and their numbers declined by about 30 percent over the first ten years. Extermination seemed imminent. When Jeremiah Curtin, a linguist, visited the Oklahoma Modocs in 1884 to record their language and history, he found "they were discontented and homesick; they wanted to go where the world was created . . . . From change of climate deaths are many. They mourn for their 'own country' (near the lava beds . . .) where each mountain, valley, and lake has a story and is connected with the religion and mythology of their tribe."[33] So many died during those first years of exile that those buried in the Modoc cemetery before 1890 did not have markers bearing their names.

Besides cremating and burying their dead, the Modocs in Oklahoma wove baskets, like the creator, using local reed or hemp grass that recalled the tule that once grew freely in profusion along the waterways of Modoc country.

GHOSTS

"There are ghosts seen over there, *hinotama*," a Japanese reported. "Greenish lights, they say, bigger than a fist. Last winter, I heard only one story of light coming out of the camp smoke above the field on a foggy morning, but now all sorts of stories are going around. We wouldn't go near too early in the morning or at night around that barrack. It's the worst place." Another told of a young girl who, upon a premonition, looked back over her shoulder. "She glanced up and was chilled by a strange glow hovering over the latrine roof. She shivered violently and hurried home to tell her mother, fully expecting her not to believe it." Her mother instead looked worried but said nothing. "The girl insisted on knowing what it was and her mother told her she must have seen *hinotama*. A few days later an elderly bedridden block resident died."[34]

Tule Lake concentration camp was a reservation for Japanese from 1942 to 1946, having undergone a forced removal from their homes in Hawai'i and the US West Coast. They, the Japanese, were in the Hawaiian Islands and on the continent because the US went to Japan to "open" its ports to US ships and goods. An armed flotilla dispatched by the president forced Japan to sign a treaty of amity in 1854. The act led to Japan's entry into the modern world-system, initially as a market and source for migrant labor. Hawai'i's sugar planters recruited them beginning in 1868 when the first group of Japanese arrived in the islands about the time of the US war against the Modocs. West Coast labor recruiters descended on Hawai'i to secure Japanese laborers for the railroads and lumber and agricultural industries. By 1908, there were over 125,000 Japanese in the islands and 80,000 on the continent.

Like the Modocs, the Japanese were aliens "ineligible to citizenship." As we saw, the Naturalization Act (1790) restricted US citizenship to "free white persons," which disallowed Indians, Africans, and Asians from membership in the nation. At the same time, Indian lands and African and Asian labor produced the citizen race. In fact, ownership of land and labor as property was the defining attribute of race (whiteness), gender (manhood), capitalism (class), and (US) citizenship.

The Second World War was waged from one side of the color line for white supremacy (discourse) and colonialism (material relations).

Imperialism was an extension of European national sovereignty. From the other side of that global color line, Third World liberation movements strived for decolonization and antiracism. Indians, Africans, Latinxs, and Asians served among the US imperial troops abroad, and at home produced for the US war machine. In resistance, Third World people warred against racism and inequality in the US while suffering, during the war years, reservations and concentration camps, ghettoes and race riots, and a Jim Crow military.

The Japanese presence at Tule Lake, thus, was unexceptional in the course of US history; it was, in fact, a central article of the nation's constitution. Removal and confinement, extermination and domestic dependencies were consistent narratives of Modoc and Indian pasts, and they linked the Lava Beds with the concentration camp.

At least since the First World War, US military and civilian intelligence had investigated the "Japanese problem" in Hawai'i where Japanese comprised about 40 percent of the population. The problem arose when Japanese, Filipino, and Puerto Rican sugar plantation workers struck for higher wages, an eight-hour workday, paid maternity leave for women, and better health-care and recreation facilities. US intelligence saw that 1920 strike as exemplary of Japan's global ambition "to amalgamate the entire colored races of the world against the Nordic or white race, with Japan at the head of the coalition, for the purpose of wrestling away the supremacy of the white race and placing such supremacy in the colored peoples under the dominion of Japan."[35] In the formulation of W. E. B. Du Bois: the problem of the twentieth century was the problem of the color line.

As early as 1936, President Franklin D. Roosevelt recommended "concentration camps" for suspected Japanese, and on February 19, 1942, issued his Executive Order 9066 that authorized the military to remove "any and all persons" and provide them with food and shelter. Justified by "military necessity," the forcible eviction of some 120,000 Japanese was, like the US War on the Modocs, a military operation for the national security.

Construction on the Tule Lake camp began April 15, 1942, and the following month, the first band of some five hundred Japanese "volunteers"
arrived to help build the facilities that would hold them. In the summer of
1943, the WRA, the civilian agency that replaced the military Wartime Civil
Control Administration, converted Tule Lake into a maximum-security
camp for "disloyals," and by the spring of the 1944 the camp held over eighteen thousand Japanese, the largest of the ten WRA concentration camps. A
"man-proof," six-foot-high chain-link fence topped with barbed wire surrounded the camp, spiked with watchtowers at intervals along the perimeter manned by soldiers with machine guns. For a time in 1943, an enhanced
military presence with eight tanks occupied the camp under martial law.[36]

The camp administrators, the WRA, encouraged the Japanese to produce
on vegetable, hog, and chicken farms for their subsistence. In October 1943,
Japanese farmworkers struck in protest over the death of a fellow laborer,
Kashima, who had been killed in a truck accident. That work action followed
on the previous year's strike by mess hall workers in July, a campaign for
higher wages in August, and two labor strikes in August and September. The
day after Kashima's death, in elections held for a representative body called
the Daihyo Sha Kai, Japanese who were critical of the WRA and its policies
won, but the camp's director, Raymond Best, ignored them and their nego-
tiating committee, casting them as troublemakers.

When the national WRA director Dillon Myer visited Tule Lake on
November 1, 1943, the Daihyo Sha Kai insisted on meeting with him by
amassing thousands of Japanese around the administrative building in
which Myer was meeting with Best. George Kuratomi, the protesters'
spokesman, outlined for Myer the people's grievances that included Best's
dishonest dealings with them, white racism among several WRA staffers,
inadequate food, and overcrowding. At base, Kuratomi explained, the Japanese asked that they "be treated humanely" by the US state.[37] Instead, Myer
expressed confidence in Best, and offered the protesters no encouragement

or promise of redress. To adjourn the meeting, the WRA called for military police on jeeps mounted with machine guns to enter the camp, and with tear gas dispersed the protesters. Soldiers then proceeded to single out and apprehend suspected leaders.

White WRA administrators feared for their personal safety, having witnessed the Japanese demonstration. The next day, November 2, after Myer and Best failed to reassure them, WRA staffers went directly to Lt. Col. Verne Austin, head of a nearby battalion of some 1,200 troops, to get his promise that the army would guarantee their safety. Best, angered over that vote of no confidence in his administration, fired two of his most outspoken critics, and within a week twenty staff members resigned.

Meanwhile, white settlers in the Tule Lake basin complained that Best, Myer, and the WRA coddled the Japanese, and the local and national press played up the November mass protest, which the papers characterized as rioting by the Japanese "enemy." White WRA staff members added fuel to the fire with comments that were, according to Emily Light, a schoolteacher, "hysterical" and exhibiting "quite vicious" attitudes toward "those Japs."[38] After a scuffle between a small group of Japanese and several white administrators, Best called in the military.

Tanks rolled into the camp on November 4, and the army declared martial law. The military imposed a 6 a.m. to 7 p.m. curfew, and arbitrarily apprehended and detained Japanese without recourse to charges or hearings. The occupation forces banned the Daihyo Sha Kai and arrested its members, required identification badges of everyone twelve years and older, and commenced a comprehensive sweep of the entire camp. On November 26, three groups of about 150 soldiers carrying full field equipment and gas masks and all officers bearing side arms, clubs, and gas grenades spread throughout the camp. The troops netted 25 tons of rice and other grains, 22 barrels of saké mash, 400 boxes of canned goods, 20 crates of dried fruit,

20 cartons of cereal, 2 saké stills, a Japanese-language printing press, 500 knives, 400 clubs, 2 public address systems, and 500 radio receivers.

To segregate their prisoners from the rest of the camp, the army erected a stockade surrounded by barbed-wire fence and guard towers, and within the stockade built two to five barracks and tents called the "bull pen" to chill out the incorrigibles. The bull pen, then, the inner sanctum, was a prison within a stockade within a concentration camp. The authority drew up lists, methodically hunted down their quarry, seized over 350 of them, and tossed them into the stockade.

Matsuda Kazue's brother, Yamane Tokio, was one of those who was arrested, beaten, denied medical attention, and locked in the bull pen for nine months. Flimsy and unheated, the tents offered scant protection from the elements that reached freezing temperatures in winter. With bunks set on the frozen ground and no extra clothing or blankets, living in the bull pen was "a life and death struggle for survival," Yamane testified. To no avail, Matsuda pleaded with the authorities to release her brother, transfer her husband who was being held in an alien detention center in Santa Fe, New Mexico, so he could see his dying mother in Tule Lake, and then, to attend her funeral. The military transferred Yamane from Tule Lake to Santa Fe despite his US citizenship.[39] Yamane was among some 1,200 sent by the military from Tule Lake to Justice Department detention camps for aliens.

Beatings, such as the one administered to Yamane, were common in Tule Lake's interrogation rooms where fists and baseball bats were the preferred instruments of reason. A former security officer recalled with delight the night of terror on November 4, the day the tanks rumbled into camp. "None of the three Japs were unconscious but all three were groggy from the blows they received, especially the one . . . hit with the baseball bat," he crowed. These, the officer explained, had been picked up and taken to the administration building where they were ordered to lie on the floor. When they refused, "I knocked my Jap down with my fist. He stayed down but was not unconscious. [Q] hit his Jap over the head again with the baseball bat." Later, during questioning, the officer had an "itching to take a sock at the Jap so I . . . hit a hard blow to the jaw with my fist. [He] went down and out. I reached down and shook him hard in an effort to revive him. I even grabbed him by the hair and shook his head. After about three minutes he came to." Meanwhile, screams could be heard coming from the back rooms. That night in all, eighteen Japanese were "severely beaten with baseball bats," according to a deposition, and some required "hospitalization for several months and the mentality of one was impaired permanently as the result of the beating he had received."[40]

Despite the military's repressive rule, an overwhelming number of Japanese continued to express confidence in the Daihyo Sha Kai through December 1943 even though the army refused to recognize them and held most of their members in the stockade, segregated from the camp population. Toward the end of December and the start of January 1944, a series of events brought the situation to a head. On the morning of December 30, Lt. Schaner, the stockade's warden, arbitrarily pulled two men, Tsuda and Yoshiyama, and ordered them to the bull pen.[41] A few days earlier, Schaner had chosen them to be the spokesmen for the others in the stockade.[42] In protest against Schaner's highhandedness, the men refused to assemble for the 1 p.m. roll call. If the men cleaned the stockade area and assembled for the evening roll call, Schaner promised, he would release Tsuda and Yoshiyama from the cage. The Japanese fulfilled their part of the bargain but by the next morning the pair had not been freed. So the men again refused to assemble for the morning roll call, and were forced from their barracks by armed troops later in the day.

Facing the assembled men, Schaner pointed to Uchida, and commanded that he join Tsuda and Yoshiyama in the bull pen. Then he challenged the Japanese: "Now if there are any more of you who would like to go with him, just step up towards the gate." After a moment's pause, one of them, Koji Todoroki, stepped forward and, according to an army eyewitness, "a murmur passed through the prisoners, followed by the entire group breaking ranks and moving in the direction of the gate."[43]

Frustrated, Schaner left the men standing in the snow for about three hours while he consulted with his commander, Austin, about his next move. "I was just waiting for that," Schaner told the men when he returned. "You men will be put on bread and water for twenty-four hours. You men will have to learn that we mean business and will not tolerate such a demonstration." Trucks then entered the stockade compound, and removed all stores of food. In addition, Schaner ordered a search of the stockade's barracks, which was undertaken "in a most unnecessary destructive method," in the words of a military observer. As a result, many personal items such as radios, pens, watches, cigarettes, and cash were stolen from the Japanese.[44]

Thus provoked, the men vowed to go on a hunger strike until the release of everyone from the stockade. Tsuda explained: "The reason the men . . . are on this hunger strike is because they know not the reason they are in the stockade. They feel they have been unjustly confined and the reason given to them is that they are the potential troublemakers and strong arm men of the colony, which they feel is not true. This is the manner in which they are trying to prove their sincerity and show that they should be vindicated."[45] The hunger strike lasted from January 1 to January 6, 1944, over the Japanese New Year, which carried religious and cultural significance, with no tangible concessions from the military. News of the hunger strike leaked out to the camp population on its third day, and instead of a general protest in support of the stockade hunger strikers, sentiment appeared to turn toward a swift end to the escalating hostilities.

Some in the camp favored accepting the army's demand that the Daihyo Sha Kai must be disbanded and a new body elected to negotiate the end of martial law. Others argued to support the Daihyo Sha Kai as the only and

Extinctions

true representative of the people. Both justified their positions with appeals to Japanese, not white values, and both regretted the split in the ranks of an otherwise united people. The Daihyo Sha Kai had not shown a "true Japanese spirit," one argument went, by not resigning when they failed to dislodge the military from the camp. "We have no other desire than to exist as a true Japanese and to return to Japan unashamed," the appeal concluded. The other faction supported the Daihyo Sha Kai for exhibiting a "true Japanese spirit" by refusing to compromise with the army. "I surely hate to see the Japanese divided," said a stockade leader, Inouye, "and hate to see them fighting with each other." Shimada explained the thinking on the outside: "Let me repeat this, the Army would not give a chance to talk about [the] release of you people [those in the stockade], unless normal condition was first returned." To which Inouye replied: "We realize all the things you people are going through and have told the men in the stockade that you people are working so hard for the common goal. We are just as worried as you people are."[46]

On January 11, 1944, Tule Lake's Japanese voted, according to the official tally, 4,893 against the "status quo," 4,120 for the "status quo," and 228 undecided. The "status quo" meant retention of the Daihyo Sha Kai. The voting might have been influenced by the army's rounding up of Daihyo Sha Kai sympathizers the morning of the vote, and some claimed voting irregularities. A Japanese report claimed a true count of thirty-one blocks (a residential unit of barracks) for "status quo," twenty-nine against, four blocks undetermined, and one block abstained.[47] Whatever the final tally, the vote showed a reluctance to repudiate the Daihyo Sha Kai and to concede the occupying army's position despite the prospect of an end to martial law and the release of the men in the stockade. On January 15, the army returned the camp, except the stockade, to the WRA, and on May 23, 1944, control of the stockade reverted to the WRA. Still, tensions remained high. A Japanese was

Part 2. Subjects

shot and killed by a guard following a minor altercation, and in June, Tasaku Hitomi, a suspected WRA collaborator, was found murdered. Finally, in August 1944, the stockade was closed.

Graffiti scribbled on a Tule Lake camp warehouse wall in Japanese:

The world is not governed fairly.
Not a land of God, nor of Buddha, nor of the stars.
Longing for the stars.[48]

And on the stockade wall, in English and Japanese:

Down with the United States.
Show me the way to go to home.[49]

REVIVAL

"Americanization" was a weapon in the arsenal of white supremacy. As an instrument of control, Americanization came to the fore during the first several decades of the twentieth century. Its importance derived from the unprecedented immigration of the late nineteenth century both in scale and ethnicity. During 1865 to 1915, some 25 million immigrants entered the US or more than four times the total of the previous fifty years, and they came not from northern Europe as was typical since the nation's founding but from southern and eastern Europe. These were of a darker hue, many not of the Protestant faith, and they comprised significant percentages of the population of major cities like New York and Chicago. Americanization, a contemporary study noted, involved Anglo-conformity or assimilation toward the core after having vacated Old World cultures for the New, followed by the scattering of those new Americans among "native" Americans to augment the category "free white persons."[50]

Americanization for Japanese and other people of color, by contrast, sought their cultural extinction and segregation from the majority. They,

Extinctions

unlike Europeans, could not meld into whiteness. As the sociologist Robert Park observed of Japanese and African Americans: "It is not because the Negro and the Japanese are so differently constituted that they do not assimilate. If they were given an opportunity the Japanese are quite capable as the Italians, Armenians, or the Slavs of acquiring our culture and sharing our national ideals. The trouble is not with the Japanese mind but with the Japanese skin. The Jap is not the right color."[51]

Americanization was prescribed for the Japanese to keep them in a state of dependency. "Do not count on education to do too much for you," University of Hawai'i president David Crawford counseled Japanese "new" Americans in 1930, "do not take it too seriously. Do not expect a college degree, an A. B. or a Ph. D., to get you ahead unduly in this world." Education was important, Crawford explained, but "it must be education in the proper sense." Three years earlier, the university president had appeared before this same group to berate them: "Too many of the young people of Japanese and Chinese ancestry consider agriculture as beneath them—they want white-collar jobs." Young people, he advised, "must be satisfied with what they can get at first and hope to work up."[52] Like the newly freed African Americans after Reconstruction, to become American, Japanese must first serve contentedly in plantation and domestic labor.

In the WRA's scheme, Americanization, like the dispersion of southern and eastern European new Americans, sought the extinction of Japanese communities. "It would be good for the United States generally and I think it would be good from the standpoint of the Japanese-Americans themselves, to be scattered over a much wider area and not to be bunched up in groups as they were along the Coast," the WRA's Myer stated during a press conference. The WRA will solve "a serious racial problem by having them scattered throughout the United States instead of bunched up in three or four states."[53]

With that end in mind, the WRA required Japanese released from the concentration camps to work or attend college to swear they would "stay away from large groups of Japanese" and "develop such American habits which will cause you to be accepted readily into American social groups."[54] Still physically distinguishable and "not the right color," Japanese might retreat into self-reproach and self-hatred. As a nisei explained to President Roosevelt in 1942: "We, who are Americans to the core, but in appearance betray our oriental ancestry feel ashamed that the people of our own race are greatly responsible for the present conflict."[55]

Especially during World War II and within the confines of the concentration camp, Americanization stressed even more the extermination of Japanese culture, which the state and many of its citizens saw as attributes of the enemy race. Shinto and Buddhist temples were closed and desecrated and their priests were among the first to be removed and confined, the Japanese language fell under suspicion and was banned for a while in some camps, and the WRA deliberately set out to pit the issei or first generation against the nisei or second generation, giving privileges to nisei who were US citizens by birth over their parents who were prevented by law from US citizenship. Within that context of repression and submission, Japanese cultural revival, like the "Ghost Dance" movement, was a means and expression of resistance. "When cultures are whole and vigorous," a sociologist explained, "conquest, penetration, and certain modes of control are more readily resisted."[56]

Oppression galvanized the Japanese as a people, and culture shaped that people's consciousness, giving them a collective sense of peoplehood. For Japanese, the concentration camps followed in a long line of anti-Asian ideas and activities, which they challenged to assert their humanity and dignity. "The historical reaction of the immigrant Japanese to instances of anti-Japanese action," a scholar wrote of the prewar period, "has been one of very strong resentment against the attitudes of white supremacy, and one motivation behind their economic struggles in America has been the aim of showing the white majority group that they are a group to contend with as equals and not to be treated slightingly."[57]

That consciousness as Japanese stemmed from their exclusion from the US people and nation as much as their love of Japan. It was that original exclusion that impelled, indeed necessitated, the re-creation, the reinvention of a Japanese people, a variety made and performed in the US. Common in everyday camp speech were appeals to the "Japanese spirit" and "we're all Japanese." Public, cultic festivals such as New Year's Day and obon to honor the ancestral dead were occasions for group solidarity and celebration through a remembrance of things Japanese.

While Yamato damashii or "Japanese spirit" was a rallying cry for Japan's militarists, the phrase acquired a different meaning within the US concentration camps. At a farewell banquet for volunteers for the US Army in Minidoka concentration camp, a nisei reminded his listeners of the cause for which they fought. "We have been kicked around and kicked around," he said. "We have lost most of what we had. We have been stuck here in these centers. And we don't feel too good about it. But we know our future will depend on what these boy volunteers will do. They have had the courage to risk their lives in spite of this. We know that they will go in there and fight and we know that they will never do anything to dishonor the spirit of *Yamato damashi* [sic]."[58]

Japanese religion, a central feature of Japanese culture, supplied a means for resisting oppression in the US by advancing a collective consciousness like the "Ghost Dance" in Indian country. A historian of Buddhism observed that the number of Buddhists and Buddhist churches surged after passage of the racist Johnson-Reed Act of 1924. The act introduced quotas based on "national origins," favoring northern Europeans and severely restricting Africans, Pacific Islanders, and Asians. "Before that event," the study noted, "some of them [Japanese] had been hesitant in declaring themselves Buddhists, considering such an act impudent in a Christian country. But the immigration law made them more defiant and bold in asserting what they believed to be their rights; it made them realize the necessity of cooperation for the sake of their own security and welfare, and naturally sought the centers of their communal activity in their Buddhist churches."[59]

By contrast, a claim to civil rights drew from European traditions and the promise of equality as guaranteed by the US Constitution. From one point of view, that assertion of rights might exemplify Anglo-conformity, while from another, we see Japanese culture as absorbing (European) Enlightenment ideas as a "Japanese" value. Buddhism, for instance, appropriated democracy and antiracism into its teachings. "The Lord Buddha believed all men to be . . . spiritual equals," Buddhists at Gila River concentration camp learned. "He attempted to break down the caste system of India . . . . Buddhism disregards race" and is against racism, and Buddhists constitute an oppressed group.[60]

Japanese religious tradition is, in fact, syncretistic, combining elements of Shintoism, Confucianism, Taoism, Buddhism, and, in the US, Christianity. Conversely, some Japanese Christians envisioned a Japanese religious community, which distinguished them from their parent, white churches that sought their assimilation. Despite the violation of their civil liberties, a Christian minister observed, and the repression of "the theology of pluralism . . . there was a feeling for it. The Japanese people had a self-consciousness as an ethnic people," he wrote of the wartime concentration camps. "They were trying to demand self-definition but their voices were not heard. They were trying to assert their dignity and humanity in the intrinsic worth of their own traditions and cultural inheritance . . . but they were being pressed down at every turn. The ministry tried to affirm their pride as a people of God, and show fidelity to their peculiar peoplehood as a part of God's intention in a pluralistic community."[61]

The Japanese patriarchal family descended from the indigenous, Shinto belief of ancestor worship, which Confucianism and Buddhism later adopted. The family consisted of both the living and dead, and the ancestral spirits dwelled in the family home together with its living members. Filial piety, Confucianism held, formed an extension of ancestor worship, and Buddhism envisioned the merging of ancestral spirits with the Buddha. "Through sutras and services the ancestor is one with the Buddha," Bishop D. Ochi, a Buddhist leader at the Gila River concentration camp, explained in his unpublished manuscript, "The Spiritual Life of the Japanese Evacuees." Moreover, he continued, "to the Buddhist in America the Buddha and the ancestors exist together as a meaningful part of the life of the individual."[62]

Pertinent to that connection between religious belief and the family, the WRA's attempt to set the second against the first generation and therewith divide-and-rule undermined Japanese culture and community. Contrarily, the struggle to keep the family unit intact adhered to Japanese cultural and religious practice. As a WRA report observed: "during their stay at the centers they [Japanese] continued their previous practices of religious worship, tried to achieve some semblance of order and dignity in their broken lives, and frequently showed an almost pathetic eagerness to hold their families together and to work back toward their prewar social and economic status."[63]

Indigenous to Japanese religious beliefs, like the Modocs, was the intimacy of gods, humans, and nature. Shintoism, a native religion of Japan, embodying history and folklore perhaps best expressed those ties as kami or "spiritual essence" that resides in all things, including mountains, rivers, rocks, trees, the wind, animals, and ancestors. As a consequence, humans must respect the world around them wherein kami dwells. Japanese arts such as bonsai, ikebana (flower arrangement), landscape gardening, the tea ceremony, haiku poetry, and sumo wrestling spring from that root of Shintoism. A resurgence of those folk beliefs and practices was a notable feature at Tule Lake concentration camp.

Marvin Opler, a WRA community analyst from 1943 to 1946, witnessed what he called a "nativistic cultural revivalism," and documented its swift decline after the camp's closing in 1946. Opler classed them as "revivalisticmagical movements" or ones in which "revival is a part of a magical formula designed to modify the society's environment in ways which will be favorable to it." At Tule Lake, according to Opler, all of the Japanese participated in that revival and movement. "Folklore which had been remembered by a handful of Issei," he noted, "and perpetuated in a small circle, was seized upon by Issei and Nisei alike in a broadening sphere where it was deemed important to strike back at administrative pressures, programs, and policies with the dignified weapons of Japanese culture."[64] The hinotama or "ghost seen as a fireball presaging death" was one of the most prevalent of those beliefs and observances.

Another folk belief popular in the camp involved the fox, cat, and badger, animals connected with the Shinto cult of the rice goddess Inari. In the camps, food sufficient and wholesome to Japanese diets was a prominent source of anxiety. A bearer of rice, which when cooked is the word for a meal (gohan), Inari descended to earth bearing sheaths of grain during times of famine, riding on a white fox. Inari worship, especially in Japan's agricultural districts from whence many Japanese migrants originated, was so widespread that it nearly formed a distinct religious practice.[65] At Tule Lake, Inari worship blossomed, and families maintained Inari shrines in their residences.[66]

The white hair of the fox on which Inari rode denotes age and wisdom and the ability to see into the future, but the fox, badger, and cat are also tricksters that can possess a person's mind and body. Only exorcism by an Inari shrine master can save the victim because possession ate away the life force or, in Japanese, the "spirit leaks out." At Tule Lake, a Japanese recalled, "I had never heard much of Fox, Badger, or Cat until this camp. Back in Gilroy, where I was born, I had heard it only once and forgot it until here. Then it was a newcomer had arrived and the old people found he kept several foxes on his farm. They talked about it until it became a choice story among the young that he could set these foxes to bewitch anyone he didn't like."[67]

Drama (shibai and kabuki), song (utai, shigen, and nanaewabushi), and poetry (haiku and senryu) flourished at Tule Lake. According to a study of camp poetry, "to understand the poetry, one must understand the people. In general, they are all, except the very young, embittered and disaffected by the journey inland"[68] to the concentration camp. Members of the Tule Lake Senryu Kai wrote 558 senryu poems between January 4 and August 31, 1943. Largely escapist, according to the study, senryu poems were part of the religious and folk revival movement that critiqued Americanization and the confining camp. Senryu poetry supplied "the refuge, the recreation, and the escape."[69] In fact and notably, poetry interrogated US democracy and its concentration camps.

> "So, the finger-pointing again!"
> See the old man's
> Bitter face
> (We are not criminals)
>
> Only in dreams
> In a world of freedom
> Earth-bounded, we walk
> (And here, the fence)

Mirroring a similar theme, the chorus of a wedding song reflects upon the seagulls that fly to Tule Lake each summer.

> The sea-birds fly inland to the dry and waterless desert.
> They stop here, but will not stay.
> Too dry, too weary here.
> They fly away.
> Even the sea-birds find no reason to remain.[70]

PILGRIMAGE

> Thirty-three years have passed since last I descended into Tule's basin.
> No seagulls to be seen that summer of 2011.
> But the tule still grows in abundance,

long after women's deft hands plucked, dried, and plaited them into
revelations of the creator's art.

From the southwestern shore where the lava flow breaks upon the lake,

Eagle can spot the Japanese concentration camp, especially their fires
at night.

And from those fires, Inari, looking toward the setting sun, must have
seen hinotama piercing the night sky.

On that western side, I chanced upon a cluster of white sage, growing
wild in the black lava beds, free.

Kintpuash lives.

Still defiant, still pungent,

He endures.

CHAPTER FIVE

Third World

I was fortunate to find housing in Westwood for a monthly rent of fifty dollars. No bigger than a walk-in closet, the modest room sat off the two-car garage of a rather comfortable home. I could have suffocated from the carbon monoxide fumes. The neighborhood was white and upper middle class, as was typical of Westwood, but it was within easy walking distance of UCLA.

It was the fall of 1967 when I entered graduate studies in African history. I lived alone and, like my father, rarely spoke. In fact, when the occasion arose, I could hardly utter the few words necessary to ask for food in the student cafeteria. Once a week on Fridays, I treated myself to a hot meal, but the event required the ordeal of speech. I mumbled and stumbled over words to the complete puzzlement of my server. I might have passed as a foreign student lost in English.

Weirder still was the troubled adolescent who lived in the big house. I knew him to possess a life of complete privilege, and yet the kid once told me I reminded him of Richard Cory of the Simon & Garfunkel song, and not the poem by Edwin Arlington Robinson. According to the lyrics, Richard Cory owned half the town with wealth to spread around. He had political connections, and power, grace, style. Cory seemed to have everything, while the song's narrator, who worked in Cory's factory, hated his life of poverty and wished he could be Richard Cory. The kid's inversion of our subject locations struck me as ludicrous as a remark by a blond, high school goddess princess in Hawai'i who assured me I looked like the rock star Rick Nelson. Perhaps, I mused, the kid connected me with the song's ending, which has Cory committing suicide.

Immersed in African history, I failed to take note of the surge of US imperial troops in Viet Nam to over half a million. In that first year of my graduate studies, some 300,000 marched in New York City against the war, and 100,000 tried to shut down the war-making Pentagon in Washington, DC. When the state reduced and then eliminated graduate student deferments from military service, I agonized over fleeing to free Canada as others had done, and then instead testified before my draft board in Honolulu to claim conscientious objector status.

Unlike too many of my generation, I managed to escape military service by enlisting in the Peace Corps, another agency of US imperialism. The corps assigned me to Frogmore, South Carolina, for training and a process of weeding called, in inimitable Peace Corps fashion, "self de-selection." In 1862, missionaries opened Penn Center in Frogmore on St. Helena Island to educate enslaved Sea Islanders,[1] and about a hundred years later the center was famous in the civil rights movement as the eye of the storm where many of the South's freedom fighters, including Martin Luther King, Jr. and members of his Southern Christian Leadership Conference, rested and plotted ungentle strategies in nonviolence to advance the cause of liberation. Penn Center was our corps' home base.

I shiver at the recollection of white men in pickup trucks with racked rifles hung prominently in their rear windows, cruising as if hunting for vermin in the center's vicinity. I was there because the Peace Corps subscribed to the liberal idea, no doubt racist, that its volunteers destined for Africa should live among rural, African Americans for "sensitivity" training and learning to live together with black folk.[2]

Third World

I experienced what the writer and critic Meena Alexander called "the shock of arrival" upon first setting foot in Frogmore, Beaufort County.[3] Given only the names of our host families, we had to rely upon our ingenuity and daring to venture out into the alien land that was rural South Carolina, amidst swamps and trees drooping moss. Ghosts peopled the countryside. Somehow, I managed to find the Singletons, African American sharecroppers, whose wooden house stood on stilts, not unlike my old, sugar plantation home in Hawai'i, above the marshy ground.

The blood rushes to my cheeks in discomfiture to this day as I recall spotting a framed diploma on the wall. "Oh," I asked, "from what university did your child graduate?" "That's a high school diploma," Mr. Singleton replied softly. Fresh from UCLA's graduate program, I had forgotten that for these African American children mired in poverty, completing high school was a signal accomplishment worthy of display. I was unmindful of my roots, narcotized as I was by Western civilization and culture. I was proud to have received an "A" in my college "Art Appreciation" course, reputedly the toughest general education class. Needless to say, art, called grandly "classical," included only European visual and musical high culture. I had to unlearn the parochialism of my education.

Teaching at a local African American high school, like living with the Singletons, returned me to my roots. The students in my biology class were wondrously bright, probing, and expectant; it was, after all, a season of youth. But the gravity of small budgets and poorly equipped classrooms encumbered learning. I had to draw my own charts and diagrams, and students had to share microscopes that barely worked. Discovering single-celled life in pond water under those conditions was particularly taxing.

Indelibly etched in my mind's eye is the sight of a young man walking to school in the morning chill, his lanky figure and misty breath bathed in golden sunshine, wearing much too large and worn leather shoes. His "kicks" were not a fashion statement but a stigma of necessity. From my education in Hawai'i, I came to recognize those students and the Singletons as my people, and the elites and their apparatuses, gun-toting racists, and inferior, colored schools as my other. Those recognitions and affiliations fortified my Freirian critical consciousness,[4] and they continue to animate and direct my personal and intellectual labors.

Dawned 1968.[5] In January the Vietnamese launched the Têt offensive, which culminated with their nation's liberation from the shackles of colonial rule. Some 47,000 Japanese students and protesters converged on the US Navy base at Sasebo, Japan, when the nuclear aircraft carrier *USS Enterprise* docked on its way to Viet Nam. In March, some 10,000 Chicanx high school students in Los Angeles organized a walkout called a "blowout" for educational equity, and students of color joined to form the Third World Liberation Front at San Francisco State College.

In April, an assassin's bullet silenced the incomparable voice of Martin Luther King, Jr., and protesters poured into the streets of over forty US cities. In China, Mao Zedong offered a statement "In Support of the Afro-American Struggle Against Violent Repression," and tens of thousands marched in the rain to denounce US racism. Later that month at Columbia University, African American and SDS (Students for a Democratic Society) students occupied campus buildings to stop the university's plan to expand into Harlem and end its contracts with the US military-industrial complex, so-named by a former Columbia president (later to be a US president).

In May, students and workers marched and erected barricades in Paris. That summer, activists and community members formed the American Indian Movement, and in August, Soviet tanks rolled into Prague to crush Czechoslovakia's uprising and planned "third way." In September, the National Organization for Women protested women's objectification at the Miss America beauty pageant in Atlantic City, and students, peasants, and workers in Mexico City demanded an end to government repression. In November, Richard Nixon captured the White House.

The world around me was in flames, although at the time I hardly knew it. In retrospect, all of those events of 1968 comprise salient elements in this telling of my life and labors.

VIET NAM[6]

Viet Nam, during my college years, was a war. Little did I know about the people of Annam or of their remarkable, centuries-long struggle against Chinese aggression and incorporation. I knew nothing about the brutality of French colonialism that began in the mid-nineteenth century or about Ho Chi Minh's 1911 exile to France, where in 1920 he helped found the French Communist Party. I was ignorant of the heroic, anticolonial struggle waged by the Vietnamese people against the French, then the Japanese during World War II, and again against the French, when the colonial puppet Bao Dai warned France's General Charles de Gaulle: "You would understand better if you could see what is happening here, if you could feel the desire for independence which is in everyone's heart and which no human force can any longer restrain." French colonialism, Bao Dai predicted, would only spur Vietnamese opposition: "each village will be a nest of resistance, each former collaborator an enemy, and your officials and colonists will themselves ask to leave this atmosphere which they will be unable to breathe."[7]

"I can't breathe," African American Eric Garner repeated eleven times before he died on a Staten Island sidewalk, July 17, 2014. A New York City police officer's chokehold and his throwdown and submission position contributed to Garner's death. Police had suspected Garner of selling single cigarettes without tax stamps. "I can't breathe" became a rally cry that enjoined an ongoing national movement against police brutality and to affirm that black lives matter.

I did not know that the Vietnamese Declaration of Independence of September 2, 1945, was modeled after that of the United States. "All men are created equal . . .," the document asserted, and "they are endowed by their Creator with certain inalienable rights." It concluded with the ringing promise: "All the people of Vietnam are determined to mobilize their right to liberty and independence."[8] I failed to understand that the US replaced France as Viet Nam's colonizer after the 1954 Geneva Conference, and reneged on that agreement's call for nationwide, democratic elections that would have established a free and united Viet Nam. I was ignorant of all that. To me, Viet Nam was a war.

The United States of the 1960s was destined to explore and map, in the words of President John F. Kennedy, "new frontiers." That language was, in fact, as old as the nation's origins and history of American Indian conquest, removal, and termination. Although Kennedy's new frontiers shifted in meaning and location during his administration and that of his successor, Lyndon B. Johnson, they included prominently the domestic frontiers of race and class and the expansions of empire abroad, including the moon and beyond.

An optimistic belief in the power of the state to right wrongs and tame wildernesses both within and without the US underwrote Kennedy and Johnson's liberalism. Their faith, enabled and encouraged by a robust capitalism, allowed for an activist government that tackled ambitious agendas such as civil rights and racial equality, a war on poverty and class uplift, and a reassertion of imperial might or, in the language of the Cold War, communism's containment. Across those frontiers of race and class trod African Americans and other people of color, women, gays and lesbians, the poor,

youth, and intellectuals, forging a liberal consensus and advancing movements for civil rights and social reform.

The nation-state's imperial ambitions, however, fractured that 1960s
liberal coalition. The US war in Southeast Asia was a prominent factor in that
breach that led to the demise of liberalism and rise of conservatism, the
presidency of Ronald Reagan during the 1980s, and the so-called "Republi-
can revolution" of the following decade. For some, the war appropriated
resources and political wills from the reservoirs of racial and class blight. As
civil rights leader Martin Luther King, Jr. noted, "the promises of the Great
Society have been shot down on the battlefield of Vietnam. The pursuit of
this widened war," he charged, "has narrowed the promised dimensions of
the domestic welfare programs, making the poor white and negro bear the
heaviest burdens, both at the front and at home." Even President Johnson
agreed with that reasoning, when he frankly admitted that the "whore" of
Viet Nam swept him away from "the lady I love," his "Great Society."[9] For
others, the war exposed and made prominent the hypocrisy of the liberal
agenda: there was no dissonance, no paradox between a policy of ostensible
racial and class uplift at home and making the world safe for democracy and
capitalism abroad. They were one and the same.

Working among African Americans and the rural poor in the US South
during the summer of 1964, a student volunteer wrote to her parents: "For
the first time in my life I am seeing what it is like to be poor, oppressed, and
hated . . . . The people we're killing in Viet Nam are the same people whom
we've been killing for years in Mississippi."[10] Antiwar activists of the Vietnam Day Committee stated: "Vietnam, like Mississippi, is not an aberration,
it is a mirror of America. Vietnam IS American foreign policy."[11] More systematic was the analysis offered by the SDS formed in 1962:

> We see the US policy in Vietnam as part of a global strategy for containing
> revolutionary change in the "Third World" nations of Asia, Africa, and Latin
> America. Rather than the result of an essentially good government's mis-

taken decisions, we see the world-wide exploitation and oppression of those insurgent peoples as the logical conclusion of the giant US corporations' expanding and necessary search for higher profits and strategic resources. That system is properly named imperialism, and we stand by and support all those who struggle against its onslaught. They are our brothers and sisters, not our enemies.[12]

In July 1965, civil rights activists in Mississippi issued "five reasons why Negroes should not be in any war fighting for America" after the death of John D. Shaw, one of their classmates, in Viet Nam. Among those five reasons: "No Mississippi Negroes should be fighting in Viet Nam for the white Man's freedom, until all the Negro People are free in Mississippi."[13] Black power advocate Stokely Carmichael memorably described the US war in Viet Nam as "white people sending black people to make war on yellow people to defend the land they stole from Red people."[14] The internationalist Black Panthers pointed to a link between the exercise of white power at home and abroad. As "the aggression of the racist American government escalates in Vietnam," the Panthers charged, "the police agencies of America escalate the repression of black people throughout the ghettos."[15]

Racism in the conduct of the war was most evident to US soldiers. In 1966, James Johnson (African American), Dennis Mora (Puerto Rican), and David Samos (Lithuanian / Italian) issued a joint statement refusing to serve in Viet Nam.

> We have decided to take a stand against this war, which we consider immoral, illegal, and unjust . . . . We represent in our backgrounds a cross section of the army and of America . . . . We speak as American soldiers. We know that Negroes and Puerto Ricans are being drafted and end up in the worst of the fighting all out of proportion to their numbers in the population, and we have firsthand knowledge that these are the ones who have been deprived of decent education and jobs at home. The three of us . . . found we thought alike on one overriding issue—the war in Vietnam must be stopped.

In that same year, over a thousand young men in Puerto Rico signed a statement refusing to serve in the US armed forces because it was an obligation, the document read, "imposed by the North American imperialism on Puerto Rican youth as a part of the colonial subjugation of our country."[16]

African American Bob Sanders described his reaction to entering an army induction center. "It looked bleak," he began. "A few guys standing around outside, but inside there was this huge sea of guys. There were sitting on benches like church pews, just like a congregation for young men only. It felt strange; here I was getting ready to be carted off. I was a black and I thought about slavery. You know, the guys were predominantly black."[17]

In a sermon entitled "Declaration of Independence from the War in Vietnam," delivered on April 4, 1967, in New York City, Martin Luther King, Jr. described the evolution of his thinking on the US war in Asia. The US military buildup in Viet Nam, King observed, showed that the country had become "a society gone mad on war," and as the war machine devoured the nation's resources its programs for the poor were "eviscerated." "So," he concluded, "I was increasingly compelled to see the war as an enemy of the poor." Further, he noted, the distant war exacted a disproportionate price on African Americans, who were denied basic rights at home. "We were taking the young black men who had been crippled by our society and sending them 8000 miles away to guarantee liberties in Southeast Asia which they had not found in Southwest Georgia and East Harlem," he explained. "So we have been repeatedly faced with the cruel irony of watching Negro and white boys on TV screens as they kill and die together for a nation that has been unable to seat them together in the same schools." What of the Vietnamese? King asked. What do they think when the US aligns itself with the landlords and not the peasants, and when this government, "the greatest purveyor of violence in the world today," tests its latest weapons on the Vietnamese people. "We must find new ways to speak for peace in Vietnam," King urged, "and justice throughout the developing world."[18]

Helicopters low on the horizon, especially when flying in formation, and the rat-tat-tat staccato beat of their rotors cause my heart to race to this day, urging me to run for cover. Images of the violence of the US war in Vet Nam were too vivid and abundant to ignore or forget. They situated me in the midst of exploding napalm and free-fire zones where everything that moved perished.

When I landed in Viet Nam for the first time in October 1999, I knew I had been there before, despite having escaped the obscenities during the US war. I remembered the warm, moist air on my skin the second I stepped off the airplane and walked down the ladder to the ground. I felt at home. I wrote in my notes that day: "Peering through the car's window as we drove from the airport, layers upon layers of green [rice] paddies, women and men bent to their tasks, hills rising in the distance, and in the city men, women, and children converging and weaving in a river of bicycles and scooters." I immediately sensed an attachment to that place, Viet Nam.

At a reception hosted by the US embassy in Ha Noi, a Vietnamese colleague greeted me. American bombs had killed his brother, he told me, and I apologized for the Japanese and then US invasion and occupation of his country. I was his enemy twice over, I said, and was overawed when this stranger turned to me, embraced me with open arms, and called me a brother.

COLOR LINE[19]

At the century's start in 1900, the African American intellectual W. E. B. Du Bois famously declared: "The problem of the twentieth century is the problem of the color line."[20] He delivered, fittingly, that prophetic announcement in

London, the seat of the British Empire on which the sun never set because at the time it encircled the globe. Imperialism closed the nineteenth century and its counter, the decolonization struggles of Africa and Asia, ushered in the twentieth century. Self-determination and antiracism or the dismantling of the ideology that justified and supported colonialism were the central elements of those liberation movements, which promised a new dispensation for humanity and, after two global wars and the Cold War's onset, world peace.

Early in the century in the midst of World War I, Du Bois explained that colonialism or the exploitation of the lands and peoples of the "darker races"—"Chinese, East Indian, Negroes, and South American Indians"—produced European empires composed of material relations of expropriation and exploitation and the discourses of religion and science. The Berlin Conference of 1884–85, he recalled, parceled out Africa, synonymous with "bestiality and barbarism," for European possession and colonization, exemplifying how racism resolved rhetorical incongruities such as (universal) declarations of human equality and paid real dividends for Europe. At stake in the present war, Du Bois wrote, were those colonies and the idea of white supremacy that warranted them. Lasting peace, he concluded, will only descend with the abolition of racism and the inauguration of a "new democracy of all races: a great humanity of equal men."[21]

Added the black, Caribbean intellectual Hubert H. Harrison, World War I ostensibly waged for democracy was never intended to include people of color. "The white world has been playing with catch-words of democracy while ruthlessly ruling an overwhelming majority of black, brown and yellow peoples to whom these catch-words were never intended to apply," he charged. At core, the war was a fratricidal conflict, "a war of the white race" over empire to possess the lands and determine the destinies of the "colored majority in Asia, Africa and the islands of the sea."[22]

For racists and antiracists alike, the problem of the twentieth century was the problem of the color line, which sustained, in Du Bois's words, the "greed for wealth and power." The problem for racists like the US journalist Lothrop Stoddard was "the rising tide of color" that threatened to swamp "white world-supremacy."[23] For antiracists like Du Bois, the problem was European colonial rule and its solution was Third World independence and an end to racism.[24]

A mere decade after Kaiser Wilhelm II of Germany exhorted Europe to rise above its parochial disputes to defend "your holiest possession"—Christianity and European civilization—against the impending threat of the "yellow peril,"[25] Japan defeated Russia in 1905. The event prompted a young Oxford lecturer, Alfred Zimmern, to put aside his lesson on Greek history to announce to his class "the most historical event which has happened, or is likely to happen, in our lifetime; the victory of a non-white people over a white people."[26]

Du Bois agreed with Zimmern's assessment: "the Russo-Japanese war has marked an epoch," he exulted. "The magic of the word 'white' is already broken . . . . The awakening of the yellow races is certain. That the awakening of the brown and black races will follow in time, no unprejudiced student of history can doubt."[27] Japan's victory, a historian concurs, broke the myth of white invincibility and influenced a regeneration of Asia broadly.[28] Contrarily, the prospect of colored resistance to white supremacy globally, as was hoped for by Du Bois and others, inspired anxieties and fears over the West's decline among those invested in imperial order and white supremacy.

RACE RELATIONS

The impending conflict of color produced a discourse and field of study, race relations, to manage the problem of the twentieth century and forestall the prospect of a race war.[29] Its purpose was to study "racial tensions" and "racial conflicts" as social problems with an eye toward ameliorating those conditions. Called racial adjustments, assimilation was evolutionary and designed to preserve the status quo of power's location by moving in a single direction, toward and in conformity with the empowered majority.[30]

In the US, the Institute of Race Relations was charged with studying natives to install "effective government" and continue their economic dependency, while the Institute of Pacific Relations, established in 1925, had as its prime objective, "to prevent a possible Oriental-Occidental war arising . . . out of an increasing bitterness over racial, religious, economic and political differences."[31] That "bitterness," however, did not emerge from "differences," but by the relations of power, involving conquest, colonization, and exploitation.

Later framed as problems, colored subjects and their agencies were at first solutions to white masters when useful to them, as in supplying efficient, pliant labor, but they caused apprehension, even dread, when they aspired to full equality and a measure of self-determination. "One speaks of race relations when there is a race problem," declared the sociologist Robert Park, one of the founding figures of the field. To illustrate, he wrote of the race problem in South Africa where "the African does, to be sure, constitute a problem."[32] Of course, from the African perspective, that is, from the San, Khoikhoi, Nguni, and Sotho point of view, the invading European might have comprised the problem.

The field of race relations thrived in the US especially during the interwar period, and it took turns particular to the US and Britain.[33] During the 1920s, revealing of the field's origins and objectives, an influential US sociology textbook likened race conflict to nationalism and the drive of subject peoples for freedom and self-determination.[34] On the eve of World War II, a "state of the field" race-relations conference cautiously diagnosed an obvious condition: "the world seems to be reorganizing to some extent along racial lines," the problem of the twentieth century.[35]

WORLD WAR II

Race figured prominently in World War II. Greater than its victory over the Russians, Japan's early advances against European colonies in Asia represented, according to a historian, "a blow to white prestige" and "heightened the degree of racial self-consciousness" in a world divided into West and East, white and nonwhite.[36] As a March 1942 commentary in the *Times* (London) noted, "Japan's attack has produced a very practical revolution in race relations."[37]

Even before the war, Japan had championed the cause of peoples under European colonial rule. At the Treaty of Paris (1918–19) and the formation of the League of Nations, Japan proposed an amendment to the league's covenant that would ensure "equal and just treatment in every respect, making no distinction, either in law or in fact, on account of their race or nationality." The colonial powers rejected that challenge to white supremacy, but Japan gained the esteem of Asian and African anticolonialists as the "logical leader," in the words of Du Bois, of "all coloured peoples."[38]

By the 1930s, Japan followed the European lead for national greatness by pursuing empire in Manchuria and North China. Despite its imperialism in Asia, on December 8, 1941, Japan issued an Imperial Rescript, which described the nation's war aims: to ensure Japan's national integrity and to remove European colonialism from and bring stability to East and Southeast Asia. As Japan's Imperial Army advanced into Southeast Asia, its generals proclaimed "Asia for Asians," and General Yamashita Tomoyuki declared his intention to sweep away the arrogance of the British colonizers and share the "pain and rejoicing with all coloured peoples."[39]

As its fortunes on the warfront diminished, Tokyo called a Great East Asia Conference in November 1943 that included representatives from Southeast Asia—Burma, the Philippines, and Thailand. There, Prime Minister Tojo Hideki declared that Japan was waging a war against "Anglo-Americans" who sought to perpetuate their colonial hold over Asia, and the conference concluded by urging cooperation based upon principles of coexistence and coprosperity, respect of national sovereignty and cultural diversity, the economic development of all, and an abolition to all systems of racism.[40]

Imperial Japan's blatant duplicity notwithstanding, its pronouncements of antiracism and self-determination resonated throughout colonized Asia, especially because they stood in opposition to the European conduct of the war. "As the war developed," India's anticolonial leader Jawaharlal Nehru observed in retrospect, "it became ever clearer that the western democracies were fighting not for a change but for a perpetuation of the old order"—the preservation of white supremacy and colonial rule. The Allies, he sadly noted, eagerly embraced the legacies of "empire and racial discrimination," and after the war, as proof, "the old imperialisms still functioned."[41]

Beyond India's borders, anticolonial leaders simultaneously condemned and cheered the Japanese advance. In British, French, and Dutch colonies, recalled Mahatir Mohamad, Malaysia's prime minister (1981–2003), "most Asians felt inferior to the European colonisers and rarely did we even consider independence a viable option." But Japan's expulsion of the British "changed our view of the world," showing that "an Asian race, the Japanese" could defeat whites and with that reality dawned "a new awakening amongst us that if we wanted to, we could be like the Japanese. We did have the ability to govern our own country and compete with the Europeans on an equal footing." Despite intense suffering under Japanese wartime occupation and "tremendous disappointment" over the return of the British after the war, Mohamad wrote, the shackles of "mental servitude" had been broken.[42] Similarly, Singapore's Lee Kuan Yew testified that Japan's defeat of the British "completely changed our world."[43]

For European colonizers, Japan threatened to upset their world and the race relations of imperial rule. Prime Minister Winston S. Churchill declared that Pearl Harbor delivered "a staggering blow" and "our prestige suffered with the loss of Hong Kong."[44] Still, he boasted, the British Empire would survive and remain intact. In early 1942, amidst widespread, mass resistance to colonialism in India, Churchill reassured Britain's House of Commons that the Atlantic Charter's provisions were not "applicable to [the] Coloured

Races in [the] colonial empire, and that [the phrase] 'restoration of sovereignty, self-government and national life' . . . [was] applicable only to the States and the Nations of Europe."[45]

Reporting on the dent to British prestige and white supremacy generally due to the loss of Hong Kong, a US journalist described the humiliation of defeat along the color line: "They [the Japanese] paraded us, the hungry, bedraggled two hundred of us, through the crowded Chinese section" for all to see. "We were the perfect picture of the Fall of the White Man in the Far East. A white man lying disemboweled in the dirt, a white woman snatched naked and gang-raped . . . these pictures delighted the Jap heart." She added: "if you in America could see your own people being marched by those little monkey men with the big bayonets, you would realize what the Japs intend to do to all the white men."[46]

Japan's wartime achievement was to capitalize on the partition of the color line and the aspirations that transgression stirred especially among the still colonized in Asia and Africa. Although Japan lost the war, a British colonial officer predicted it created conditions in Southeast Asia so revolutionary that there would be no easy return to white rule.[47] Among the war casualties were the mutually constituting discursive shams of white superiority and Asian inferiority, together with the colonialism they sustained.

B. V. A. Roling of the Netherlands, one of the eleven judges presiding over the Tokyo War Crimes Trial, pointed out: "It was quite different in Japan [in contrast to the Nuremberg trials]. The Japanese defended the action of Japan in this Asian land and in the world, to liberate Asia and to change the world. And they had a case, in this respect." Whereas "Nuremberg was a clear case of aggression to dominate the European continent."[48] Moreover, along the color line, Nazi Germany affirmed the doctrine of white supremacy while Japan undermined it.[49]

There is a tendency within European historiography to deny significance to the anticolonial struggles of the Third World. Such histories credit

Europeans with gifting independence to their former colonies and providing them the scaffolding for the modern, nation-state. They belittle postindependence nation-building by referencing tribalism, ethnic and religious conflicts, corruption, and ineptitude as the consequences of decolonization.[50] Some of those writings share a nostalgia for colonialism and the apparent order it imposed over unruly, untutored subjects. An author, for example, described the era of European colonial rule in Asia as "the most peaceful and stable period the East had ever known," and without that "stabilising" influence of the West, Asia gained so-called "freedom" and "independence" [author's quotes] while sinking into "a morass of debt" and communist insurgencies.[51]

Those defenders of colonialism slight anticolonialism's efficacy along with the racism, which endorsed white expansion and rule. In fact, a scholar observed, academic discourses virtually ignore the salience of European and American racist language when addressing the white identity, race, and racism. "The greatest influence on racial thinking," he continued, "was the emergence of resistance to Western domination" and fears of the decline of the West.[52] Japan and nationalist leaders in the Third World played key roles in that realignment of the color line by articulating solidarities of race—white and nonwhite—an invention of the West and deployed by the rest in "Africa for Africans" and "Asia for Asians," and by punctuating the contradiction between the West's rhetoric of equality and freedom and its practice of colonial and neocolonial subjugation.

I should have studied world history more closely when first I entered UCLA's graduate program in African history. At the time, I understood Japan's attack on Pearl Harbor as the trigger for the mass removal and confinement of some 120,000 Japanese in Hawai'i and along the US West Coast. Like most historians, I believed that World War II experience descended from the preceding, decades-long history of anti-Chinese and then anti-Japanese hatreds in the US. The worldwide problem of the twentieth century seemed to us unconnected with the anti-Asian racism in the US that led to the concentration camps of the "good war."

African Americans like W. E. B. Du Bois had a better understanding of world and US history. From their perspective, many black intellectuals held Japan in high esteem because it seriously challenged white supremacy, and they knew that the international and national arenas formed correspondences. Racism at home advanced white supremacy abroad, and white supremacy in the periphery reinforced racism in the core. Even the conservative, anticommunist African American journalist George Schuyler praised Japan for deflating "white supremacy and arrogance in the Orient. Where white men once strutted and kicked coolies into the street," he reported, "they now tread softly and talk in whispers." The Second World War was "wonderful," Schuyler maintained, because it retarded white supremacy and incited aspirations for racial equality within and without the US.[53]

In that light, both Du Bois and Schuyler criticized the government's forced, mass eviction and detention of Japanese in the US. Du Bois was one of the few African Americans to sign the socialist Norman Thomas's open letter to President Roosevelt, condemning him for the internment of Japanese Americans, and he saw the president's Executive Order 9066, which authorized that action, as "conclusive proof of the racial origins of the Pacific war."[54] Schuyler warned that the Japanese American precedent threatened African American rights. The Native Sons of the Golden West, Schuyler observed, pressed for the Japanese removals along with the vacating of African American citizenship, thereby taking away the rights of both people of color.[55]

In the 1960s, along the century's color line emerged a new generation of Third World students.[56]

THIRD WORLD STUDIES[57]

In his revolutionary anthem, *The Wretched of the Earth* (1961), Frantz Fanon described the cosmos or order created by European colonizers, which segregated the colonizer and colonized into different worlds, separate and unequal. That divide and hierarchy of race and class involved white, capitalist expansionists from the First World over colored, native workers of the Third World. The former were humans and individuals; the latter, nonhumans and the faceless masses. Because of those conditions bred by colonialism, Fanon wrote, Third World decolonization is necessarily a revolutionary process, replacing a certain "species" with another "species" of men and altering the consciousness of both the colonizer and the colonized.

That renewal of the world order is not merely destructive, Fanon explained, it is also a work of creation. The revolution gives birth to "new men" with a "new language and a new humanity." We, the colonized, Fanon urged, must "change our ways" from a "nauseating mimicry" that copies the European example and pattern. "Leave this Europe," he exhorted, move "in a new direction," fashion "the whole man," and thereby, as Third World people, begin "a new history of Man."[58]

The Third World, conceived about mid-century and composed of Africa, Asia, and Latin America was, in the words of Fanon, a project by the periphery to solve the core's problems of imperialism, wars, and systems of bondage.[59] The Third World's historic turn, Indonesian president Ahmed Sukarno told the 1955 Bandung Conference of newly independent African and Asian states, was directed at "the liberation of man from the physical, spiritual and intellectual bonds which have for long stunted the development of humanity's majority."[60] Bandung promised the equality of all races, respect of national sovereignty, international cooperation, and lasting world peace.

Indeed, the Third World's rise and with it the end of formal European empires marked a turning point in some four hundred years of world history. That achievement along the color line was sweeping and revolutionary.

In 1968, the students of the Third World Liberation Front at San Francisco State College had that in mind when they demanded a "Third World curriculum."[61] The TWLF, its founding statement declared, consisted of Third World students in solidarity with Third World people. "We adhere to the struggles in Asia, Africa, and Latin America," the document explained, "ideologically, spiritually, and culturally." Because of racism in the US, the TWLF declared, "we have decided to fuse ourselves with the masses of Third World people, which is the majority of the world's peoples, to create, through struggles, a new humanity, a new humanism, a New World Consciousness."[62]

That "New World Consciousness" drew from anticolonial intellectuals like Fanon and Albert Memmi who denounced the erasure of the colonized from history and their resulting "cultural estrangement" from self and society. Colonization "disfigures," wrote Memmi, and requires a restoration of "a whole and free man"; Fanon urged the creation of "a new humanity . . . a new humanism."[63]

Moreover, students of the TWLF, aligning with Fanon in his call for a Third World revolution, explained:

> We offer a positive program. We are not anti-white; we are anti-white-racist-oppression and it is this powerful and just determinant that is the genesis of our movement, but the growth of the movement is affirmative; an affirmation of our humanity, our strength, our beauty, our dignity and our pride. Our programs are working programs. Our direction is revolutionary. Our method is organization. Our goal is Third World Power. Our essence is a New World Consciousness of oppressed peoples.[64]

Third World students understood the revolutionary, global nature of their demand for Third World studies. Barbara Williams, an African American student at San Francisco State, wrote: "We are conscious of our blackness, brownness, redness, yellowness and are moving with that knowledge back into our communities. We intend to reveal to the world our own place in this world's history and to mark our place in space and time." George Murray, a graduate student and part-time English department instructor at San Francisco State and the Black Panther Party's minister of education, added: "When we talk about becoming free, we have to talk about power, getting all the goods, services, and land, and returning them equally to the oppressed and enslaved Mexicans, Blacks, Indians, Puerto Ricans, and poor whites in the U.S. and to the rest of the oppressed and hungry people in the world."[65]

Across San Francisco Bay at the University of California, students organized Berkeley's Third World Liberation Front to demand Third World studies on that campus. Such Third World consciousness can be seen in *Asian Women*, a 1971 foundational text edited by a collective drawn from a UC Berkeley course. A prominent section was devoted to "Third World women." The editors, in selecting chapters for that section, observed the connections among women in America and Asia forged by the common threads of resistance and liberation against oppression and exploitation.

Pivotal for the *Asian Women* collective was the Indochinese Women's Conference held in Vancouver, Canada, in April 1971 that brought together Third World and women's liberation concerns and engaged over 150 Canadian and US activists with a six-woman delegation from Viet Nam.[66] "As Third World people," a report from that conference claimed, "we share similar struggles in fighting racist conditions and attitudes in our communities and our everyday lives. Our people—Blacks, Chicanos, Asians, Native Americans, and Native Hawaiians—have had our land ripped off by the whites, our women raped, our homes plundered, and our men drafted to further this country's imperialist ventures into Third World countries." Accordingly, "we see a need for learning about each other's history as Third World people and of informing each other about our movements for self-determination."[67]

Turning Third World studies into "ethnic studies," which transpired in the fall of 1968 and spring of 1969 at San Francisco State and UC Berkeley, trivialized that declaration of a global solidarity with the liberation and antiracist struggles of Third World peoples. That co-optation not only domesticated an international alliance and movement; it reduced its revolutionary potential and power by grafting it onto the trunk of race relations and ethnic studies as sociology at the University of Chicago had prominently promulgated.

ETHNIC STUDIES

Chicago sociology's ethnic studies hearkened back to the pre–World War II race relations of the colonial era. At its core, its ambition for race relations and ethnic studies was to distinguish American from European sociology by focusing on social processes believed to be unique to the US environment. Further, Chicago sociology advanced the new concept of ethnicity over race, which had dominated US sociology since the late nineteenth century pioneered by sociologists such as George Fitzhugh, Henry Hughes, William Graham Sumner, and Lester Frank Ward. Those saw race as a natural state and racial hierarchies as permanent and necessary for social order.

Sociology in the US mirrored its context of the late nineteenth century, a swirling sea of domestic, social currents. Urbanization and immigration from southern and eastern Europe, unprecedented in numbers and color, language, and religion, and their attendant problems, including housing, sanitation, poverty, ethnic and labor strife, social disorganization, and crime and juvenile delinquency, prompted the rise of the social gospel and various reform and nationalist movements such as "Americanization." During the 1880s and 1890s, the first courses offered by US sociology addressed social "pathologies" as studies directed at problem solving.[68] Sociology was thus a science of society and its management.

Robert Park, a central figure in establishing an American brand of sociology at the University of Chicago, was especially concerned with the

"Negro problem" and "Oriental problem" as samples to test his general propositions about American modernity. As he observed: "The study of the Negro in America, representing, as he does, every type of man from the primitive barbarian to the latest and most finished product of civilization, offers an opportunity to study . . . the historic social process by which modern society has developed. The Negro in his American environment is a social laboratory."[69]

The consequences of Chicago sociology were both paradigmatic and far-reaching. Its students and faculty, notably Park and William I. Thomas, who had recruited Park to Chicago, conceived of race relations and its subjects—"problem" minorities—as case studies to understand and offer cures for the ills of urbanization. The focus, thus, was on US cities and modernization broadly, and African and Asian Americans, like European ethnic groups, were mere transients and experimental subjects in the laboratory of progress.[70] Chicago sociologists, thereby, saw their studies as a subset of urban and spatial orderings of individuals and groupings. Additionally and importantly, Franz Boas and his colleagues and students had separated race from culture[71] whereby ethnicity bore the prospect of problem solving and social change through cultural assimilation.

Within that flattened world of the modernizing, homogenizing city, ethnicity or culture displaced race, and European ethnic, immigrant groups constituted the model for the progressive cycle of immigration, contact and interaction, competition and conflict, and accommodation and assimilation. African Americans from the rural South in the urban North and Asian migrants in the agrarian West were like Polish peasants in northern cities, according to a version of the Chicago school. The civilizing modernity of the urban environment dissolved the affiliations of race, enabling a single frame of reference and direction for disparate peoples.[72] The durability of racism, called "racial prejudice," as was shown in the experiences of African and Asian Americans ultimately diminished that initial optimism.

Perhaps pivotal in that regard was the Chicago race riot of July 1919 that lasted over a week and resulted in the deaths of 15 whites and 23 blacks, injuries to 537, and left over 1,000 homeless. The Chicago riot was the worst of several instances of racial violence during that summer of 1919 in which 120 people died. In its aftermath, the state's governor appointed a commission to study its causes and make remedial recommendations.[73] Charles S. Johnson, an African American sociology graduate student at the University of Chicago, led the commission's research staff and was the principal author of the final report, *The Negro in Chicago*.[74] Although the Chicago school's race relations cycle that predicted assimilation formed the organizing framework of the study, *The Negro in Chicago* documented the persistence and deleterious effects of racism on African Americans revealed in inferior housing, schools, and recreational facilities, poverty, and unstable family life. It was clear to the commission that the African American experience in Chicago failed to fit the European ethnic model.

The 1924–26 Pacific Coast Survey of Race Relations headed by Robert Park similarly tested the applicability of the race relations cycle to a non-European group. The assumption was that the problems of Europeans in northern cities and Asians in the West were similar enough to sustain comparison. Instigated by the Institute of Social and Religious Research in New York City, the Race Relations Survey sought to ascertain the causes of anti-Japanese hatred on the Pacific Coast. Instead, Park conceived of the project as a study in assimilation, especially of second-generation Japanese.

As was shown in later studies, notably by Emory Bogardus, a former Chicago sociology student, social distance and discriminatory laws retarded assimilation's advance, resulting in some amalgamation but also segregation. Even members of the so-called assimilated Chinese, Japanese, Filipinx, and Mexican second generation, Bogardus found, were partially alienated from both American culture and that of their migrant parents, resulting in the "marginal man."[75]

As Park himself came to acknowledge, "Japanese, Chinese, and Negroes cannot move among us with the same freedom as the members of other races because they bear marks which identify them as members of their race." That fact of race isolates them. In his formulation, segregation and isolation leads to prejudice, and prejudice to isolation and segregation.[76] Because of their "racial badges," Park went on to explain, "Negroes" and "Orientals" were unable to assimilate; "the chief obstacle to assimilation of the Negro and Oriental are not mental but physical traits," he concluded. That racial distinctiveness constituted, in the language of race relations, the "Negro problem" and "Oriental problem."[77]

Exceptional, then, were African and Asian Americans to the primacy and general rule of ethnicity, the ethnic cycle, and eventual triumph of assimilation.[78] They belonged to the field of race relations. European immigrants, by contrast, affirmed the ideas of ethnic studies. They sustained the foundational narrative of the US as a nation of immigrants. African and Asian Americans could not assimilate with whites because of their color and white race prejudice, which, Park held, was "a spontaneous, more or less instinctive defense-reaction." Segregation and even slavery, accordingly, were "natural" solutions to the race problem because under slavery and Jim Crow, both groups, masters and servants, knew their places. When racialized minorities claimed democracy's promise, demanding equality with whites, they became problems for the normative majority.[79]

Sustaining those ideas of "natural" and "instinctual" responses to racializations was the Chicago school's analogy of social relations with evolution, natural selection, and biological competition, thereby procuring the endorsement of science. Thus, in the language of ecological succession, the "invading race," in Park's terms, whether black, brown, or yellow, posed the problem and not white supremacy or the ideology and material conditions that sustained it.[80] Biological determinism, unlike cultural change, was a key feature of race relations, and human nature rather than institutions made by humans held the answer to the race problem.

Race thinking, it appears, fell out of favor when Third World elites claimed the allegedly universal values of European humanism and emulated their white supremacist rulers by crafting identifications and solidarities along race lines. The demands of "Africa for Africans" and "Asia for Asians" made by the decolonization movements in Africa and Asia employed racialized categories made in Europe, and their powers threatened to disrupt the race relations of empire. White supremacy and its eugenicist "final solution" taken to its logical, obscene end by the Nazis during World War II spelled the final demise of race relations and the turn to ethnicity.

Culture or ethnicity did not have the sharp edges of race and racism, and assimilation offered a gentler means of absorption or subjugation by another name. French colonizers were particularly adept at this paternal siring and policing of dependent subjects through the education of a native elite, creating an "ex-native," in the words of philosopher Jean-Paul Sartre. In his preface to Fanon's *Wretched of the Earth*, Sartre penned an acid critique of that violation:

> Not so very long ago, the earth numbered two thousand million inhabitants: five hundred million men, and one thousand five hundred million natives. The former had the Word; the others had the use of it. . . . The European elite undertook to manufacture a native elite. They picked out promising adolescents; they branded them, as with a red-hot iron, with the principles of Western culture; they stuffed their mouths full with high-sounding phrases, grand glutinous words that stuck to the teeth. After a short stay in the mother country they were sent home, whitewashed. These walking lies had nothing left to say to their brothers; they only echoed. From Paris, from London, from Amsterdam we would utter the words, "Parthenon! Brotherhood!" and somewhere in Africa or Asia lips would open ". . . thenon! . . . therhood!" It was the golden age.[81]

Third World

Assimilation produced that "colonized mentality," in Albert Memmi's words, and "mis-education," as described by the African American educator Carter G. Woodson, was the means by which to ensure hegemony. Schooling, Woodson found in his *Mis-education of the Negro* (1933), inspires the oppressor and crushes the spirit of the oppressed by teaching that whites possessed great civilizations and blacks had produced nothing of significance. "Lead the Negro to believe this and thus control his thinking," he wrote. "If you can thereby determine what he will think, you will not need to worry about what he will do. You will not have to tell him to go to the back door. He will go without being told; and if there is no back door, he will have one cut for his special benefit."[82]

In 1968, a member of the Latin American Students Organization and TWLF at San Francisco State College applied Woodson's concept of mis-education. Schools, that student explained, purposefully excluded certain peoples and their cultures and histories from the curriculum. "It's a process of mis-education," he explained. "It has a purpose . . . . One is to teach us not how to change our community, or even live in it, but how to escape it by denying that we are a part of it . . . . The condition of black people, brown people, yellow people, and red people is essentially that we are all oppressed systematically as individuals and as a people by society."[83]

ETHNIC STUDIES REDUX
While the students of the Third World Liberation Front at San Francisco State demanded a unified Third World curriculum, administrators and faculty made a distinction between black studies, which they treated as race relations, and Asian, Mexican, and Native American studies, as ethnic studies. Those faculty and administrators might not have been fully aware of the intellectual genealogy of or even the discourses surrounding race relations and ethnic studies, but many, I suspect, understood "Third World" to conjure notions of revolution and possibly the specter of communism.

Students were susceptible to the claimed prerogatives of administrative and faculty governance, and to the authority of academic language and bureaucracy. As Roger Alvarado, a member of the TWLF, observed of that process of mystification: "You go to someone's office, they tell you to go elsewhere. You go there, this cat explains how this function is really a little different from what that cat said, so he can only do this much for you, you got to go somewhere else . . . it's the way the institution is laid out, man." Alvarado concluded insightfully: "Anyone can do whatever he wants to as long as he doesn't make any changes in the institution."[84]

Black studies supplied the opening for Third World studies. As early as 1965, sympathetic San Francisco State faculty sponsored black studies as experimental courses, and the Black Students Union (BSU) organized courses through the Experimental College and high school tutorial programs such that by March 1968 they enrolled nearly three thousand students. On February 9, 1968, college president John Summerskill appointed Nathan Hare, a Chicago sociology PhD, "to help design a curriculum of Black Studies." In April of that year, Hare proposed a "Department of Black Studies," while the Third World Liberation Front demanded an increase in minority student admission and "the establishment of a Third World curriculum, along the lines of the Black Studies Program." Meanwhile, the college academic senate considered its instructional policies committee's recommendation regarding a "Program of Ethnic Studies."[85]

In April and May 1968, library student workers struck for union recognition, Third World students demanded influence over admissions and the hiring of more faculty of color, and the SDS demanded the eviction of the Air Force ROTC from campus. Summerskill called the San Francisco tactical squad to remove student protesters from the administration building, and in the skirmish, police arrested twenty-six students and injured at least eleven. More sit-ins, demonstrations, and arrests rocked the college for days, and on May 24, 1968, the students reached an agreement with the administration.[86]

On that day, Summerskill resigned, and on June 1, 1968, Robert Smith assumed the presidency. In August 1968, the trustees considered a proposal for a black studies major, and the following month, Smith announced the formation of a Department of Black Studies and appointed Nathan Hare as its chair.

On November 6, 1968, after the dismissal of George Murray, the part-time English department instructor, the BSU launched the strike that even-tuated in a School of Ethnic Studies.[87] As the Black Panther Party's minister of education, Murray had expressed the party's vow to fight until "colonized Africans, Asians and Latin Americans in the United States and throughout the world have become free . . . and that is the historic duty of black people in the United States to bring about the complete, absolute and unconditional end of racism and neocolonialism by smashing, shattering and destroying the imperialist domains of North America."[88] The immediate demands of the strike, however, were for a larger black studies program and Murray's rein-statement. Other student organizations of the TWLF joined the BSU a few days later.

Meanwhile, in the November 4, 1968 issue of the official college newslet-ter *On the Record*, President Smith issued a "Statement on Black and Ethnic Studies" in which he refers to "black and ethnic" students, including "young adults of minority racial and ethnic backgrounds" and "Spanish-speaking cultural backgrounds." Thereby, Smith made a distinction between race in reference to blacks, and ethnicity, to nonblack people of color. A December 1968 academic senate report reinforced that differentiation when it endorsed the implementation of a "Black Studies Program" and the creation of a task-force to study the feasibility of "non-black ethnic programs" and "to explore policies and procedures for ethnic studies."[89]

Student activists mirrored the distinction between black studies and ethnic studies, which some called "ethnic area studies," reflecting, ironi-cally, the wider academic convention since the Cold War of African, Asian, and Latin American area studies. Of course, the Cold War also implicated the term "Third World," but anticolonial revolutionaries had appropriated the name to serve their purposes. Since June 1968, a position paper stated, the Third World Liberation Front had been organizing to implement "ethnic area studies" at San Francisco State and institute "a school of ethnic area studies" to respond to Third World needs.[90] Although inclusive of American Indians, the TWLF's ethnic area studies excluded indigenous peoples in the US insofar as area studies referenced regions outside the nation-state.

There were two sets of demands that followed the initial demands to expand black studies and rehire George Murray. The first came from the BSU's "10 Demands," which addressed the amplification of black studies but did not include a provision for Third World or ethnic (area) studies. The second, "Third World Liberation Front Demands," proposed that a "School of Ethnic Studies for the ethnic groups involved in the Third World be set up with students in each particular ethnic organization having the authority and control of the hiring and retention of any faculty member." Among the TWLF's five demands was a provision for fifty faculty positions for a School of Ethnic Studies with twenty of those set aside for the Black Studies Program.[91]

When the BSU and TWLF signed the joint agreement on March 18, 1969, that ended the longest student strike in the history of US higher education, they settled for the language: "THAT A SCHOOL OF ETHNIC STUDIES FOR THE ETHNIC GROUPS INVOLVED IN THE THIRD WORLD BE SET UP WITH THE STUDENTS IN EACH."[92] The name "ethnic studies" remains at San Francisco State in the School of Ethnic Studies that opened in the fall of 1969, although some students and faculty continued to employ the term "Third World" through at least 1970.[93]

Thus it was that ethnic studies came to designate my field of study even as Third World remained my intellectual work and subject position. For years, I wondered about that name change, but only began to study the question in 2008 when the National Museum of Singapore asked me to deliver a keynote lecture on the contemporary meaning of World War II. Research for that paper compelled me to consider anew the global, as opposed to the national, consequences of the war, which led me to a reacquaintance with the Third World. Prior to that opportunity, I had written about World War II solely from a domestic, US perspective. Seen from the Third World, the war appears a continuation, rather than a break as most Western historians claim, and an extension of European sovereignty to its colonial possessions in the periphery.

The real contest, the historic rupture in the course of world history, was the anticolonial struggles of Africa and Asia for self-determination and antiracism, the selfsame causes of the Third World students at San Francisco State College in 1968. How then, did Third World studies become ethnic studies in the course of the field's institutionalization was my question and problem. I knew ethnic studies to have descended from Chicago sociology, and I suspected, but did not have the evidence for, a sleight of hand on the part of college faculty and administrators.

I wrote to an old colleague, James Garrett, the most prominent student leader of San Francisco State's Black Students Union at the time, according to a government report on the 1968 Third World strike.[94] Garrett recalled political and educational leaders, in collaboration with "careerists," seeking to soften the student demands for black and Third World studies by conceptualizing them as ethnic and diversity or multicultural studies.[95] His recollection confirmed my suspicion and led me to the archives and then (2011) still formative strike collection at San Francisco State.

As I now understand it, having searched the strike collection, San Francisco State's administrators racialized African Americans and labeled American Indians, Asians, and Mexicans ethnic or cultural groups. As we saw, college faculty referenced "ethnic studies" when students demanded "Third World studies," and students deployed "ethnic area studies" to link the condition of Africans, Asians, and Mexicans in the US with the peoples of Africa, Asia, and Latin America—the Third World.[96] In the end, "ethnic studies" became the term chosen by members of the Black Students Union and Third World Liberation Front to designate its subjects—African Americans, American Indians, Asians, and Latinxs. And insofar as cultural nationalism defined the field, ethnic studies was a variant of Chicago ethnic studies.

Nathan Hare, hired by Summerskill to develop San Francisco State's black studies curriculum, submitted his proposal on April 29, 1968. In his introduction, Hare acknowledged that the impetus for black studies at San Francisco State came from African American students and the BSU. The idea for black studies, Hare wrote, "not only reflects their cries—echoed by others across the country—for relevant education; it also represents the greatest and last hope for rectifying an old wrong and halting the decay now gnawing away at American society."[97] Like Chicago sociology, in Hare's conception, black studies was designed to solve social problems in the US.

A key component of the black studies program, Hare added, again like Chicago sociology's studies of (urban) communities, was its focus on "community involvement . . . to inspire and sustain a sense of collective destiny as a people and a consciousness of the value of education in a technological society." The academic program would constitute "a cultural base" for the black community to celebrate "black holidays, festivities and celebrations." Black information centers would increase awareness within black communities, and distribute "propaganda" aimed at black children to motivate them to complete their education.[98]

Proposed classes in Hare's black studies major included four core courses on black history, black psychology, black arts and humanities, and a method and theory course in the sciences. He proposed a black arts concentration, composed of music, writing, literature, painting, and sculpture, and a behavioral and social sciences concentration, involving black politics, sociology, geography, counseling, leadership, and community. The only course transcendent of the US that might have gestured toward the Third World was a course on "Black Consciousness and the International Community."[99]

Black studies graduates, Hare believed, would share a commitment "to the struggle to build the black community," and those employed outside the black community would possess "a keener sense of security as individuals and would be better equipped to present the black perspective. This would benefit the black community indirectly," Hare concluded, "and perhaps assist those members of the white community who, like the black studies program, seek, in a roundabout way, a better society for all of its members."[100]

Black studies, so conceived, was directed at African American uplift through community development and a collective sense of peoplehood. Black or national culture, black ethnicity, was central to that project, which featured the nation and its black and white communities. Seeking "a better society for all of its members," black studies mirrored the problem solving and culture of Chicago sociology's race relations and ethnic studies and not the self-determination and antiracism of the Third World liberation movement or the internationalism of Third World women and Third World Liberation Front.[101] In May 1967, a year before Hare's proposal, college deans considered black studies as a place "wherein the Negro student could get something to help him find his place in American society."[102] It was that version of black studies that Hare endorsed, college president Smith approved, and the academic senate considered, blending Chicago sociology's race relations with ethnic studies.

Absent in that institutionalization discourse is the revolutionary movement, ideology, and language that transformed over four hundred years of world history wrought by the struggles of Third World peoples. The nation-state and nationalism, in the San Francisco State proceedings, led principally by men, eclipsed Third World consciousness and solidarity. Likewise, in the Third World, nationalist leaders, again mainly men, veered away from the internationalist spirit of Bandung and nation building became their primary goal. Neocolonialism descended as soon as independence dawned, and in our time, amidst transnationalism, imperialism and capitalism thrive in a world-system of nation-states.

Terry Collins, a member of the central committee of San Francisco State's Black Students Union, reflected on that drift to nationalism and patriarchy. In the spring of 1968, Collins recalled, a handful of "dominant personalities . . . tyrannically reigned over the other students" in the movement. "Factionalism was rampant, potential revolutionary brothers were disillusioned, sisters were used and abused in the name of 'blackness.' It was the era of bourgeois cultural nationalism." The cults of personality and authenticity, nationalism and culture, Collins noted, divided and diverted the focus of black students from "the real enemy."[103]

THIRD WORLD WOMEN

Still, there was a moment in 1968 when talk of freedom was in the air and hope seemed fresh and eternal. Third World women showed the way in their break from the iron cages of nationalism, patriarchy, heterosexism, and capitalism by conceiving and articulating a more liberating language, ideology, and practice based upon their lived experiences as women of color.

A founding figure in that liberation movement was Frances Beal, a former NAACP (National Association for the Advancement of Colored People) youth leader and a member of SNCC's (Student Nonviolent Coordinating Committee) international affairs commission. At a 1968 SNCC meeting in New York City, Beal presented a paper on the impact of racism, sexism, and capitalism on the lives of African American women, and proposed a black women's caucus to explore those particular concerns.

Capitalism, Beal pointed out, exploits all workers, but white workers can subscribe to a false consciousness of racial superiority and black men, a feeling of dominion over black women. Capitalism relegates women workers "to a state of enslavement," and black women to the bottom of the ladder of class, race, and gender. Moreover, Beal argued, the state's sterilization campaigns exert control over black and Puerto Rican women's sexuality, and the white women's movement, largely a middle-class project, excludes the masses of black women whose struggles are against gender but also class, racial, and sexual oppressions.[104]

Beal formed with others the Black Women's Liberation Caucus, which split from SNCC in 1969, and changed its name to the Black Women's Alliance (BWA). Widening its purview and circle with the recognition that, in Beal's words, "the complexities of intersecting oppressions [were] more resilient than the distinctions of the particular groups," the BWA established solidarity with other women of color, including American Indians, Asians, and Latinxs. That opening led the BWA to rename itself the Third World Women's Alliance, which stated as its goals: "to make a meaningful and lasting contribution to the Third World community by working for the elimination of the oppression and exploitation from which we suffer" and to create a socialist society free from "the pressures of racism, economic exploitation, and sexual oppression."[105]

Perceiving a similar marginalization from the civil rights and white women's movements, African American women formed the Combahee River Collective (CRC) in 1974. Sisters Beverly and Barbara Smith, with Demita Frazier, crafted the statement that articulated most persuasively the case for what later became theorized as intersectionality. As Barbara Smith recalled years later, "we wanted to integrate a race / class analysis with an antisexist analysis and practice. And we didn't just want to add on racism and class oppression like white women did."[106] The statement begins with an explication of the CRC's politics: "we are actively committed to struggling against racial, sexual, heterosexual, and class oppression, and see as our particular task the development of integrated analysis and practice based upon the fact that the major systems of oppression are interlocking. The synthesis of these oppressions creates the conditions of our lives."[107]

The ideologies and practices of the Third World Women's Alliance and Combahee River Collective work at the multiplicities and intersections of race, gender, sexuality, and class, unlike other African American women's organizations that might have stressed race and gender but glossed sexuality and class.[108] The interlocking systems of oppression, their synthesis, became a basis for legal and critical race scholar Kimberlé Crenshaw's foundational 1989 essay, "Demarginalizing the Intersection of Race and Sex," in which she named the "multidimensionality of Black women's experience" "intersectionality." "Because the intersectional experience is greater than the sum of racism and sexism," Crenshaw wrote, "any analysis that does not take intersectionality into account cannot sufficiently address the particular manner in which Black women are subordinated."[109]

Other African American scholars expanded upon the intersections of gender, race, and nation like the sociologist Patricia Hill Collins,[110] and other women of color deployed the intersections of race, gender, sexuality, class, and nation.[111] Not simply ethnic studies (Chicago or San Francisco State) or the US racial formation,[112] Third World women understood, the conditions of their lives involved the totality of power relations wherein theory and practice converged. Moreover, while traditional intellectuals claimed intersectionality as theirs, organic intellectuals were the first to name the multiple, interlocking systems of oppression that infringed upon their daily lives.[113] My theory of social formation, articulated elsewhere,[114] is an offspring of that intellectual and activist work by Third World women.

Third World studies, not ethnic studies, is my intellectual home and cause, my life and life's work. Third World studies locates my subject-self within world history and society. My field of study did not begin in 1968 at San Francisco State but at the century's start with the problem of the twentieth century. Third World and not national liberation was the aim of the Third World Liberation Front, and its affiliations and commitments were not restricted to the US but embraced the expansive Third World. The oppressed are the subjects of Third World studies, and the discourses and practices of imperialism are the instruments of their subjection. Third World women's analyses arising from the conditions of their lives exposed those ruling powers as a whole network of solitary, multiple, and interlocking oppressions that moved in space / time and that required, consequently, theories and practices equally complicated and nimble.

> In movement,
> Inhabiting and traversing space / time,
> Ceaselessly,
> I situate my subject-self and project
> Within that imaginary called
> The Third World.

CHAPTER SIX

Antipodes

An imaginary straight line through the earth's core connects my points of origin. The antipode of Hawai'i, the islands of my physical birth, is Botswana, the landlocked nation of my intellectual birth. Antipodes are oppositional but also, corresponding; Hawai'i and Botswana cohere in my life and life's labors. Another fanciful line marking the tropics brushes Hawai'i to the north and Botswana, the south. Those latitudes segregate and integrate the planet's tropical and temperate zones. Although situated squarely in the middle of the African continent, Botswana, at the time of my arrival, was an island of black rule encircled by a sea of white supremacist states—the renegade Rhodesia to its north, the client state South-West Africa to its west, and, dominating the entire region, apartheid South Africa to its east and south. Islands and continent, conjoined by the artifice of antipodes, Hawai'i and Botswana are, like all of earth's landmasses, islands.

During a stopover at Johannesburg's airport in 1969, the only notable act of defiance I could muster against racial segregationist South Africa was to urinate in the "For Whites Only" toilet. Like a scene in a bad movie, a white man in a trench coat with a folded newspaper tucked under his arm trailed me. I was merely adhering to the apartheid regime's policy whereby Japanese were classified as "Honorary Whites." The importance of commerce with Japan vacated racial segregation in which white was the color of money. The problem, though, for that lurking shadowy figure was to ascertain if I was nonwhite Chinese or white Japanese.

Thankfully, Air Botswana delivered me from Johannesburg's stifling transit lounge to the freedom of sprawling Gaborone, Botswana's capital. Independent since September 30, 1966, Botswana escaped absorption by its apartheid neighbor to the south as one of the three British High Commission Territories, which included the Bechuanaland Protectorate (Botswana), Basutoland (Lesotho), and Swaziland. Seretse Khama married a white, British woman, thereby offending the British colonizers but endearing him to many Batswana (Tswana people) who elected him their first president of that largely arid, agricultural country that danced to the rhythms of the pulsating, spreading Kalahari Desert.

Dominant, that vast, flat landscape was interrupted only by occasional islands of rock mounds. The Kalahari easily occupied one's spatial and temporal senses. Over its generous surface, grasses and trees once grew in profusion, prodigious herds of elephant, giraffe, wildebeest, and zebras roamed, and in their tracks followed women and men who gathered and hunted. These were the first people, later called Sān, on that land. In a gendered division of labor, women were the main providers of daily sustenance, roots and bulbs, leafy vegetables, and fruits, while men supplied animal protein from the hunt. For economy, Sān bands were small, mobile, and fluidly organized, and moved with the pattern of game migrations and seasonal variations of rainfall and plant life.

Having thus described the Sān as a homogenous, unchanging people, surely a caricature, like my static description of the Modocs, I know the Sān to be a diverse people economically and socially. As historical peoples, the Sān and, indeed, all of Botswana's peoples are multiply constituted and shifting; they defy positivist classifications as we find in the writings of structural-functionalist anthropologists. Because of innovation and interaction, language, economic activities, ethnic and gender relations, beliefs and ideologies, and social organization are fluid and subject to change.[1]

Unlike the kinship tribes of foundational anthropologists, most of Botswana's Sotho-speakers (Batswana) were ethnically diverse migrants from the east and south during the nineteenth century, overwhelming and scattering bands of Sān and loose groupings of Bangologa, Babolaongwe, Bakgwatheng, and Bashaga. The latter, inaccurately and pejoratively called Kgalagadi,[2] are Sotho-speakers and descend from the same people that became the Batswana. The land was marginally suited for the large-scale agricultural economies and settlements from whence came those nineteenth-century Batswana migrants. Consequently, they adapted to the new environment like the Sān and Sotho-speaking people before them.

Over the course of the century, however, and largely as a result of warfare and economic necessity, the newcomers coalesced into large towns under a single ruler (kgosi) to form nations (merafe) that the British subsumed under the Bechuanaland Protectorate in 1885. The colonizers essentialized Batswana merafe to "tribes," signifying kin-based societies, and reduced their towns that numbered in the tens of thousands to mere "villages." Batswana towns were aggregations of dozens of households and lineages, and they remained distinctive features of the Protectorate.

The Peace Corps stationed me west of Gaborone along the Kalahari's edges among the Bakwena, a Batswana subgroup identified as the "people who dance to the crocodile" (ba bina kwena). In the Bakwena capital, Molepolole, I taught science and health classes at Kgosi Kgari Sechele II Secondary School for three years, from 1969 to 1971. Dialoguing with students who were destined to lead this democratic, black-ruled nation was exhilarating and, at the same time, depressingly colonizing. Britain remained in Botswana's education in the textbooks, curricula, and final examinations, and the schools, as key apparatuses of the state, interpellated the nation's people to render them into suitable subjects of the neocolonial state. I, alas, participated in producing that "colonial mentality" in my teaching.

As aspects of that colonizing project, the life of learning moved to the hourly ringing of the bell and its five-day school week, and students wore clean, neatly pressed uniforms to enter angular, fabricated classroom structures at odds with the environment and physically and ideologically separated from the spaces in which they lived. In addition, most of the white "expatriates" who taught at Kgari Sechele occupied the then two rows of government-issued houses on the fenced-off school property. The chain-link fence distinguished the world of the foreigners from the Bakwena, and apart from contact with their students and servants who cleaned, washed, and cooked for them, expatriate teachers circled the familiar and rarely leaped full-bodied into Setswana society. Despite avoiding much of the excesses of expatriate comity by socializing mainly with Batswana in the town, I failed to appreciate the extent of my alienation from the land and its people.

Only when I removed myself physically and intellectually from the school grounds to live in the oldest and most venerable of Molepolole's sections (metse), Ntloedibe, did I come to realize the spatial and temporal distinctions of life under colonialism and apart from (if possible) neocolonialism. That extrication beyond the fence happened in 1975 after my Peace Corps tour of duty, and after my return to UCLA to resume my graduate studies.

In Molepolole for my dissertation research, I rented a sprawling house and compound in Ntloedibe. There, the sun determined most of my activities; I can appreciate its veneration by my ancestors. I sensed a cadence at variance with the colonizer's clock and workweek culture that can narcotize knowing subjects to the environment and its agencies. In Ntloedibe, the sound of roosters crowing and dogs barking, the clanking of cattle bells and bleating of goats and sheep, and far-off voices in the night signaled my risings and settings. The early morning lines of girls and women, heavy water buckets on their heads, balancing their way along trails homeward bound, and young boys steering their herds of animals, including cattle with impossibly long horns, to boreholes and then distant pastures marked the start of my days. The sun's heat energized me in the winter and enervated me in the summer, and the evening's clarity and its unfamiliar skies alerted me to my location in the southern hemisphere. Voyaging here required recalibrations.

Words fail to describe the temporal and spatial reorientations I felt, but they were pervasive and profound nonetheless. That new consciousness of space / time impressed upon me the powers of imperialism and its discourses as well as its limits when exposed to its alternative, which I sensed in Botswana. Grasping those elemental, experiential truths, however, required both an unlearning and a deliberate cultivation. Herein, I am reminded of the British geographer David W. Harvey's admonition to academics to "untrain" themselves to think outside the boundaries of disciplines, which control and counter revolutions, "to confront the realities around them" and become "active participants in the social process."[3]

CONFESSION[4]

When I began my dissertation research in 1975, I was armed with the tenets of science and the looking glass of positionality. Science demanded "objective" history while my subject position prescribed Afrocentrism or history from the African, not European, point of view. I had, during my graduate years, immersed myself in the now ancient but then current "substantivist" and "formalist" debates in economic anthropology, and was eager to affirm my formalist assumptions with the evidence I was positive I would find in the field. I had rejected the ideas of Bronislaw Malinowski, Karl Polanyi, George Dalton, and Marshall Sahlins, whose distinction between redistributive and capitalist economies failed to sway my conviction that humans were economic and not social beings at base, although their counterargument that formalists subscribed to an "obsolete market mentality" and were parochial in their universalism resonated with my distaste for Eurocentrism and the imperial sciences.[5]

I found compelling Raymond Firth's understanding of economics and his critique of Malinowski, and cheered the antiracist project of Melville Herskovits who, in his *Economic Anthropology*, stressed the rational choices exercised by people in all societies. Edward W. LeClair, Jr. and Harold K. Schneider clarified and confirmed my original impulse, and the peerless micro-studies of Polly Hill, a self-described "economist turned economic anthropologist," begged emulation.[6]

I entered fieldwork with other verities. I would show the ingenuity and benign nature of precapitalist, peasant producers and the social and environmental dislocations caused by capitalism's spread based on my readings of equilibrium, ecosystem, and ecological succession theories,[7] and I was alert to the social changes wrought by contact and technological innovation.[8] Marxism's excavation of society's materialist base, and its focus on precapitalist societies and the rise and development of capitalism, complemented my intellectual and political affiliations, and the modifications of neo-Marxists and their critiques of liberal economics and "neo-Smithian Marxists" alike pointed a way out of the "crisis" in the social sciences during the 1960s and 1970s.[9] The major question posed by Maurice Godelier, Emmanuel Terray, Claude Meillassoux, and Pierre Philippe Rey—how kinship intersects with precapitalist modes of production given their assumption of kinship's centrality in the reproduction of social relations—led to a split between those who favored the study of precapitalist formations for their own sake and those for whom the articulation of precapitalist formations with capitalism and the world-system was paramount.[10]

The influence of those ideas was far-reaching as revealed in southern African historiography. Colin Bundy's essay, "The Emergence and Decline of a South African Peasantry" (1972), and Robin Palmer and Neil Parsons's collection, *The Roots of Rural Poverty in Central and Southern Africa* (1977), drew from underdevelopment theory and moved the literature in the direction of imperialism and articulation. Although precapitalist modes of production and ingenious African farmers were essential to their interpretation, African producers were clearly secondary to the agency of European expansionists. Afrocentrists like Terence Ranger scored them for their implicit Eurocentrism.[11] By the 1980s, precapitalist modes of production and social history shifted the focus away from macro-processes and structures and toward the details and complexities of African chiefdoms and individual actors to develop what Timothy Keegan has called "a more credible picture of the black rural economy."[12]

Despite that return to what Leonard Thompson had called "the forgotten factor in southern African history"—African agency—and despite the works of historians like Shula Marks and J. B. Peires, precapitalist modes of production constitute the baseline, but not the pivot, for many others like William Beinart, Colin Bundy, Peter Delius, and Stanley Trapido.[13] Their themes of accumulation, dispossession, and resistance have contributed much to our understanding of peasant and agrarian history, and they have shown us the complexities of capitalism's articulation with indigenous formations. William Beinart and Colin Bundy posited the promising proposition that local struggles for self-determination helped shape modern, mass social movements for liberation in South Africa.[14]

Most of that excitement over dependency and underdevelopment took place after the completion of my research in Botswana. I failed to benefit from that conversation when I planned and carried out the work that resulted in my *A Social History of the Bakwena* (2000). My study, nonetheless, mirrored my times. Like the generation of historians in the 1980s who were influenced in their choice of subject matter and theoretical frames by the epic struggle during the final days of apartheid, I identified with my generation's cause—the liberation of Third World people within and without the US. I strived to expose history's complicity in endorsing the ruling class and to conceive of novel historical formations from which to navigate more liberating futures. I determined to position Africans at the center of my narrative, to let them speak, to advance an African history and not the deeds of Europeans in Africa.

Despite my commitment to self-determination, when I sat to pen my revisionist history, with my fingers frozen by the cold that seeped through the stone walls of my makeshift study in the Orkney Isles, I knew I was imposing my will upon the vital, vibrant past, making it unrecognizable to those who had so generously shared with me their histories. Like the alien traders, missionaries, colonialists, and anthropologists who had preceded me, I presumed to represent my subjects and profited from that imperious transaction. As a Motswana oral historian pointedly asked me: "What will you do with the information we provide, and who will benefit from that endowment entrusted?" In addition to my ethical responsibility and incalculable debt, I was certain the unruly, three-dimensional lives of my subjects defied discipline and containment within the two-dimensional surface of words on paper. Uprooted from its environment, the lived African past withered and died in my representation. With that realization and while in the act of writing, I felt a tightness in my stomach, a gagging in my throat. For years, that nausea afflicted me. I wept, long ago, over my betrayal and infidelity.

HISTORY LESSONS[15]

"Tell me about the Bakwena past (ditsho)," I began my meetings with the elders in my attempt at historical recovery. I recall well those tortuous hours, day after day at the kgosi's kgotla (meeting place). Painful they were because these learned men and a few women summoned by the kgosi appeared to know precious little about their nation's history. There was no master narrative, no sweeping account of origins and destinies, no king lists, battles waged, lands conquered and lost, technological and economic advances. From my readings of nineteenth-century European travelers and twentieth-century anthropologists, I secretly and arrogantly thought, I knew far more of the Bakwena past than these oral historians of the nation. After a particularly excruciating session, I blurted out in desperation: "Okay, tell me something about yourself, your genealogy."

That patronizing and ignorant, as it turned out, request unleashed a torrent of insights into self and society and history. Astonishing were their memories that recalled genealogies reaching back thirteen and more generations. Tutored as I was in the notion of "objective" history, my lead and vague question into the "Bakwena past" was my attempt not to color or predispose my informants' responses. The problem, as I came to learn, was that history (ditsho) is a personal account and possession, vital for the location of subject-selves within society, and the nation / people, the Bakwena, was a flexible, mobile entity unlike the sovereign state and people of the European variety since the Peace of Westphalia (1648).

My discovery lay bare some of the troubling assumptions I had held about the Bakwena past, and set me on a different path to historical reconstruction. The Bakwena, I assumed, were a unitary tribe or kinship group with a national history or variant thereof. I believed the Bakwena, like other Sotho-Tswana peoples, always lived in large, permanent towns composed of thousands of people as was faithfully described by nineteenth-century European travelers and by many ethnographers. I believed the Bakwena pursued a mixed economy of cattle herding and grain cultivating. Bakwena genealogies led me to question and ultimately reject my fanciful, bookish assumptions.

My renewed research design, pursued for nearly an entire year, shifted from collecting data to fit my formalist economics to gathering the genealogies of every lineage in all of Molepolole's sections. With that information,

I was able to see the Bakwena in their entirety and when and how they stitched themselves together into the garment called the nation (morafe). My tireless teachers disabused me of some of the rules and processes by which groups separated and joined that I had absorbed from non-Africans who had studied and codified African behavior into sets of laws and customs.[16] Tradition, my Bakwena tutors made me see, often serves the ends of its creators, and tidy generalizations become complicated and messy on the ground where humans, historical agents, walked and left their footprints.

I am reminded here of Michel Foucault's idea of genealogy and history. Genealogical research, he cautions, is meticulous and "patiently documentary," demanding a "relentless erudition" because it involves detours and complications of "invasions, struggles, plundering, disguises, ploys." A genealogy is neither a linear nor singular, unidirectional guide to a destination. "On the contrary, to follow the complex course of descent is to maintain passing events in their proper dispersion; it is to identify the accidents, the minute deviations—or conversely, the complete reversals—the errors, the false appraisals, and the faulty calculations that gave birth to those things that continue to exist and have value for us; it is to discover that truth or being does not lie at the root of what we know and what we are, but the exteriority of accidents." Instead of terra firma, genealogy consists of moving ground, "an unstable assemblage of faults, fissures, and heterogeneous layers that threaten the fragile inheritor from within or from underneath."[17]

Genealogical research, as Foucault perceptively observed, uncovered for me surprising truths not of my design or choosing. From my reading, the "people of the crocodile" or Bakwena organized themselves spatially and socially into makgotla (plural of kgotla) and metse (plural of motse) or sections and settlements. Senior sons determined by primogeniture and their mother's standing as first, second, or third wife, customary law held, inherited their father's office, the bogosi or "chiefship," and kgotla and maintained the right to separate and establish makgotla of their own.

Contrary to those rules, my Bakwena teachers revealed, there were instances when juniors formed makgotla, showing that law and custom offered guidelines, not unchanging, rigid rules, which were situational and elastic. When the Bakwena kgosi, Sechele, appointed Mosimane to serve as his counselor (ntona), he moved Mosimane's kgotla, Senyadima, from the section of Ntlheng-ya Tlhase to Kgosing, Sechele's section of the capital. Perhaps because of that transfer and his heavier responsibilities, Mosimane divided his kgotla, and handed over a portion named Sekamelo, from go sekama meaning "to recline one's head" or "to rest," to his junior brother, Mmutlanyane.[18] In that way, Mosimane established a kgotla headed by a junior.

Seniors, in other instances, deferred to their juniors. Legojane, the founder of the kgotla Goo-Ra-Mmoopi, had two sons, Mosimanegape and Mmoopi. Legojane's heir, Mosimanegape, chose not to succeed his father, and handed over the bogosi to his junior brother. Henceforth, Mmoopi's descendants became the "owners of the kgotla" as reflected in the kgotla's name, Goo-Ra-Mmoopi or "the people of Mmoopi."[19]

In other instances, kgotla members made succession choices. During the early nineteenth century, a mass assembly in the kgotla Matlhalerwa demanded the installation of the junior Ikalafeng over the heir, Sebekedi, ostensibly because Sebekedi's mother was a Bangwaketse, a people living to the south of and junior to the Bakwena, while Ikalafeng's mother was a Mokwena (singular for Bakwena).[20]

Women also "owned" makgotla contrary to the prerogatives of patriarchy. Tumagole, the junior brother of the Bakwena kgosi, Sebele a Sechele (or Sebele, son of Sechele), was kgosi of the kgotla Senyadimana. Tumagole had two daughters and no sons. Phetogo, the older daughter, inherited the kgotla from her father, but chose not to administer its affairs and willed it to her sons. Senyadimana is accordingly known as a kgotla ya dipitsana or "inherited kgotla" generally through a woman. Phetogo married Kealeboga, heir of her uncle Sebele (a Sechele), and her senior male descendants in turn became the Bakwena dikgosi and head of her kgotla. In 1975, kgosi Bonewamang "owned" Senyadimana by virtue of his grandmother, Phetogo.[21] This inheritance pursues a matrilineal thread running through a patrilineal society.

Population increases, driven by reproduction and the absorption of immigrants, led to kgotla formation. In marked contrast to the prevalent notion of tribes conceived of as kinship aggregations, immigrants comprised the majority of the Bakwena of Molepolole from the time of Sechele, circa 1831, to 1975, the year of my research. "Baagedi" were Bakwena immigrants, whereas "badichaba" were non-Bakwena immigrants, indicating their greater distance from the Bakwena as non-kin and foreigners. The large numbers of immigrants and foreigners relative to the core group of Bakwena and their descendants profoundly affected the population size, the physical layout of the Bakwena capital, and the locations and relations of economic, political, and social power.

Most of the baagedi and badichaba in Molepolole joined the Bakwena during the first half of the nineteenth century. A distinctive feature during that period was immigration in large groups as opposed to individuals and families,[22] who were mainly fleeing the difaqane and Afrikaner predations in the Transvaal.[23] Their arrival, between 1820 and 1860, more than quadrupled the Bakwena population.

Although the estimates of European travelers must be tempered with some skepticism, they give an indication of relative size.[24] In 1843, British missionary David Livingstone reported 300 people among Sechele's Bakwena at Tshonwane and 350 among Bubi's Boo-Ra-Tshosa section of a divided Bakwena morafe. Six years later, he estimated that the rejoined Sechele and Bubi sections at Kolobeng numbered 2,384, an increase that must have included absorbed immigrants. Later that same year, about 1,236 Bakaa arrived and settled with the Bakwena, and in 1857, just fourteen years after Livingstone's first census, Sechele's capital at Dithubaruba contained roughly 20,000 inhabitants.[25]

Although equally imprecise as those nineteenth-century estimates in terms of absolute numbers, my enumeration of Molepolole's makgotla showed the magnitude and timing of immigration together with some of its causes. In 1975, there were twenty-one major Bakwena makgotla as compared with thirty-seven major baagedi and badichaba makgotla. Among all immigrant makgotla, seven were formed before Sechele's rule, twenty-two during Sechele, five during Sebele (a Sechele), two during Kealeboga, and one during Sebele (a Kealeboga). Fifteen of the baagedi and badichaba makgotla resulted from the difaqane and Afrikaner disturbances, while only five arose from internal disputes and three because of wars among Batswana groups.[26]

Immigrants as individuals or family groups generally attached themselves to members of a kgotla with whom they had a chance encounter, were related, or were friends. By far, the Bakwena kgosi's section, Kgosing, absorbed the largest number of immigrants. In 1975, Molepolole consisted of five sections. I found twenty-three major immigrant makgotla in Kgosing, eight in Ntlheng-ya Tlhase, four in Ntlheng-ya Godimo, two in Ntloedibe, and none in Mokgalo. Kgosi Sechele probably designed that pattern in Kgosing to surround himself with immigrant makgotla to protect him from Bakwena competitors and claimants to the throne on the basis of kinship. Immigrants lacked kinship privileges, and they were indebted to the kgosi for their standing. In addition, Sechele elevated servants by creating a kgotla, Difetlhamolelo, composed of "Bakgalagadi," and he appointed Segakisa, a "Mokgalagadi" (singular of "Bakgalagadi") and son of a servant, as his ntona or counselor.[27] After his elevation, Segakisa invited Kgalaeng, a son of his father's master, to join him in Difetlhamolelo. In that way, Segakisa and Kgalaeng reversed the roles of master and servant.

Immigrants and contacts with non-Bakwena introduced novel ideas, cultures, and institutions. The nation (morafe) when constituted by kinship contained forces favorable to integration but also separation. To centralize authority and reduce divisions, Sechele introduced the ntona system, which he might have borrowed from the Makololo or Ndebele.[28] Sechele appointed four ntona to oversee each section of the capital. Segakisa headed Kgosing, Mosimane supervised Mokgalo, Ketshabile, Ntlheng-ya Godimo, and Magogwe, Ntlheng-ya Tlhase. With the exception of Mosimane, all of the dintona (plural of ntona) were immigrants, and all thus owed allegiance to Sechele for their powers. They reported to the kgosi daily, erected their homes within the kgosi's section, Kgosing, and received a share of the annual tax (sehuba) collected in their sections.[29]

Immigrant makgotla, unlike most Bakwena makgotla, commonly arose from factors other than kinship. A "makatlanathapong" kgotla, from katlana, meaning "to adhere, to stick together" and thapo or "string,"[30] was one such makgotla. Dikgori, a makatlanathapong kgotla in Goo-Ra-Tshosa, consisted of three unrelated lineages of Bangwaketse and Bakgatla, cousins of the Bakwena. The earliest to arrive were the Bangwaketse Boo-Ra-Koosentse and thus their senior status in Dikgori, and the later arrivals, Bakgatla refugees of the difaqane, became their juniors.

In addition to adhesion by disparate groups, Bakwena dikgosi (plural of kgosi) shaped makatlanathapong makgotla. Kealeboga, for example, created the kgotla Goo-Ra-Letlamma for his son by fusing three immigrant makgotla, Goo-Meje, Goo-Ra-Molefe, and Ga-Mangwato, into one. Letlamma, kgosi Kealeboga's son, built his household within the circle of the Goo-Meje, the most senior lineage of the three. When Letlamma died without an heir, the three makgotla drifted apart and formed a voluntary association while keeping their integrity as distinct makgotla.[31]

Immigrants arriving in large groups sometimes formed their own makgotla, like the Goo-Modibedi kgotla in the Ntlheng-ya Godimo section of Molepolole.[32] Well-organized and ambitious immigrants, however, posed potential threats to the stability of the morafe, and thus Bakwena dikgosi often divided and scattered them. When the Bakwena of Kgabo (ya molelo), a collection of well-disciplined, tightly organized soldiers, fled to Sechele's Bakwena at Tshonwane as a result of the difaqane and Afrikaners, Sechele separated the senior from junior lineages. He allocated the seniors to the Ntl-heng-ya Godimo section of the capital, and absorbed the juniors into his Kgosing, thereby favoring the juniors over their seniors and reducing the likelihood of rebellion.[33]

As my Bakwena teachers revealed, rules and customs circumscribed the social processes set in motion by historical actors, but those constraints, unlike rigid laws, were susceptible to human intervention.[34] The rapid and large increase in the numbers of immigrants presented challenges and opportunities for nation building. Kinship and hereditary hierarchies located social relations, while immigration supplied novel solutions to the age-old problems of competition, conflict, and separation. Immigration also pointed toward external historical forces like the difaqane and Afrikaner depredations in the Transvaal that influenced and inhabited the internal workings of the Bakwena morafe.

My naïve question about individual pasts prompted answers that altered fundamentally my understanding of Bakwena history. My great discovery, of course, was obvious to my Bakwena mentors. History and the nation, they knew, are situational and changing, forged by collections of diverse peoples, ideologies, and institutions that converge and depart at different times and places. Moreover, they taught me, history is not some distant, objective nar-ration; rather, ditsho helps to apprehend the human condition, of self and society, biography and history, the subject and the world. The past was immediate and personal, but also broadly capacious and deep.

After those history lessons, things fell into place. I came to understand that when the Bakwena set out to establish their nation, perhaps in the early eighteenth century, they were a small group of immigrants making their

Antipodes

way westward to the Kalahari Desert. Their numbers diminished greatly when their juniors, the Bangwato and Bangwaketse, left them about the mid-eighteenth century. While reproduction increased their ranks, immigration as early as before 1770 was the most significant factor in the population changes, particularly in the mid-nineteenth century, that resulted in the large, sprawling settlements of town dwellers and farmers believed to have been typical of the Sotho-Tswana.

The Bakwena nation was a federation of diverse ethnicities and not a tribe of kin groups as was so neatly arranged and described by the rules and processes of anthropologists.[35] Contrary to those imperial scripts, I found numerous instances of trespass, pointing to African agency.

My new understanding of the Bakwena social formation required, in the first instance, a quieting of my academic training and a listening to the voices of history's subjects and agents. It also, I firmly believe, demanded a recalculation of body and mind to the spatial and temporal rhythms of the land and its biotic communities, including humans and all other life forms. Moreover and thankfully, there were other lessons that awaited me as my Batswana guides led me through remarkable worlds past.

When I began my research in 1975, I knew, from my reading of nineteenth-century European accounts and twentieth-century ethnographies and histories, that the Sotho-Tswana distinguished themselves from their neighbors—the gathering and hunting Sān and the mainly pastoral Nguni—by settling in stable and sprawling, kin-based towns enabled by a mixed economy of grain cultivation and cattle-keeping. That surety became unmoored in the swirling, daily engagements with my Batswana teachers who displaced me as quickly as my mind was settling down. Sometimes I was just plain lucky.

My stumble onto genealogical research was my first big break. Assembled, the genealogies provided the scaffolding to reconstruct Bakwena demographic and social history. Although I knew that demography constituted and, in turn, was constituted by the social formation, I had not yet fully grasped the economic consequences of population changes. At the time of my research, I did not have the benefit of C. C. Wrigley's suggestion that the underlying dynamic and motive force in African history resided in the quiet, ordinary processes of birth and death, or of Georges Dupre and Pierre Philippe Rey's challenge to Meillassoux's lineage mode of production by arguing the centrality of demography in shaping the means of production.[36] Once again, I got lucky.

We, a group of Bakwena historians and I, were discussing house building. I asked them to tell me about the gendered division of labor in house construction, the amount of labor required, and the materials used in the structure. They began with the familiar Bakwena rondavel built by women and men of mud bricks, wooden posts, and grass thatching. Selebatso Masimega, my translator, goaded them to speak frankly of the Bakwena house "a long, long time ago." The men appeared hesitant, and as they pondered the implications of Masimega's charge, there was an awkward moment of silence. Finally, one of them blurted out that it was safe to speak about the mutibelagatsi or early home of the Bakwena. The men's hesitance, I surmised, was a product of white racism and a colonial mentality, which denigrated impermanent, rudimentary forms as primitive and uncivilized especially as represented by their former servants, the Sān.

The mutibelagatsi, at its simplest, consisted of a framework of branches and twigs set into the ground and covered with grass. Later, the ntlo ya moraro or "house of three things" or just moraro replaced the mutibelagatsi. The name described the three elements of the house, a roof of wooden rafters covered with grass, supported by upright wooden posts, and an intertwined wall of bushes within the circle of roof posts. Eventually, the moraro was supplanted by the ntlo or "house" that had a wall made of mud bricks smeared with a smooth coating of cow dung, and a roof that used a thicker, more durable variety of grass that was carefully thatched and trimmed.

Bahurutshe immigrants introduced that final refinement, thatching and trimming, about the same time the plough pulled by oxen found its way into the Kweneng.[37]

At last, I made the connection. What the Bakwena historians were recounting, I realized, was not merely the changes in house construction, but also the accompanying transitions in their economy. I had not seriously considered, because they contradicted my long-held assumptions, their earlier references to the centrality of hunting and gathering among the first Bakwena in the Kweneng. Now, it all made sense. Rational economic behavior explained the Bakwena responses to the evolving, desiccating Kalahari Desert and dramatic demographic changes in the varieties of house construction and the shifting modes and relations of production.

HERDING, GATHERING, AND HUNTING, CA. 1700–1831[38]

Throughout the eighteenth century, the Bakwena probably numbered less than a hundred people, who possessed herds of short-horned Setswana cattle and settled in temporary villages along the fringes of the Kalahari Desert, alternating among sites like Mochudi, Shokwane, Molepolole, and Dithejwane. Having come from the better-watered Transvaal, the Bakwena probably found the desert to be a barrier at first, but also discovered the Molepolole vicinity, with its perennial pools and streams, its high, defensible hills, and its plains that teemed with a variety of game, generous in supplying for their material needs.

They employed labor principally in herding, gathering, and hunting. Plant cultivation was clearly secondary to those forms of production. Bakwena fields were small and the leading crops, several kinds of beans (dinawa) and melons (marotse), were short-season and drought resistant, making them ideal for the nomadic life of hunting, herding, and gathering and for the semi-arid surroundings. Similarly, the mutibelagatsi or simple house of twigs and grass was an economic structure that complemented the requirements of production and the environment.

The Bakwena obtained animal protein from the milk and meat of their livestock and from hunting, which was for the most part a collective effort beyond the capacity of a single household. Requiring about forty men a month to build, the game trap (gopo) was a common way of procuring meat and other products from the hunt like skins and hides. The gopo consisted of a trench or pit of variable size, two bush fences that opened like widening arms from the pit to over a kilometer in length. Upright, sharpened stakes lined the pit's floor, which was covered with sticks and grass. Men, women, and children circled the countryside to drive the game toward the gopo. The hunters built traps in valleys near saltlicks that were frequented by game animals to the north and south of Molepolole. Although gopo represented considerable labor investments in their construction and upkeep, they were utilized repeatedly and were an efficient way to hunt as long as game could be found in the vicinity.[39]

The sudden and large infusion of immigrants into the Kweneng during the early nineteenth century resulted in a decrease in game and edible fruits and roots around Molepolole, even though David Livingstone reported that the Kolobeng area during the 1840s still had an abundance of game, including buffaloes, and herds of elephants roamed the valleys behind Molepolole.[40] Still, the substantial increase in human population soon overtaxed the fragile, borderland environment, and drove game into the less densely peopled Kalahari.

In addition, the difaqane and Afrikaner disturbances brought raiders into the Kweneng, both African and European, who preyed on Bakwena cattle. The net effect of those influences led to declines in hunting and herding and increases in plant cultivation and the importance of women's labor. Another factor in that transition was the immigration of premier agriculturalists from the Transvaal like the Bahuruthse and Baphalane who preferred grain cultivation and supplied the required labor and skills. Those refugees, together with the immigrant Bakaa who were skilled ironworkers, lay the foundation for grain cultivation as stressed and practiced by the Bakwena throughout the twentieth century.

GRAINS AND GENDER, CA. 1831–1885

Because of the threat of foreign invasions, nineteenth-century Bakwena generally chose to settle on the summits of rocky, defensible hills, while their agricultural fields spread on the plains below. The cultivators selected their field sites based on proximity, vegetation, and soil. To reduce effort and travel time, agriculturalists preferred field locations within easy walking distance from their homes. Accordingly, their fields generally lay just beyond their makgotla and section (motse), producing the familiar pattern of Batswana towns ringed by arable lands.[41]

Besides proximity, the vegetation that grew on the land affected the location and choice of field. Cultivators, for instance, invariably avoided plots on which grew the motlwa grass during this period of hoe cultivation. Motlwa is hardy, tenacious, and possesses a spreading root system that entangles itself with the roots of garden crops, making it impossible to weed without uprooting the food plant at the same time. If left to grow, the motlwa will draw moisture and nutrients, stunting and strangling the crops. Even fields cleared of motlwa risked being overtaken by the grass, rendering them unproductive within three years. Only after the introduction of the iron plough, which turned the soil to a depth sufficient to uproot completely the motlwa, was it possible for cultivators to clear a field of the weed.[42]

Bakwena agriculturalists considered soil type in the selection of a field site.[43] They recognized three main varieties of soil suitable for their crops: seloko, a black, brown soil found in valleys; mokata, a red soil found in open plains; and chawana, a sandy mixture of seloko and mokata. Sorghum (mabele) grew best on seloko, but beans and other crops like groundnuts (ditlou) thrived on mokata. Chawana was the best overall for most Bakwena food crops.[44]

During the eighteenth century when fields were small, a woman and her husband cleared and prepared the land. Clearing (go reza) involved cutting smaller bushes, ringing and burning larger trees, and burning the heaped vegetation on the field, leaving the ashes to fertilize the soil. When plant cultivation increased during the nineteenth century, the women of a kgotla worked collectively to clear the fields. Those labor units moved from one field to another, clearing the ground for all the members of the collective. The field's owner was responsible for feeding the women workers that day. As the cost of labor and value of agricultural products rose and as social stratification became firmer and more pronounced, households organized work days, entered into contract agreements (tumalano) with hired workers, or deployed their servants, bound laborers, to clear and prepare the field for planting.

Households sponsored workdays (malaletsa) and paid the laborers with the parts of slaughtered cows. The tumalano system involved an agreement between an employer and worker with the negotiated rate based on the field's size, the vegetation that grew on the plot, and so forth. Circa 1910, a goat was the price for clearing one Sekwena acre or twelve paces square, a sheep for clearing two acres, and a cow for larger areas.[45] Throughout most of the nineteenth century, the servant or batlhanka system involved the use of Basarwa (Sān) and "Bakgalagadi" labor by Bakwena masters who were only obliged to supply them with food for their upkeep.[46]

Bakwena cultivators employed similar systems of labor for the planting and caring of their fields. The season opened with rainmaking and the first rains about mid-October when the kgosi called for letsema (from tema, "a piece of cultivated ground") and closed near the end of December. The kgosi, with the advice of his rainmaker (moroka wa pula), exercised authority in determining the start of the agricultural season, which conformed with the usual pattern of rainfall, but the practice was also intended to even the social relations by requiring everyone to begin at the same time. Still, with more resources and labor on hand, the wealthy maintained their advantage over the poor.

A typical day began about makuku or the second crowing of the roosters, when a woman awakened, and by o dinaka tsa kgomo or when it was light enough to make out the horns of the cattle, she was out in her field and working. She labored until about motsegare wa sethobolo or midday when the sun was at its hottest. Stopping for a rest, a less ambitious cultivator returned home to cook and eat, while an industrious woman remained in her field, ate her packed lunch, and quickly returned to work. The less ambitious cultivator resumed her labors and continued until lephirima or sunset, but an industrious woman quit only after she could no longer see, around maabaneane, and even worked into the night if there was moonlight.[47]

The Sekwena method of hoe cultivation was to till the soil and plant the seeds in one operation. The cultivator marked off a rectangular or square area by notching the ground, thereby delimiting a temanyana (diminutive of tema). She then filled a letlatlana, a cone-shaped container made of woven grass with a capacity of five liters or more, with a mixture of seeds, mainly sorghum (mabele), and also one or two handfuls of beans (dinawa), and a handful of another legume variety (letlhodi), melons (marotse), pumpkins (maputse), maize (midi), and watermelon (mahapu). She mixed the seeds thoroughly in the letlatlana and broadcast them evenly over the marked field (temanyana). Using her hoe, the cultivator then turned the soil, uprooting weeds and covering the seeds at the same time. She repeated the process, marking, seeding, and cultivating other, equivalent areas (temanyana) until the day's end. The amount of ground planted that day formed a template for subsequent days until the entire field, the tema, typically about four to six Sekwena acres or about 2,000 to 5,000 square meters, had been planted.[48]

Working in teams helped to relieve the loneliness and monotony of solitary labor, taught inexperienced workers new techniques and skills, and was probably more efficient than individual effort. Nkwane Gaealafshwe of Goo-Ra-Tshosa recalled how in 1906, when she was a young girl, her grandmother initiated her into agricultural labor. A wealthy woman, her grandmother employed about ten "Bakgalagadi" servants to cultivate her field. The "Bakgalagadi" formed a line, and her grandmother placed Gaealafshwe and her sisters between those experienced workers. In one day, Gaealafshwe remembered, she and her sisters learned valuable skills, and the group completed about two Sekwena acres.[49] "All of them held native hoes," a nineteenth-century European visitor wrote of Bakwena women outside Tshonwane, "and standing in a line, raised their tools, and worked in time, humming a drawling, monotonous song as a guide to their operations."[50]

The implement used in cultivation was the Sekwena hoe (sechele), which consisted of an iron blade set at an acute angle into a wooden handle.[51] Before the iron-working Bakaa joined them in 1849, the Bakwena probably purchased iron hoe blades from the Balete and Bakgatla with livestock and skins.[52] After the arrival of the Bakaa and other metal workers from the Transvaal, the sechele was produced locally.[53] The sechele was small and comparatively thin before the arrival of European traders because iron was neither plentiful nor cheap. During the second half of the nineteenth century, however, Bakwena metal workers obtained large pieces of iron from Europeans, resulting in broader, heavier hoes that lasted longer than the earlier versions but were also clumsier, especially in weeding, and required greater effort to wield.

As the rains fell, weeds invariably sprouted in profusion. The Sekwena hoe was incapable of reaching the required depth to uproot certain weeds completely. Weeding started after the mabele had reached a height of about twelve centimeters, about two weeks after germination, when they could be more easily identified and distinguished from weeds. Moreover, the waiting period allowed the crops to take root, and permitted buried weeds to emerge and show themselves. During the weeding season, generally from January to

February, a worker with a hoe was able to weed, on average, about one Sekwena acre every two days.[54]

Besides weeding, women horticulturalists thinned the seedlings to prevent their overcrowding. They thinned mabele to about thirty centimeters between plants, and beans, melons, and pumpkins, about a meter apart. However, if the soil was fertile and the season promised abundant rain, the cultivators crowded their plants to maximize yields.[55] In that way, the cultivator decided from among several options after having considered the relevant variables and risks.

Between February and March, with the flowering of the mabele plants and fruiting of melons and beans, birds flocked to the fields to feed on the maturing grain. Mainly younger children drove off the birds, while women prepared the storage facilities and threshing floor (segotlho) made of cow dung along the field's borders. Women, sometimes with their husbands' help, then erected a drying rack (serala) from which to hang sorghum and maize next to the segotlho.

As they ripened, beans and melons were harvested and eaten, and by April all of the beans would have matured, been picked, eaten, and the excess mixed with ashes and goat dung and stored. In April and May, the air changed and a cold, drying wind from the west caused the grain to ripen. Women cultivators harvested and hanged on racks the mabele until about June when the harvest was complete. Using sticks, they threshed the grain, dislodging the sorghum seeds from their husks, and spread the grain over the threshing floor for a final drying. When thoroughly dry, women carried the mabele from the fields to their mothers' households (malwapa), where they treated the grain with a mixture of ashes and cow dung and stored it in woven grass granaries (desigo)[56] in the home of each cultivator's mother.

Grains supplanted beans and melons as the principal food crop beginning around 1831. That dietary change, enabled by the productive labor of women, altered the social relations between women and men. Within the Bakwena gendered division of labor, men controlled most of the products of hunting and the milk and meat drawn from livestock and the capital they represented. During the eighteenth century, gathering and cultivating, mainly but not exclusively women's work, were secondary in the provisioning of Bakwena households. But for most of the nineteenth century, Bakwena political consolidation and nation building enabled by the huge population increases together with large, stable settlements were made possible, in large measure, by an expansive agricultural base that was the work of women, primarily.

At the household level, women's control over grains, underscored by their storage at the home of the cultivator's mother, allowed women to escape patriarchal controls, possess capital in the exchange-value of grains, and therewith access and wield a measure of power. Men still maintained authority over the distribution of land, including arable fields, and cattle were the principal currency and means of exchange. Additionally, with the introduction of the oxen-drawn plough, men exacted claims on women cultivators because they owned the oxen and plough.

Under the system of hoe horticulture, women exercised near-exclusive control over the products of their labor with grains matrilocally stored.[57] After the plough's introduction, that one-field system was supplanted by a two-field system wherein women cultivated a larger field for themselves called tshimo a mosadi or "woman's field" and a smaller plot for her husband called tshimo a monna or "man's field." Their products were stored, respectively, at her mother's home and her husband's home, and the cultivator's harvest provided for the daily sustenance while the man's was generally reserved for special occasions. Some women, to gain greater independence under the two-field system, used hoes to cultivate their own garden plots in addition to their two ploughed fields. Although requiring additional labor, those gardens generated yields that belonged to the cultivator alone.[58]

Contrary to the laws and customs codified by Europeans, Bakwena gender relations as exhibited in the relations of production were flexible and were neither timeless nor absolute. Men's control over hunting, herding, felling and hauling trees, and mining did not preclude women's labor in hunting, herding, fencing, erecting rafters, and roof thatching. Conversely, men joined women in basket making and weaving, producing objects like granaries (desigo), and in sewing skins and pelts to make clothing, rugs, and blankets. Producers consumed their goods, and exchanged them in trade. When women's labor fell short, men assisted women in cultivation, from clearing the land to harvesting, and women, besides men, drove the teams of oxen to plough. Clearly, productive forces affected and modified Bakwena gender spheres and their manifestations.

Changes in the means and relations of production led to other alterations in the composition of labor. The move from individual to collective labor, taking place during the transition to grain cultivation in the nineteenth century, resulted in a more efficient organization of agricultural labor. Working in a group provided incentives for greater productivity, and skilled cultivators taught less experienced laborers better techniques. Even efficient planters might not be equally adept at the different requirements of farming such as weeding, harvesting, and storing. All benefitted from the knowledge and skills of fellow members of the work group.

The time needed to complete certain tasks was often crucial because optimal conditions lasted for a limited time. Cultivating and planting, for example, had to be completed between mid-October and December because of the length of time required for crops to mature and the changes in the weather. The spring rains loosened the ground for cultivation, and caused the seeds to germinate and grow. The cool winds of fall were essential for drying the harvested grain before the hail and frosts of June. Work groups, rather than solitary planters, were more likely to complete those tasks within the window of seasonal opportunities and constraints, especially during the transition to larger fields and greater reliance upon grains.

The efficiencies gained through the reorganization of labor had their limits and were dependent each season upon the variables of individuals, the collective group, and the wider social and environmental contexts. As their reliance upon grain cultivation increased, the Bakwena found new sources of labor to raise the level of production. Men, hunting less with the flight of game into the Kalahari, worked alongside women in the fields,[59] and the Bakwena exploited "Bakgalagadi" servants as in kgosi Sechele's large fields at Midie, about thirty kilometers northeast of Molepolole. There, groups of possibly Bakgwatheng resided and cultivated the kgosi's extensive fields of sorghum throughout the second half of the nineteenth century.[60]

New technologies, like the plough used by the Bakwena about or just before 1885,[61] further boosted agricultural yields by enabling larger, more productive fields. The plough had consequences for gender relations and the division of labor, and more acres under cultivation exhausted greater tracts of land at a faster rate, and necessitated extending the farmlands far beyond the contiguous perimeter of the capital. Those distances precluded daily commuting between one's home and field, and led to the building of temporary, seasonal homes in areas called "the lands" (masimo). With population increases and congestion in the capital, some farmers preferred living permanently in the countryside, abandoned their houses in Molepolole, and invested in more substantial dwellings adjacent to their fields. Finally, labor saving devices like the plough might have resulted in labor surpluses and temporary unemployment. To cope with that problem, it appears, Kgosidintsi, a kgosi, directed a return to the labor-intensive method of hoe cultivation.[62]

The Bakwena modified the European plough or mogoma wa sekgoa to make it affordable for the masses. Commanding a price of 20 pounds (sterling) in the Bakwena capital in 1849, only the elite could purchase the mogoma wa sekgoa.[63] Seizing that market opportunity, Bakwena artisans fashioned two varieties of the "people's plough" or mogoma wa Setswana. The first was made entirely of wood, while the second, more-costly model employed an iron share with wooden handles. Although the "people's plough" broke more often when hitting rocks or roots and could not turn the soil as deeply as its European counterpart, it was affordable and was an advance over the sechele or Sekwena hoe. When the price of the European import declined, Bakwena cultivators switched to that plough.[64]

Greater numbers and a more efficient organization of laborers, along with new technologies, allowed horticultural production to keep pace with population growth and yielded surpluses that were used in trade. During the time of Sebele (a Sechele), the Bangwato, Bangwaketse, and Bakgatla exchanged cattle for grain at Molepolole. Four sacks (each sack having a capacity of about sixty liters) of mabele purchased a one-year-old cow (mwalolelo), five sacks bought a two-year-old cow (magatelo), and six to six-and-a-half sacks, a three-year-old cow (moroba).[65]

Women, as producers, engaged in that grains trade. Bangwaketse women brought to Molepolole a red stone (letshoko), which the Bakwena wanted and did not have. Rubbing letshoko on a pot's surface gave it a lovely red sheen. Such was its value that Bakwena women paid four to six measures of sorghum for a single measure of letshoko. In turn, Bakwena women traveled to Manyana with sacks of mabele to buy large pots made famous by potters like Mma Morobeng, who created a style named after her, mmamorobeng, and whose earthenware pots were renowned for their strength and fine quality. At Manyana, a pot generally fetched its capacity in sorghum. Through the grains trade, Bakwena women were able to accumulate chickens, herds of goats, and even cattle, which became their sole property.[66]

In addition to the commerce in grains, the Bakwena cultivated two important export crops: tobacco (motsoko) and cannabis (motokwane). Although both women and men produced those valued goods, men monopolized the trade and its profits. Growing tobacco and cannabis was a completely separate activity from grain cultivation, and those crops became prominent only toward the end of the nineteenth century. Bahurutshe immigrants might have introduced the plants and method of cultivation to the Bakwena.[67]

The Bakwena grew two varieties of tobacco, the short-leafed (magonotwane) and the long-leafed (motsoko wa Setswana or tsebeditelele), from seed each year to produce plants with leaves that were rich and strong in flavor. Farmers planted the seeds in August, and transplanted the seedlings in September or October, usually into plots that had a loose, rich soil called lerotobolo or soil that had been fertilized with manure (mosotelo). They chose locations along the banks of a spring or stream to allow for an easy irrigation of the plants.[68] Cultivators watered tobacco twice daily, ideally in the morning and at sunset, and grew them through May. As the leaves matured, the farmer picked, graded, and cured them.[69]

For the Kalahari trade, Bakwena classified tobacco leaves into three grades. The top-grade leaves they placed in a heap in the sun and covered the pile with a skin mat. If it rained, they hanged the leaves individually inside their homes. After about a week and while the leaves were still pliable, they rolled them into a cylindrical bundle called a togwa of two standard sizes: a larger roll of about thirty centimeters in length by eighteen centimeters in diameter, and a smaller roll about half that size. The larger togwa fetched a cow (mwalolelo), while the smaller roll, a goat. The medium-grade leaves growers crushed with stones while they were still green and placed them in a container to dry. About five teacups of that crushed tobacco purchased a goat. The poorest grade leaves were simply sold in heaps primarily for small items like chickens, but larger heaps could get goats and sheep.

Prices varied, depending upon the quality of the articles of trade, the bargaining ability of the trader, and scarcities and the available quantities. For instance, during kgosi Sechele's rule, a single cup of cannabis bought a cow (mwalolelo), but by the time of Kealeboga, Sechele's grandson, a cow (mwalolelo) commanded the inflated price of a large pillowcase of cannabis.[70]

CATTLE AND CLASS, CA. 1831–1885

Cattle—and with them, men's ascendancy—accompanied the transition to grain cultivation. Cattle supplied animal protein, in place of game, and were a valued, scarce resource. They were thus accumulated, appropriated, and (re)distributed within and without the Bakwena social formation. Cattle, accordingly, comprised capital and were a key instrument of gender and class formation and stratification.

Cattle transfers took place in several ways. In individual households, fathers willed to their children cattle as gifts called kgomo ya boswa or "cattle of the inheritance" while they were still minors, and the cattle and their offspring became those children's property. A son, as he matured, received from his father "herding cattle" or dikgomo tsa madisa (from go disa or "to herd"), indicating the cattle belonged to the father but were placed under the stewardship of his son. As the owner's estate, those cattle were distributed, upon his death, by the men of his kgotla to his dependents.[71] Husbands gave to their wives cattle (kgomo ya letsele) as an outright gift but managed jointly while the man was alive. Upon his death, the kgomo ya letsele became his wife's property.[72]

All of those transactions redistributed but retained cattle within a family group, except for daughters who married out. Accordingly, the proverb, ngwana wa rrangwane nnyale, kgomo di boele sakeng ("child of my paternal uncle marry me, so the cattle may return to the cattle fold"), advised daughters to preserve the family's wealth by marrying within the kin group.[73]

Whether within family groups or the nation, concentrations of cattle generally established the loci of power. Further, owners consolidated and expanded their influence by distributing cattle. The mafisa system, widely practiced in the nineteenth century, was a principal means by which cattle-owners enhanced their standing within the social formation. Under mafisa, owners loaned their cattle to dependents referred to as kala ("branch") or tsala ya me ("my friend"), who herded and cared for the cattle in exchange for the milk and use of the animal(s). Mafisa cattle thereby created and solidified a social relationship, and alleviated envy and conflict over access to a means of production. Bakwena rulers employed the mafisa system to attract and ensure the loyalty of immigrants, many of whom came to the Kweneng devoid of stock. Further, the system provided owners with essentially free labor, and lessened the risk of disease wiping out their entire herd by having their cattle distributed over a wide area.

The system, however, held potential perils for the owner and openings for the kala. The terms mafisa from go fisa or "to burn," "cattle that burn," the name of mafisa cattle, and tshukudu or rhinoceros, a dreaded beast, for the cattle owner point to the vexed relationships within the mafisa system. A kala might lose cattle or allow them to grow lean and sick, he might not report the births of calves, and he had ample opportunities to hide from the owner the true status of his cattle because of the long distances that separated the owner from his mafisa cattle. A kala, thus, could slaughter the animal and report that it strayed or was killed by wild animals, and he could keep for himself the offspring of mafisa cattle instead of adding them to the owner's herd. The mafisa system, thus, was simultaneously a way of control and of resistance.

Besides cattle, Bakwena rulers had other means of accumulating wealth and preserving the hierarchies of power. A ruler's prerogative was the taxing of labor and goods. The kgosi's ability to summon a letshomo or royal hunt was particularly important during the period before circa 1831 when hunting, besides herding, provided the main source of protein. The hunt produced food and skins, some of which the kgosi kept and others he distributed to his people.[74] The kgosi mobilized mephato or age regiments for cattle raids on neighboring peoples, and he dispatched them into the desert to secure some of its products. Some of the gains he retained; the remainder, he allocated to the participants.

Sechele, for instance, ordered the Maganamokgwa mophato to Ga-Tawana to collect elephant ivory for him during the late nineteenth century.[75] Gaealafshwe, kgosi of Ntlheng-ya Godimo, organized a letshomo and sent his men into the Kalahari to acquire meat and skins for him about the turn of the twentieth century. Workers called makata cultivated the kgosi's field in a labor tax that probably gained prominence only after the rise of grain production. The makata were usually men thereby allowing women to cultivate their own fields, and they worked the full agricultural cycle from planting to harvest.[76]

In addition to taxing labor, Bakwena rulers taxed goods known collectively as sehuba. While compulsory, sehuba did not entail a specific amount, but taxpayers had incentives for generosity. A pleased ruler might reward his subject with mafisa cattle, a political title and office, servants and immigrants, or even a kgotla.[77] Maybe because of the multiple occasions for tax collecting by the kgosi and heads of sections, Sechele installed a systematic way of collecting taxes by appointing his collectors in each section of the capital. Gaealafshwe in Ntlheng-ya Godimo, for instance, usually collected sehuba in pelts during the winter when furs were thickest and at their peak. Under his watchful eye, Gaealafshwe counted and selected about ten percent of the taxed pelts and sent them to Sechele while keeping the remainder for himself. Gaealafshwe in addition received a fraction of the sehuba collected by his juniors.[78]

Perhaps the most important source of economic power for the ruling class throughout the nineteenth century was its virtual monopoly over the labor of servants (batlhanka). This labor system, instituted by kgosi Moruakgomo and modified by Sechele, supplied rulers with an enormous supply of workers to cultivate their fields, herd their cattle, and bring them sehuba in skins, ostrich feathers, and ivory. The batlhanka were primarily "Bak-galagadi," peoples who fled the Bakwena and other Batswana by retreating into the desert, and to a lesser degree, Sān, who were conquered or drawn into the orbit of Bakwena overrule. They, like cattle outposts, were a part of the territorial properties carved out of the desert for certain members of the elite, and like cattle, were allocated from father to child and from kgosi to loyal subject.[79]

Toward the end of the nineteenth century, Sebele (a Sechele) declared an end to this system of master and servant for the ruling class as a whole. At the same time, he strived to establish his sole hegemony over the peoples of the Kalahari. He failed in that attempt, but his actions influenced a defection of over half of the Bakwena to Kgari, Sechele's junior brother, who led the secessionists into exile.[80] The formal demise of the batlhanka system, how-ever, ended the virtual monopoly held over access to the desert and its labor and products by Bakwena rulers and opened those resources of the Kalahari to all.

POSITIONS

Despite the excitement of change in the midst of a historiography adrift in the doldrums of Eurocentrism during my graduate years, my economic his-tory of the Bakwena would have assuredly differed had I centered the "Bak-galagadi" and located the Bakwena as their other. The view from the Sān shore might have discovered the "Bakgalagadi" and Bakwena as beached strangers to their desert island and home.[81] Had I chosen to unravel system-atically the connections among labor, capital, production, and reproduction in the manner of Margaret Kinsman or Jeff Guy, my account would have been less descriptive and offer a more precise explanation of the diversity and unity of economic and social relations.[82] Had I recognized gender relations as the central pivot and dynamic of precapitalist formations, as argued persuasively by Belinda Bozzoli, Margaret Kinsman, and Jeff Guy, I would have seen as fundamental the domestic sphere and the struggle over the appropriation and control of women's productive and reproductive capacities.[83]

Somehow, despite my presuppositions and arrogance, I discovered (old news to my African teachers) the Bakwena did not always live in large towns and carry on a mixed economy of cattle-herding and grain cultivation, but began as small, mobile groups of herders, gatherers, and hunters. I learned that the lineage mode of production could not have predominated, at least since the late eighteenth century, because kinship was not the adhesive that held fast the fractious Bakwena social formation. Immigrants predominated, and their insertion into the morafe was a central feature of nation building. I came to understand that seniors did not always dominate juniors, men, women, masters, servants, and I realized that birth, class, gender, and "race" were not always fixed categories but were constantly contested and struggled over, conferring agency to history and individual lives.

From those positions and seen from the intellectual genealogies from which I descend, I readily confess that my imposition, my version of the Bakwena social formation, comprises but a slender, indeed pitiful slice of the desert and the vast and variegated past inhabited and shaped by the peoples who dance to the crocodile.

On the day of Botswana's independence from its former colonial master Great Britain in 1966, Hawai'i's governor John Burns attended the ceremonies in Gaborone, the nation's capital. Because of Hawai'i's geographical location as the only US state with a landed antipode, Botswana, President Lyndon Johnson selected Burns to represent the nation and give to President Seretse Khama its gift, a light airplane. That same day in the islands, Botswana's flag flew over Hawai'i's Iolani Palace, which was once the independent kingdom's seat of government before the US takeover, and the Royal Hawaiian Band played a "Hawai'i and Botswana" march in honor of the occasion. Decolonization in the Third World was observed in a still colonized Hawaiʻi. Since that day, dozens of Batswana have studied in the islands.[84]

Because a single ocean clothes most of the skin of our planet earth, there are few landed antipodes. So positioned, Botswana and Hawaiʻi share connections as landed antipodes and as the borders of the tropics. Their spatial orientations reveal the seamlessness of islands and continents, the tropical and temperate zones. As Lindiwe Molomo, one of the Batswana students who studied in Hawaiʻi observed, rather than posing oppositions, Hawaiʻi and Botswana form correspondences in that they are "so similar" and "more like home."[85]

Antipodes

CHAPTER SEVEN

History

History and geography are imperial discourses insofar as they order and discipline space / time. Imperial powers installed those regimes in the making of empire. During the sixteenth century, Spain, Portugal, and Britain calculated longitude variously. Established in 1676, the Greenwich Observatory became Britain's prime meridian during the late 1700s, and at the International Geographical Congress held in Antwerp in 1871, twelve nations agreed on the Greenwich meridian as zero longitude. By the late nineteenth century, modern nations agreed that "universal time" was useful for science, industry, railroads, posts, and telegraphs. Attended by twenty-five nations, the International Meridian Conference held in Washington, DC, in 1884, the year before the Berlin Conference divided Africa among European colonizers, agreed on Greenwich as the prime meridian or zero degrees longitude, and that the twenty-four-hour day began at Greenwich mean midnight. Greenwich Mean Time (GMT), also known more grandly as Universal Time, Terrestrial Time, and Cosmic Time, was thus, like a species of history and geography, an instrument of imperialism.[1] Centered upon London, the heart of the British Empire marked the starting point of spatial order on the planet and time zones as "ahead of GMT" or "behind GMT."

SPACE / TIME[2]
Movement requires and thus implicates space and time. In the social world, movement is agency, which is power, while in the physical world, movement

202

is energy.[3] Human experience as perceived, the US mathematician and physicist Brian Greene writes, "takes place in some region of space during some interval of time." We, humans, understand our reality in space and time, he continues, and consequently science has been struggling to apprehend space and time as they "actually are."[4]

Newtonian physics sees space and time as constant, immutable entities that structure and govern the universe as laws. Einstein's theory of relativity jarred that positivist dictum of classical physics by postulating that space and time are not separate, independent entities but exist in relation to one another and can warp and curve in a dynamic, writhing, and flexing "revolutionary dance."[5] Relativity, for instance, explains why objects fail to move in straight lines in gravitational fields because gravity bends space and time, rendering them elastic.

An object like the sun with its gravitational field warps the space around it, and time slows down and speeds up under gravity's influence. Relativity shows unchanging, universal time to be merely "an artifact of life at slow speeds and weak gravity," which evaporates at the speed of light and in powerful gravity fields.[6] In fact, moving at the speed of light denies the possibility of time, and space and time, although distinctive, are bound to one another as relational consorts such that they constitute "spacetime," in Greene's rendering, or space / time.

While relativity operates well at the extremes of light speed (movement and time) and the expanding universe (movement and space) propelled by the "big bang," Einstein's physics breaks down at the level of atomic and subatomic particles and their behaviors. Quantum mechanics works best in this world, which operates on the German physicist Werner Heisenberg's uncertainty principle. It is impossible to determine simultaneously the location (space) and speed (time) of particles, Heisenberg discovered. That indeterminacy, quantum reality maintains, is not a consequence of inadequate equipment or practice; determinacy is unattainable in principle because of the "quantum state" of particles.[7]

Instead of solid particles that make up atoms and molecules as posited by classical physics, superstring theory hypothesizes particles as strings that vibrate to produce different behaviors and properties. As in quantum mechanics, accordingly, because of the variable qualities of those strings, their quantum states, predicting behaviors and properties can only approach approximations and probabilities. In that sense, reality can be multiple, not necessarily singular, and ambiguous and the outcome of chance. Rather than a universe governed by predictable laws, thus, we can conceive of multiverses of random possibilities.

We now realize that movement, space, and time only have meaning in a relational sense as appearing in the eye of the beholder and a matter of perspective. Like the Polynesian navigators in my *Island World*, voyaging canoes remain stationary while islands move by. Because of relativity, there is no absolute, frozen past, present, or future; there is only time wherein all moments dwell without flow or direction. There is no now, which is already the past. Moreover, because it takes time for light to travel, what one sees has already happened. The present, then, exists in the past. In fact, all events, past, present, and future, exist for all time, affirming Einstein's contention that the physical world comprises a relativistic reality.[8] Like motion, it all depends upon perspective, resulting in different conceptions of space / time.

Time and space have no meaning in a canefield.[9]

Those ideas of indeterminacy and flux, of relations and standpoint positions of the physical world, inhabit the social world. Judith / Jack Halberstam describes "queer temporality" as untethered from the biological clock that moves from birth to death, reproduction and family life.[10] The AIDS pandemic, s / he explains, has compressed time, expanding the potential of the moment while shrinking the prospect of any future. Queer time fosters an erotic present, imminent mortality, and expectation of the contingent, transient, and fleeting. Queer time, Halberstam concludes, departs from "the temporal frames of bourgeois reproduction and family, longevity, risk / safety, and inheritance."[11] That queering of normative temporality scrambles assumptions of time, disrupts linear and continuous development, and intervenes in the narratives of time that presume to capture reality and articulate what it means to be human.

The "longue durée" stands at the other end of the spectrum of manufactured time. A construction of the French *Annales* school of history in the first half of the twentieth century, the longue durée features the long term during which historical structures evolve and explanations become clearer and more comprehensive. The grand scale presents history in its fullest. Fernand Braudel, in the second part of the century, extended that canvas temporally and spatially, which, like capitalism and its career, grew to encompass and structure the entire world.[12]

For Karl Marx, geological time, another longue durée, inspired his idea of social formations, which he understood as the form (space) and stage (time) of society as excavated by Duan Zhongqiao. In his *German Ideology* (1846), Duan reports, Marx describes the "form of society" as the product of human interactions, and the term "social formations" first appears in his *The Eighteenth Brumaire of Louis Bonaparte* (1851) to indicate the form and stage of social development.[13] The idea for social formation, Duan speculates, comes from Marx's readings in geology as witnessed in his notes taken in 1851 on J. F. W. Johnston's *Lectures on Agricultural Chemistry and Geology*. Rock strata constituted "formations," the agricultural chemist explained, with each stratum unique unto itself, but the strata together, one layer atop another, revealing changes over time. Marx assimilated those scientific ideas into his writings that followed his reading of Johnston as shown in the passage: "Just as one should think of sudden changes and sharply delineated periods in considering the succession of the different geological formations, so also in the case of the creation of the different economic formations of society."[14] Intent on a science of history and society, time and space, Marx summoned geology to perform that work of authority.

South Asian historian K. N. Chaudhuri argues not against a stratigraphic, linear, or well-ordered succession of time, but for "different classes of time" on the basis of unequal frequencies and power. The suggestion that power differentiates time calls to mind the force of gravity fields that warp and curve space / time. Like the *Annales* historians Braudel and Lucien Febvre, Chaudhuri insists that history is "the totality of social life" involving "different levels, time spans, different kinds of time, structures, conjunctures, events" interacting in a constant flux and dynamic structuralism. From that perspective of history, Chaudhuri describes space as "a more fundamental, rational and *a priori* dimension for social action than time-order and succession."[15] That suggestion is at odds with conventional histories, which are organized around chronology or time.

As in Marxism's contradictions and dialectics that generate ceaseless changes that move back and forth but toward an end, Claude Lévi-Strauss, as a structuralist (space), understood the advancement of knowledge as "an unbroken movement of thought" (time) wherein "beliefs and superstitions dissolve" and "ethics gives way to history, fluid forms are replaced by structures and creation by nothingness." Still, Lévi-Strauss saw the social not simply as structures but as a restless, endless turning through space / time: Somewhat mystically, Lévi-Strauss continued: "As he moves about within his mental and historical framework, man takes along with him all the positions he has already occupied, and all those he will occupy. He is everywhere at one and the same time; he is a crowd surging forward abreast and constantly recapitulating the whole series of previous stages. For we live in several worlds, each one truer than the one it encloses, and itself false in relation to the one which encompasses it."[16]

The "epoch of space," the twentieth-century continental philosopher Michel Foucault pronounced, has replaced the nineteenth century's "great obsession" with history and its themes of development, crisis and cycle, and an ever accumulating past "of dead men and the menacing glaciation of the world." In our time, Foucault notes, spatial simultaneity, juxtaposition, and the near and far, side by side, and dispersed produce elements and ensembles that connect on "a temporal axis" to reveal a structuralism that does not deny and is attentive to time. The multiplicity of spaces we inhabit, Foucault envisions, forms a "cluster of relations" in which space constitutes subjects and societies in a relational sense.[17]

Oddly, Foucault was unaware of his reliance on geography until it dawned on him during a journal interview published as "Questions on Geography." The editors of *Hérodote* considered space to be central to the philosopher's work, and persisted in questioning him about that. Foucault resisted that suggestion until the end when he conceded: "Geography must indeed necessarily lie at the heart of my concerns." Foucault's excavation of the formation of discourses and genealogy of knowledge not as consciousness or ideology but as the tactics and strategies of power expresses that centrality of space: "Once knowledge can be analysed in terms of region, domain, implantation, displacement, transposition, one is able to capture the process by which knowledge functions as a form of power and disseminates the effects of power."[18]

One of Foucault's teachers, Gaston Bachelard, meditated on "the poetics of space." As a philosopher of science, Bachelard begins, he had to forget his learning and break from his habits of philosophical research in order to apprehend "the problems posed by the poetic imagination." In this environment, he writes, "the cultural past doesn't count." Instead, one must be receptive to "the image at the moment it appears . . . in the very ecstasy of the newness of the image." That poetic figure has a dynamism, a power of its own, inducing "sudden salience on the surface of the psyche" and, not unlike superstring theory, "reverberation."[19]

The poetic image, Bachelard continues, exists in relation to its reader, and excites through communion or communication. Of great ontological significance, that trans-subjectivity can only be understood through a "phenomenology of the imagination," and its psychic repercussions involve variations and a "creative consciousness." Not requiring scholarship, Bachelard concludes, "the duality of subject and object is iridescent, shimmering, unceasingly active in its inversions," and the novelty of the poetic image, its creation, is "the origin of language."[20] The poetic image, the poetics of space, enables language and consciousness and is thus a discourse in the making.

Like Bachelard, the Marxist philosopher and sociologist Henri Lefebvre examined the intimacies of space in the everyday life of home and city to show that the spatial is socially produced. Spaces are creations, historical, as well as processes in formation. Social spaces are lived and actualized before they are theorized, and they emerge from the relations of production. Lefebvre's achievement represents a break from the mathematical and geometrical concept of space as an empty domain that requires filling, whether in the Aristotelian and Kantian tradition of space as a category of the physical senses or in the Newtonian and Cartesian representation of space as an absolute object. Mathematics abstracted space from social life, and philosophy theorized mental space as sets and ensembles with their own logic, coherence, and regulation. Missing was the human, Lefebvre points out, and the relation between the subject or mental space and object or social space.[21]

Contemporary, postmodern geographers have been especially attentive to the requirements of space and the hegemony of time as was recognized by

Foucault and others. That dominance of the temporal, the US urbanist Edward W. Soja writes, has obscured a recognition of "the spatiality of social life," following Lefebvre, and the construction of human geographies. Critical theory and its consort, historicism, Soja continues, have centered genealogy and time and marginalized context, society, space, and geography. Scholars must, he contends, confront "the fatal intersection of time with space" and account for "the simultaneity and extension of events and possibilities." That spatial consciousness, he proposes, develops a critical sensibility, presents an entirely new way of seeing, expounds a poetics of space, and revives an awareness of personal political responsibility to inequalities and injustices.[22]

We think of space as a crossing and as an object of conquest, writes the British geographer Doreen Massey. "The imagination of space as a surface on which we are placed, the turning of space into time, the sharp separation of local place from the space out there; these are all ways of taming the challenge that the inherent spatiality of the world presents," explains Massey. Instead of comprising a closed system, space is constructed and in process and flux, it is constituted through relations, and it is the sphere of complex multiplicity and coexisting heterogeneity. Space remains open and contingent, and denies politicized discourses of progress, development, and modernity. In space, in its negotiations of relations among multiplicities, the social is constructed. Space is not a void without movement; it is as lively, dynamic, and full of political possibilities as time.[23]

Like Massey, British geographer David Harvey writes against the separation of social processes from spatial forms, and the staging of the former onto the latter as if space simply provides a platform for the social. Rather, he explains in a relational way, spatial forms "contain" social processes even as social processes are spatial. Moreover, space is not philosophical or absolute. Instead, "the proper conceptualization of space is resolved through human practice with respect to it." Space and social justice are human practices. The "geographical imagination," Harvey proposes like C. Wright Mills's "sociological imagination," supplies a recognition of self and place as transactions among individuals and objects, the spatial and the social. That social space "is made up of a complex of individual feelings and images about and reactions towards the spatial symbolism which surrounds the individual." Both familiar and bounded, social space, Harvey concludes, varies over time from individual to individual, society to society (space).[24]

Three-dimensional space, Yi-Fu Tuan observes, is a human apprehension of the senses and of learning and experience, but spatial constructions are also conceptual and cultural. The Sioux, for instance, understand space as circular and see spatial organization in its roundness from birds' nests to the transit of stars in the heavens. Pueblo Indians conceive of space in rectangles, and see that organizing principle in nature. The upright human body apprehends space as front and back, head and feet, human-built environments follow spatial conceptions, and language embodies those social values of stature and status of forward and backward, high and low (base), great and small. In addition, those spatial orientations of front and back implicate time wherein what lies before us is the future and behind us, the past. For Hopi Indians, "the long ago and far away" conjure the connection between spatial distance and remote, past time.[25]

South Asian historian Sugata Bose contends the scales of time and space hold explanatory meaning. Global models like world-systems analyses, he contends, "are too diffuse to take adequate account of the rich and complex interregional arenas of economic, political, and cultural relationships," while local perspectives, such as celebrated in subaltern studies, neglect "broader comparisons." Instead of dividing the world into regional spaces carved out during the Cold War by areas studies like the Middle East, South Asia, Southeast Asia, and East Asia, Bose proposes an "interregional arena," such as the Indian Ocean world, tied together by "webs of economic and

Part 2. Subjects

cultural relationships . . . [with] flexible internal and external boundaries."[26] Still, for Bose, unity, contact, and coherence are what characterizes inter-regional arenas of economy and culture.

Contrarily, it is possible, indeed useful, to imagine incomparable, unrelated spatial configurations that constitute subject matters, and where there is dissonance, chaos can reach dynamic states of regularities "that repeat themselves globally."[27] Amidst the cacophony of globalization and cosmopolitanism, the US anthropologist Clifford Geertz lectured on "local knowledge" or "the small imaginings of local knowledge and the large ones of cosmopolitan intent," steering between "overinterpretation and under-interpretation, reading more into things than reason permits and less into them than it demands." The discipline of anthropology, Geertz explains, is "the interpretive study of culture," which is "an attempt to come to terms with the diversity of the ways human beings construct their lives [space] in the act of leading them [time]." Local knowledge, Geertz holds, is an attempt "to define ourselves by locating ourselves among different others," including incommensurable, dissimilar others, and making sense of "particular things in particular places" such that they take "particular form and have particular impact."[28]

Because of its indeterminacies, C. Wright Mills writes, history should be "one of the most theoretical of the human disciplines." The shadow cast by Heisenberg over history, Mills points out, arises from the uncertainty of how lives intersect with social structures, the contingency of biography and history, and the broad range of possibilities in the selection of evidence, events, and their explanations. Despite the quantum state of the discipline, Mills observes, historians for the most part are oblivious to the need for theory, which makes it "all the more impressive" and "unsettling."[29]

Poetic knowledge is born in the great silence of scientific knowledge.[30]

TRANSLATIONS

Whether the global and local form dialectics or map correspondences as in homogenization or fragmentation, oppression or resistance, both spatial categories exist in relation to one another and, for many, comprise dialogical and interlocking spaces.[31] That idea of a global / local assemblage and synergy[32] informs my trilogy on space / time. I write against the "myth of continents"[33] in my *Island World* by foregrounding islands and positing the planet's spatial arrangement as the earth's mobile, tectonic plates that support the planet's lands and waters in their fullness. I reorder the binary, spatial configuration of core and periphery of the world-system[34] in my *Pineapple Culture* to conform more closely with W. E. B. Du Bois's twentieth-century global color line marked by the tropics.[35] The pineapple, I show, in its transits in violation of the tropical and temperate zones points to the falsity of those divides and to the union of the earth's lands, whether continent or island, surrounded by a single world ocean that flows unbounded.

In constant motion, historical formations take flight on the wings of the imagination. Like the location of self within society as proposed by C. Wright Mills and of the self within space / time as articulated by David Harvey, the historical imagination writes the subject-self into history. The historical formation soars above the mundane, freed from the gravity of time / space, like the Ashochimi ashes of the dead flung into the air and carried on the Moaʻe Lehua (trade winds) from California to Hawaiʻi, continent to island, temperate to tropical zones. The formation defies the imperial dictates of space / time and, upon landing, it inspires regeneration. Storytellers and listeners, from their respective vantages, engage and concoct new talk stories.

Those renewals, nonetheless, are transplantations and as such, translations of the original form. The Roman orator Cicero in 46 BC advocated the tethering of texts to rhetorical models, to have translation serve the purposes of speech, of free style to convey the full force of language.[36] In 1813, the German philosopher Friedrich Schleiermacher lectured to the Berlin

Academy of Sciences on the ideal translator who creates an "image" to produce a sense of foreignness because to the home-staying reader, the text is in a foreign tongue. That distancing, that othering, he hoped, would in turn create and enhance a German language, literature, and nationalism.[37]

Schleiermacher's "image" calls to mind Bachelard's poetics in which "the very ecstasy of the newness of the image" produces sudden salience. And that newness, that rendering of one's language as foreign, is a queering of the familiar, rendering it alien and strange. An achievement of poetry, after all, is its gift of new light upon old worlds. Enchantment, a queer mix of delight and disturbance.[38]

Walter Benjamin, the literary critic and philosopher, argued in a 1923 essay for the autonomy of translations as texts in their own right, derivative but also possessing the integrity of a work of signification.[39] Whereas to postcolonial critic Gayatri Spivak, translation is "a simple miming of the responsibility to the trace of the other in the self."[40] Part of that responsibility, Spivak maintains, is the learning of other languages; another is the acknowledgment that translation, as an intimate act of reading, bears a mere "trace of the other" emerging from the self. In that act of tracing the other by the self, concludes the translation theorist Lawrence Venuti, translation is a form of imperialism and reveals "the imperialistic impulse that may well be indissoluble from translation."[41]

History, at core, is a translation. As such, we understand written history as the historian's representation of the past. Even first-person accounts, commonly considered primary documents by historians, are translations. The Palestinian revolutionary Leila Khaled, referenced earlier, dictated her autobiography to her editor, George Hajjar. In July 1971, Hajjar spent more than thirty hours with Khaled over a five-day period to record her account of her life in struggle. Then in September and October 1972, Khaled and Hajjar discussed those notes. As Hajjar describes the process and final outcome: "I wrote this book as told to me by Leila Khaled." During the initial conversation, Hajjar put Khaled's oral rendition to paper as notes, which they negotiated orally, and finally Hajjar converted those oral transactions into a written narrative. Accordingly, when told in the first person, "I come from the city of Haifa, but I remember little of my birthplace" and "I swear by my revolution, by my humanity, that we shall return the Palestinians to their home and we shall recover our lost humanity!"[42] readers should be aware of the joint authorship of the "I" and their claim to speak for Palestinians in the "we" and "our."

Like Khaled's autobiography, a testimonio is a narrative told in the first person to an interlocutor who records, transcribes, and edits the account. The process transforms a living, oral testimony into words on paper.[43] In that way, a testimonio is a translation, a mediated text. Testimonios give voice to subalterns or those not heard, and they speak back against the othering discourse of imperial texts, which objectify colonial subjects. As such, testimonios resist erasure and appropriation, and because they, unlike biography and autobiography, speak for the people and not just the self, testimonios represent "a collective self engaged in struggle."[44] Testimonios, in fact, skirt the margins of the spoken and written word, and question the very idea of literature as written texts, as produced by a single author, and as expressions of the elite. Moreover, testimonios are quintessentially women's writings.[45]

Drawing authority from the collective and not the individual voice, Bolivian Domitila Barrios de Chungara declares through her translator: "I don't want anyone at any moment to interpret the story I'm about to tell as something that is only personal. Because I think that my life is related to my people. What happened to me could have happened to hundreds of people in my country." Her subject-self, Domitila points out, exists in relation to and for the uplift of her people. "I don't just want to tell a personal story. I want to talk about my people. I want to testify about all the experience we've acquired during so many years of struggle in Bolivia . . . . It's for them that I agreed that what I am going to tell be written down."[46]

Those interstitial works, between the spoken and written word, mediated and unmediated texts, single and multiple authors, and individual and collective voices, inform my historical understanding and formation in this writing of my (subject-)self into history. As Raymond Williams reminds us, authors are never solitary; they are located in space / time. From Marxism, he writes, we perceive the individual and society as "radically unified" because humans are social beings.[47] The distinctions between self and society are, indeed, social constructions while blurring them, making them writhe and flex in a revolutionary dance, destabilize their assumed autonomy, solidity, and surety.

Even as testimonios are antiliterary insofar as literature constitutes a dominant form of legitimation and colonization, historical formations are antihistorical within the canon of imperial history. Confronting colonial subjectification in which the colonizer interpellates the colonized, the subject resists by struggling "toward voice, history, and a future."[48]

RAINMAKER[49]

But can the subaltern speak? ponders Gayatri Spivak in a celebrated essay.[50] Subaltern speech within imperial discourses aside, translation can make it even more difficult to hear the voice of the colonized subject. During my dissertation research in Botswana, I recorded the Mokwena rainmaker Timpa Mosarwa. As was my practice, I wrote notes during the interview and later checked them against the tape recording. Not only a fluid conversation between two persons,[51] the interview involved the mediation of my translator, Selebatso G. Masimega. Accordingly, in the version below, Timpa Mosarwa narrates (oral) through my transcription (written) of his translated voice. Additionally, for the sake of narrative flow, I reorganized the interview and removed Masimega's voice. My notes are within brackets and italicized. Through those multiple layers of interventions, then, can we hear Timpa Mosarwa speak?

I am not a trained rainmaker (moroka wa pula). I learned this trade by observing and copying my father who was a trained rainmaker. I was the rainmaker for kgosi Kgari. My father, Mosarwa, was the rainmaker for Sebele II. My grandfather, Ntshwabi, was the rainmaker for Kealeboga. My great grandfather, Midiyamere, was the rainmaker for Sebele I. Finally, his father, Baji, was the rainmaker for Sechele I. [*Mosarwa's rainmaking genealogy follows the line of Bakwena dikgosi from Kgari (1931–62) to Sebele II (1918–31) to Keale-boga (1911–17) to Sebele I (1892–1911) to Sechele I (ca. 1831–92).*]

A rainmaker summons rain by digging different roots (digwere). He crushes and places them into a large earthenware container. The kgosi (ruler) sends young girls, virgins, to fetch water after the first rains have fallen. The water must be from the first rains. The rainmaker fills the earthenware pot with that water, stirs it with the mixture of roots, and the resulting potion is medicine for rain.

The pot remains at the kgosi's house the entire year. If the contents dry up, the kgosi will ask virgins to collect more water to refill the pot. The next year, in September, the rainmaker will put new digwere into the pot. He never removes the old ones, and yet, roots never seem to fill the pot. Usually, by September, the mixture dries up. This coincides with the fall of first rains anyway, in time to refill the pot.

The digwere come from the dithejane, mogaga, and mosimanwa trees. In addition to the roots, rainmakers concoct mokgao powder from the leaves of a tree found in the hills. They dry the leaves and grind them into a powder, and then mix that with eland fat.

Mokgao powder can induce rain to fall despite death, which could stop the rain from falling over the place of misfortune. When a man or his wife dies, the surviving spouse will ask the kgosi for mokgao powder to smear on his or her feet. The man or woman departs for the family's lands [*fields*] with the root of a mogaga plant [*an onion-like bulb*]. Along the way, he or she must peel off a layer from the mogaga, and drop it along the path. Upon reaching the fields, the widow or widower should place the remaining mogaga root into a pot with water, and mix that with the mokgao powder. The person should then sprinkle that mixture over the family's fields and cattle outpost to ensure that rain will not bypass the lands and pastures.

Another method for summoning rain is to collect digwere and fry them until they are burnt. The rainmaker then mixes that with eland fat, and shapes it into a black tsidi or molded form. [*Mosarwa's finger movements indicated a cube about an inch square.*] The kgosi kept the tsidi in his house, and carried and administered it as needed. When out at the lands, for example, the kgosi could burn the tsidi, causing black smoke to rise, forming dark clouds that bring rain.

I do not know what stops the rain from coming these days. When our dikgosi (plural of kgosi) were rainmakers, the rain fell in abundance. When the kgosi was the rainmaker, the work of the moroka wa pula was to collect leaves, grind them, and make mokgao powder, which he presented to the kgosi. The kgosi then distributed the mokgao powder freely to those who wanted it.

The identity of the moroka wa pula was always kept secret. The kgosi was the head rainmaker. He alone authorized the moroka wa pula to collect the roots and dry and crush the leaves. If the rains failed to come, the kgosi bore the blame.

[*During the agricultural phase of Bakwena history beginning with Sechele, the role of the kgosi was to provide for his people. Rain was essential for grain cultivation and for the large herds of cattle. It was important, thus, that the kgosi remained the chief rainmaker, and the moroka wa pula, anonymous. In addition, a rival kgosi might want to abduct or steal away a successful rainmaker.*]

The kgosi maintained only one moroka wa pula who was also in charge of his cattle. [*Like mafisa cattle*], the moroka wa pula was free to use the kgosi's cattle to plough for him or to carry loads. Besides cattle on loan, the kgosi paid his rainmaker in goods.

During the months of February to June, Bakwena must not cut the mogonono, mokgalo, morutlare, and mosetla trees or the rain will stop falling in the Kweneng.

[*In reply to my question, "Do Bakwena believe in rainmakers?"*] Very much, yes, a lot.

DIPHEKO TSA GO NESA PULA GA KGOSI TSA BAKWENA

To remove a layer of translation while adding another, I offer the following, which is a transcription of the February 12, 1975 interview with the rainmaker Timpa Mosarwa. As noted, I tape-recorded the interview, and some forty years later, Teresa Rantao Ogle listened to Mosarwa's voice (oral) and transcribed (written) what she heard. That hearing and transcription are different forms of translations but translations, nonetheless, as a voicing and writing of Timpa Mosarwa through Rantao Ogle. My translator's (Selebatso G. Masimega's) interjections are in italics. As Gayatri Spivak advises, responsibility requires learning other languages and the recognition that readings by the self, even in the other's language, bear a mere trace, not the fullness, of the other.

Part 1

Gone go dirwa jaalo, gobe go tshelwa metsi a pula ya sepha ya nthla. Go be go tsewa basetsana ba iseng ba ye sesading, ba be ba neelwa dinkgwanyana tse dincha gore ba ye goga metsi a o a pula ya ntlha ya sephai, ba be ba tlatsa nkgo e tona tona. Go be gotlhakanwa le digwere. Digwere tse o, ebong, thejwane le mogaga le mokhao le mosimao.

Mokhao o ne o silwa o be o tlhakangwa le mafura a tlou le a phofu gobe go fuduiwa ka leswana la morula. Digwere tseo di epiwa ngwaga le ngwaga, Mosadi fa a swetswe ke monna kapa ngwana kwa mosimao, a be a neelwa mogaga le mokhao.

Motlholagadi o tla neelwa mogaga le mokhao, a be a tshasa mokhao mo dinaong tsa gagwe. A be a tsamaya a nna a farotsa mogaga a latlhela diphatsana tsa mogaga mo tseleng. Fa e fitlha kwa merakeng a be a gasa mokhao mo merakeng eo, le mo masimong.

Dinkgo tseo, di nna fela ko kgosing. E tlaare ka kgwedi ya Tlhakole, gonne go fuduiwe nkgo eo.

Go tle go dirwe jang fa nkgwana eo e ka kgala?

Digwere di a epiwa ngwaga le ngwaga. Go bidiwa basetsanyana ba ba iseng ba bone sesadi gore baye go ga metsi mangwe le mangwe, ba tlatse nkgo eo, go tlhakangwa le digwere tse di ntseng dile mo teng. Go be go tshelwa mafura a tlou le a phofu, go be go huduiwa ka lone leswana la morula. E tlaare ka kgwedi ya Tlhakole, e tlaabe e wela. Go be go tshelwa bopi ja mokhao, go tlhakangwa le mahura o ne ao a diphologolo tse pedi tseo e bong a tlou le a phofu.

E tlaare ka kgwedi ya Tlhakole, mokhao o ne o sireletsa gore pula e seka ya kalela. Mosadi wa motlholagadi o ne a neelwa mogaga le mokhao. O ne a ya masimo go gasa mokhao gore pula e seka ya kalela. Ka kgwedi ya Phatwe nkgo e tla fufula.

E tla tsaya lebaka le kae gore e tlale?

Ka kgwedi ya Tlhakole, e tla boa e wela. Digwere tsa mogaga le thejane le mosimao le mokhao le mahura a diphologolo tseo, go be go tlhakangwa gotlhe. Mokhao o a silwa, fa e le mosadi wa motlholagadi, mokhao o thelwa mo dinung tsa gagwe a be tsaya mogaga a be a eta a o farotsa a o latlhela mo tseleng. Mokhao o ne a be a o gasa mo merakeng le mo masimong gore pula e seka ya kalela.

Ke kgosi fela e nesang pula. E raya ngwana wa yone e re, ngwaka, a e re kamoso mosong, re phakele re ye go leka go nesa pula. Motlholagadi fa a fitlha teng koo, a be a tlhapa dinao.

Fa kgosi e sa nese pula, ke mang yo o tla e nesang?

Bosigo fa batho ba sa robetse, kgosi e tsamaya e ya go nna e tlopola molora mo di thuthubung tsa batho, e be tlhakanya melora e o le digwere tse di mo nkgo e tona-tona eo.

A rrago o ne atle a go rute go nesa pula?

Nnyaa, nna ke ne ke tsaya malebela fela.

A Bakwena ba ne ba a tle ba dire jaalo?

Nyaa, kgosi ke yone fela e e neng e leka go nesa pula.

Kgosi e ne e tle e bitse mongwe wa lefatshe le sele gore a tle go leka go nesa pula? A kgosi e ne e tle e re, ngwanaka dira jaana? A batho bane ba atle ba duele kgosi?

Batho ba ne ba tle ba ntshe ponto, kapa kgongwana e le gone go leboga se kgosi e se dirileng.

Yo o nang le thata ya go nesa pula e ne e le mang?

Ka ngwao ya rona, kgosi ke yone fela e e neng e ka dira pula.

A rrago o ne a go ruta go nesa pula?

Nna ke ne ka itseela malebela fela mogo rre gore o dira jang.

A gone gole moroka a le mongwe fela?

Kgosi e ne e tle e bitse mongwe wa lefatshe lengwe gore a tle go nna moroka wa pula.

A digwere di ne di etle di besiwe gore mosi o ye kwa godimo gore maru a pula a koke gore pula e ne?

Jaanong rrago o ne a tshela ka eng?

Kgosi e ne a na le dikgomo. A lema ka tsone. E re fa thobo e mo ratile, a be a rekisa a kgona go bona madi. Jaalo he, e ne e le kafa molao o neng o ntse ka teng.

Gone go epiwa digwere di be di silwa di be di tsenngwa mo nkgong e tona, tona. Gobe go tseiwa basetsanyana ba iseng ba e sesading. Ba be ba neelwa dinkwanyana tse dintsha tse di iseng diresiwe. Ba be ba tewa gotwe ba ye go ga metsi a pula ya sephai. Fa ba goroga ka o ne metsi a o, a be a be a tshelwa mogo yone nkgo e tona eo. Go be go huduiwa ka leswana la morula go tlhakatlhakangwa.

Mokhao o ne o neelwa mosadi yo o swetsweng ke monna kapa ngwan wa mosimane. Mosadi wa motlholagadi o ne a neelwa Mokhao go dira gore pula e seka ya kalela. O a ne a neelwa makhao. A be a neelwa le mogaga. Ke gone kafa bo-rraetshomogolo ba neng ba laela kateng.

Dinkgo tseo dine dinna fela ko kgosing.

Go ka tweng fa e kare ngwaga e ise e fele nkgwana e o ya be e kgala?

Go boiwa gape go tseiwa basetsanyana ba iseng ba e sesading gore ba ye go gelela metsi mangwe le mangwe gore go tle go tladiwa nkgo eo. Go epiwa digwere, di be di silwa di be di tsenngwa mo go yone nkgo e e kgadileng eo.

Go epiwa mogaga, le thejana, le mosimao. Go be go latlhelwa bopi ja mokhao go be go tlhakangwa ka leswana la morula. Go be tshelwa mahura a tlou le a phofu. Mathare a mokhao a a silwa a be a tlhakangwa le mahura a diphologolo, tseo Mokhao gase wa batlholagadi fela.

Motlholagadi o dirang ka mokhao fa a o tsaya?

O tsaya mogaga, a boye a tseye mokhao, a o tshase mo dinaung tsa gagwe. A be a a ya ko merakeng a eta a latlhela phatsana tsa mogaga mo tseleng nngwe ka bongwe. Gone go dirwa jaalo dikgosi di sa tshidile.

Kgosi yone e ne e le yone e neng e nesa pula. Ene yo o nang le go nesa pula ke mang?

Ke kgosi, o raya ngwana wa gagwe a re. A e re phakela ka moso re tsogelle re ye go leka go nesa pula.

A rrago o ne a go ruta go e nesa?

Nyaa, ke ne ka tsaya malebela fela gore o dira jang.

A kgosi e ne e ka bitsa mongwe wa lefatshe le sele gore a tle go nesa pula?

A digwere tse, di tle di besiwe gore mosi o tle o ye kwa godimo gore maru a koke, go re pula e tle e ne?

Ee, ba ne batle ba dire jaalo. Digwere tseo dine di tlhakangwa le mahura, mosi obe otlhatlogela kwa godimo, pula e be e na.

A Bakwena ba ne ba tle ba dire jaalo?

Nyaa, gone go dira kgosi ka namana.

A batho bane ba tle ba duele kgosi ka go nesa pula?

Kgosi e ne e tle e neelwe ponto kapa kgomo e le sekai sa tebogo fela ka tiro e kgosi e e se dirileng.

Rrago o ne a tsaya kae madi, le dikgomo?

Kgosi e ne ya tle e neelwe ponto, kapa kgongwana. Kgosi e ne e na le dikgomo tsa yone.

Dikgomo di ne di tlhokomelwa ke motlhanka wa kgosi. Kgosi e ne lema, e re ka dinako tsa ditlala e be e rekisa mabele e bona madi.

Dikgomo tsa matimela le matlakala, kgosi e ne e laola gore di neelwe mongwe?

Part 2

Dilo tsotlhe di ne di ntshiwa ke kgosi.

Go raya gore fa rrago e ne e le ngaka ya pula, a o ka gakologelwa maina a dikokomane tsotlhe tsa gago?

Bane bale mo lelapeng la ga Sechele.

Bo rragomogolwana e ne le bomang?

Rre e ne e le Mosarwa, a be tsalwa ke Mediyamere go be go tla Kealeboga go be go tla Baji, e ne e le rremogolo. Mosarwa, o ne a nna mo lapeng la ga Sebele wa ntlha.

A go ne go a tle go rengwe ditlhare e bong, mokgalo, mosetlha, le morutlhare, le mogonono?

Ke tsone ditlhare tse e neng e le moila. Gotswa kgweding ya Lwetse. E re ka kgwedi ya Setebosigo, moila wa go rema di tlhare tseo o be o tsholediwa.

A go tsoma gone go na le moila mongwe?

Nyaa, go tsoma go ne go letlelelwa fela ka nako tsotlhe.

Mo bogologolong, batho ba ne ba ka letlelelwa goya go tsoma. Dinama tseo di ne di isewa ko magaenng, tse dingwe di ne di abelwa mong, ebong kgosi.

A ga o rute ope mo sebakeng sego, phekola go dira pula?

Kgosi e ne e ya go reka selepe, le boleke, e be e neela motlhanka wa yone more e be e mo neela le thobane, le thipa, e be e moraya e re tsamaya o fete o ne e le mang mang dikgomo.

Rre go ne gotwe Mosarwa. Baji o ne a le mo lelapeng laga Sechele. Mabukwana, ditlhare tse di sa rengweng ka kwedi ya Motsheganang e ne ele mokgalo le mosetlha.

A go na le meila e mengwe e o e ntseng jaalo?

Nyaa ga a ke itse epe meila.

Kana bogologolo, e ne e a re batho ba santse ba robetse, kgosi e ye go tlopola molora mo dithuthubudung tsa batho, molora oo, o be tlhakangwa le mere eo e mo nkgwaneng.

A go tsoma go ne go na le moila mongwe?

Nyaa, go tsoma gone go sena moila ope. Batho ba tle ba e go tsoma ka nako tsotlhe.

A ga o rute ope ngwana wa gago gore a tle a nese pula?

Jaanog he, ke ne ke botsa gore a go tswa mo tlhaloganyong ya kgosi gore e tlhophe mongwe gore a leke go nesa pula. Ga ke rute ope ka jaana le nna rre ga a ka a nthuta. Ke ne ka tsaya malebela fela gore rre o ne dira jang.

A ga ba ka ke baya kgaolong nngwe go senka mongwe yo ka dirang pula?

Jaanong kgosi e ne e ka mo neela kgetsanyana ya mere gore a e tlatse. Kgosi ngwe le ngwe, e ne e dira jaalo.

Rre o ne a tla go nna le Sebele. Fa Sebele a sena goswa, gabe go tla Kgari. Sengwe le sengwe se a neng a se tlhoka, se ne se tswa mo lapeng la ga Kgari. Rrago ke Mosarwa, a be latelelwa ke Baji, o ne a le mo lapeng laga Sebele wa ntlha. Ba kgosi e sena go swa, go ne go diragala gore kgosi e e e salang morago e be e leka ka bojotlhe go leka go phekola pula.

Fa mmedi o santse o gola, gone go sa rengwe, mosetlha, le mokgalo le morutlhare le e e leng o ne mogonono. Go tla go fitlha ka kwedi ya Sete-bosigo,o Fa di ka rengwa ka yone nako e o, go tla nna sefako se se golo fela thata sa tshenyo e kgolo thata. Fa e le letsomo, batho ba ne ba letlelelwa go ya go tsoma ka nako tsotlhe, ba bolae diphologolo, ba tsise dinama mo gae, ba abele mong, ebong kgosi, dirwe dingwe.

A kgosi e ka leka go ruta mongwe go ithuta go nesa pula?

Ee, kgosi e ne e ka dira jaalo.

Rre e ne ele kgosi Mosarwa, Sechele, a latelelwa ke Kealeboga. Go be go tla Moji. Moji, e ne e le rre mogolo.

Gore pula ene, go ne go epiwa digwere di be di silwa di be di tsengnwa mo nkgong e tona-tona. Fa kgosi e sena goswa, e e mo latelang e ne e le yone e etla salang e leka go nesa pula.

A go raya gore bo rrago mogolo botlhe e ne e le ba dira pula?

Ka bo rremogolo ne e le dikgosi, botlhe e ne e le badira pula.

Basetsanyana ba ba iseng ba robale le banna ba ne ba neelwa dinkgwan-yana tse di ntsha, tse di iseng di dirisiwe. Mokhao o ne o neelwe mosadi yo swetsweng ke monna kapa ngwana wa mosimane, a be a neelwa mogaga le mokhao, gore a tsamaye a farola mogaga a latlhela le tlape la o ne ka bongwe mo tseleng. Mokhao o ne a be a o tshasa mo dinaung tsa gagwe. A be a tshela mokhao mo merakeng le mo masimong, e re fa a refitlha, a be a be a tlhapa dinao.

A o kile wa utlwa fa digwere tseo di ne di a tle di besiwe gore mosi oye kwa godimo gore maru a koke, gore pula e tle e ne? A ke ka fa Bakwena baneng ba a

tle ba dire ka teng? Fa rrago a sena go nesa pula, batho ba ne battle ba neye
kgosi eng?

Kgosi e ne e na le dikgomo tsa yone. Kgosi e ne e tle e laole gore dikgomo tsa matimela letsa matlakala di neelwe mongwe. Digwere tseo, di ne di nna fela mo nkgong fela kwa kgosing.

Gone go tseiwa leswana je le tona-tona la morula, go be go fuduiwa go tlhakatlhangwa digwere le metsi a pula ya sephai. Fa e sena go bowa e wela e be e fufula, e ne e e fuduiwa gape go be latlhelwa bopi ja mokhao mo teng.

Yo o nang le thata ya go nesa pula e ne e le mang? Gape pula e ka kalediwa keng?

Digwere tse gotweng mogaga, le thejane le mosimao, di ne di tlhakangwa le mafura a tlou le a phofu, go be fuduiwa ka leswana je le tona la morula go tlhakangwa mere le metsi a o a pula ya ntlha ya sephai.

Mosadi wa motlholagadi o ne a tshasiwa ka o ne mokhao oo mo dinaung. A be a eta a farola mogaga a latlhela letlape la o ne ka bongwe mo tseleng. Fa a fitlha ko merakeng, le ko masimong, a be a gasa mokhao le mogaga gone koo.

A gone go ka diragala gore kgosi e ka bitsa mongwe wa lefatshe lengwe gotla go leka go nesa pula?

Ee, gone go e tle go dirwe jaalo.

Gone go tseiwa digwere tseo di be di tlhakangwa le mafura a tlou le a phofu. Kgosi ka namana ke yone fela e e ne e tle e leke go nesa pula.

A go dira pula e ne e le mo lapeng laga Sechele?

Ee, Sechele ne e le modira pula.

Fa e re motho yo o senkilweng go tla go leka go nesa pula, a fa pula e ka gana go na? A kgosi e ne e ka mokoba?

Nyaa, go ne go lekwa kgapetsa-kgapetsa go fitlhela gore pula e be e ne.

A batho bane ba dumela gore kgosi e ka nesa pula?

Ee, batho ba ne ba dumela ka botlalo gore kgosi e ne le yone fela e neng e ka nesang pula.

ISLAND STORY

In the summer of 2010, Taira Tsugiko of the Haebaru Town Museum on Okinawa Island kindly agreed to work with me to sponsor a poster contest featuring the work of students at the lone junior high school on Yonaguni Island. The farthest south of the Ryūkyūs, Yonaguni rises within sight of the island nation, Taiwan. The plan was to have the students represent "A Yonaguni Island Story," which I wrote based on my readings of several texts, written and oral.[52] Yamazato Katsunori, at the time, of the University of the Ryūkyūs translated my English account, and passed his translation to Yoneshiro Megumu, a noted Yonaguni Island historian, for his comment. Yoneshiro "changed some parts" of his translation, Yamazato reported, especially my claim that a man "from the Philippines" found an island rising from the sea.[53]

Taira and I flew from Okinawa to Yonaguni Island on December 8, 2010, and that evening we selected six prizewinners from among the forty-seven submissions. The following day, the day of the awards ceremony, excitement ran high among the students, teachers at the junior high school reported to us. Starting at 8:15 in the morning, Taira and I announced the winners and presented them with certificates and gifts.

Later, we visited an awamori factory (it was still much too early to drink but the brewmaster insisted and the distilled liquor in its large, ceramic pot appeared so darkly tranquil), a garment center, and a tiny museum run by an old woman who refused to stop talking, she had so much to say. After searching for a place to have lunch, we returned to a tiny yaki niku café we had passed earlier.

A single woman ran the place, and after querying us, she discovered we were the visitors who had sponsored the art contest at the local school. Her daughter, Itokazu Kanna, attended the school, she told us. She was elated when we told her Kanna had won second prize. She told us her good friend's daughter, Tajima Shihori, also attended the school. Shihori, we reported, won first prize. While cooking our lunch, the woman called her friend, Shihori's mother, to tell her the good news. A few minutes later (it was a small town), Shihori's mother appeared at the restaurant's door. The two mothers then told us their stories.

They were not Yonaguni Islanders, the women confessed. Itokazu was a Korean from Tokyo who had married a Yonaguni man and moved to the island. She told us she missed Korean culture and food, and taught her daughters, despite Japanese prejudice against Koreans, to be proud of their Korean mother. Tajima was from Osaka, and she enjoyed drawing. Both women said they were excited when they learned of the contest, and urged their daughters to enter. Tajima even took Shihori to the beach to have her observe and really see the ocean's water, its movements, colors, and shimmer in the changing light.

Both mothers, non–Yonaguni Islanders, were proud of their daughters who were island born and their representations of "A Yonaguni Island Story," which is a history of origins as told by me from a variety of sources, as translated by Yamazato Katsunori and modified by Yoneshiro Megumu, and as depicted by Itokazu Kanna, Nemoto Daisuke, and Tajima Shihori—authors and historians all. Those histories, those representations, written and painted, in English and Japanese translation, assembled and altered, map three-dimensional activity over time onto a two-dimensional plane.

1. A BEGINNING. A man from the Philippines found an island rising from the sea. "There is nothing on the island," he thought. "I will shoot my arrow to the shore."

2. Later, he returned to discover that his arrow had caused grasses and trees to grow and fill the island. "I will bring my family to live here," he said.

3. The man and his family were happy on the island. They ate wild berries and grew crops. They fished and gathered seaweed and shellfishes. And they multiplied and became the "people of Yonaguni."

4. AN END AND A NEW BEGINNING. But one day, the clouds darkened, turned pitch black, and hid the sun. And then it rained and rained for months, flooding the land and killing many people.

It rained for months, flooding the land and killing many people. By Itokazu Kanna, Yonaguni Junior High School, 2009.

5. Finally, the rain stopped, and through a small opening in the sky, a ray of light from the sun hit the ground. On that spot, the survivors built a shrine they called Tidan Dukuru or "place of the sun," and they became the "people of Yonaguni."

6. AN END AND A NEW BEGINNING. Again, the people multiplied and were happy.

7. But one day, the sky turned yellow, then orange, and finally an angry red. Fire fell from the heavens, and scorched the land and the people. The fires killed everyone, except one family who hid in a cave.

Fire fell from the heavens, and scorched the land and the people. By Nemoto Daisuke, Yonaguni Junior High School, 2009.

8. When the fires finally cooled, the family came out of the cave and started a farming village they called Dunada Abu. They became the "people of Yonaguni."

9. AN END AND A NEW BEGINNING. Once again, the people multiplied and were happy until a huge tidal wave swept over the island and destroyed everything.

10. A woman and two children she held in each hand managed to escape the tidal wave by running to the middle of the island. But the waves rose and she could save only one child. "I will sacrifice my own daughter," she

But the waves rose, and she could save only one child. By Tajima Shihori, Yonaguni Junior High School, 2009.

decided, "and save my brother's son." As soon as she gave her daughter to the angry waters, the tidal wave ended.

11. The woman and her brother's son became husband and wife, and their children became the "people of Yonaguni."

与那国島物語[54]

1. 島の始まりのお話し。<u>南の方</u>からやってきた男が海の上に<u>小さく盛り上がった形</u>を見つけました。「<u>ここ</u>にはまったくなにもないな」と男は考えました。「浜辺に向かって<u>ヤドカリをつけた</u>矢を放ってみよう」。

2. しばらくして男が戻ってみると、その矢で放ったヤドカリが増え、大きな島になり、草や木も生えていました。「家族を連れてきてここに住むことにしよう」と男は思いました。

3. 男とその家族は島に住み始め、幸せに暮らしました。野に生えている草の実を食べ、作物を育てました。魚を釣り、海草や貝を集めて拾いました。その家族はだんだんと増えていきました。やがて「与那国の人々」が誕生しました。

4. 島の終わりと新たな始まり。でも、ある日、空が暗くなりました。雲は真っ黒になり、太陽を隠しました。それから何ヶ月も雨が降り続き、洪水が起こり、たくさんの人が死んでしまいました。

5. やがて雨が止むと、雲に小さな穴があき、そこから太陽の光がまっすぐに差してきて地面を照らしました。生き残ったひとびとは、この光の差した地面にティダンドゥグル（「太陽の場所」）と呼んで崇 (あが) め、みんなの大事な事を話し合う所に決めました。それからそのひとたちは「与那国の人々」になりました。

6. 新しい島の始まり。人々の数がまた増え、幸せに暮らしはじめました。

7. でも、ある日、空が黄色になり、それからオレンジ色になり、最後に怒ったような赤い色になりました。天空から火が降ってきて、あっという間に島と人々を焼きました。ドゥナダアブという洞窟に隠れた一つの家族以外は、全員が火で死んでしまいました。

8. 火がおさまると、その家族は洞窟から出てきて新しい村をつくりました。そのひとたちが「与那国の人々」になりました。

9. 次の新たな島の始まり。また、ひとびとの数が増え幸せに暮らしました。しかし、ある日、津波が島を襲い、またすべてをこわしてしまいました。

10. 二人の子どもを腕に抱いた女が、島の真ん中に走っていって津波を逃れました。でも、波が高くなって襲いかかってきたので、子どもは一人しか助けることができません。「自分の娘を犠牲にして兄弟の息子を助けるしかない」と女は考えました。女が娘を荒れる波に流すやいなや、津波はおさまりました。

11. 女とその兄弟の息子は一緒に生活するようになりました。そしてその子どもたちは「与那国の人々」になりました。

AFFILIATIONS

On June 19, 2011, Lydia Juliana Ama de Chile, our gracious host in Izalco, El Salvador, surprised my wife, Marina, and me by taking us to visit Barrio Cruz Galana. Located in the western part of the country, Izalco is the site of the brutal 1932 massacre of some ten to forty thousand peasants, mainly Pipil Indians, by the government of President Maximiliano Hernández Martínez. His well-armed army easily crushed the peasant insurrection, and under the deception of negotiation and clemency, the military proceeded to kill suspected rebels and all Indians or Náhuatl speakers in what can only be described as a genocide.[55] Appropriately, people refer to that attempt at extinction as the Matanza or "the slaughter." Doña Juliana's granduncle, Feliciano Ama, was one of the Indian leaders hanged in the uprising, and the state commemorated his execution with a postage stamp as a warning against rebellion.

Izalco graced a hillside and below the town, across a busy highway, sprawled Barrio Cruz Galana. The barrio's indigenous inhabitants, Doña Juliana explained, were in the midst of the Cofradia de Padre Eterno, one of the two annual first-fruits ceremonies held in thanksgiving to tuteku or god for the harvest. When we arrived, a line of cheering women greeted us in undulating, high-pitched registers. Holding baskets of flowers, they proceeded to shower us with petals. Like the rains from the heavens that blessed the earth, purple, red, yellow, and orange blossoms fell from the skies, glanced off our heads and shoulders, and came to rest on the ground, marking our path to the home where the figure of Padre Eterno awaited.

The sole man, Alonso Garcia, swinging a smoking censer, led the way. Inside, band members on a marimba, guitar, and trumpet played quietly in the back of the room as we, the somber guests, sat on chairs facing Padre Eterno. Garcia's mother, the famed curandera Juana Garcia, who had died earlier that year just short of her one-hundredth birthday, stared down on the proceedings from her perch on the wall of her house. Beneath her weathered photograph, old women, sacred women, the barrio's curanderas with healing powers positioned themselves. They, each one, searched us with their penetrating gazes.

Padre Eterno sat behind cascades of flowers, mainly red ginger, and palm fronds, and I immediately thought about Hawai'i where red ginger grew in profusion, and Okinawa where palm fronds marked sacred sites. The row of curanderas looked the world to me like the sacred women of Okinawa's Kudaka Island, although these were not dressed in white. Truth and wisdom lined their ageless faces, and I could not help looking twice; one caught me staring at her.

After welcome speeches by Doña Juliana and Alonso Garcia, an elderly woman presented me with a gift from the barrio—a round, sweet pineapple still on its stalk tied with a string of dried banana fibers. The offering might have come to me because of patriarchy, but it blew my mind, having just completed the book *Pineapple Culture*, the second of this trilogy on space / time. Fiction could not have contrived a more perfect union. Choking back the tears, I knew I had come home.

In Barrio Cruz Galana, on ground made sacred by the blood of martyred Indians, on the eastern shore of the Pacific Ocean, I found peace and communion. The pineapple, a fruit of the tropics and gift to the world, enabled that affiliation. Handcrafted by American Indians likely along the present-day border of Argentina and Brazil at least four thousand years ago, the pineapple is as indigenous to America as the Pipil Indians of El Salvador.

The migrating fruit traveled along the Amazon River highway to the Atlantic and then Caribbean, where in 1493 Callinago Indians presented to Spain's Christopher Columbus the prized pineapple. The conquistador promptly plucked a few of them, including enslaved Indians, for his patrons, King Ferdinand and Queen Isabella, as objects of plunder. By that time, the fruit had already made landfall in Central America.

Doña Juliana told us that this first-fruits ceremony, the Cofradia de Padre Eterno, featured the pineapple as an offering to tuteku, and its eating by the

History

barrio's residents affirmed their community membership. The next morning, we gratefully enjoyed the fruit, which in its assimilation and embodiment united us with the Indians of Barrio Cruz Galana.

Doña Juliana, like her patriotic granduncle, engages and shapes history. As principal of an elementary school, she taught children the Náhuatl language, which Spanish-speaking colonizers had suppressed and denigrated as the language of the uneducated, downtrodden masses. At her school in Izalco, children spoke and sang in Náhuatl, and they dressed in and danced to indigenous colors and sounds. My Salvadoran-born wife, Marina Amparo Henríquez, supports that movement of language and cultural regeneration, and students sang her praise at Doña Juliana's school for her contributions. After retiring from the elementary school, Doña Juliana taught a class of young students the Náhuatl language on the very ground of the Matanza. In that act of transmission, the peasant revolution lives.

First-fruits celebrates life's regeneration and the movement and passage of time from wet to dry season. Extinction is not an option for El Salvador's Náhuatl speakers who survived, despite genocide, as a people and culture. Women like Barrio Cruz Galana's curanderas, Doña Juliana, and Marina Henríquez, men like Alonso Garcia, and the schoolchildren who study under a tree whose roots reach deep into the bloody earth have determined otherwise.

In the last instance, those elemental forces of human resolve and creation moving across space / time, from Okinawa to El Salvador, inspire this writing of my (subject-)self into history.

MULTIVERSES

In this, my consideration of history, space / time, I am drawn to Gaston Bachelard's "poetics of space," involving a "phenomenology of the imagination," which leads to discovery, sudden salience, and is the birth of language. It seems possible, as Julia Kristeva sought in prosody, that new language and its epistemology might afford an opening for other ways of knowing not of or from the master's toolkit. Moreover, bodies marked by space / time through experience and the imagination can, in the words of the structuralist Claude Lévi Strauss, occupy all space for all time. Because, he writes, "we live in several worlds," the immediate more pertinent than the old and the new impertinent to its successor. They form, in the sense deployed by Michel Foucault, ensembles and a "cluster of relations," and quantum states, as superstring theory might argue. Those relations, their reverberations suggest a single universe unlikely, and point to the liberating prospect of multiverses.

The Ryūkyū Islands, situated near the western terminus of our Oceania, and El Salvador, a stretch of the American continent along the expansive water's eastern shores, are my places of generation within the welcome embrace of the Third World, postcolonial Botswana and colonial Hawai'i. I so designate them. As extremities and points of origin, they find dialogical communion within the subjective—me—and are not oppositional, situated as they are an ocean and International Date Line apart and distinguished by places named, in a flexing of imperial power, islands and continents.

The Black Stream, the Kūrōshio current flows past the Ryūkyūs, transporting warm, tropical water teeming with the larvae of corals, grubs and worms, starfish, sea cucumbers, sea urchins, and oysters and mussels, seaweed and fishes. Moving in a gyre, the river flows northward, skirting Japan, toward the North Pacific current that bends down the west coast of America to become the California stream. Rotating clockwise in the northern hemisphere around the earth's ocean, the waters kiss El Salvador's shore, and return to the Ryūkyūs, completing the circle of life.

Rising mid-ocean are the islands of Hawai'i, another place of my constitution, which during the early twentieth century was the distribution center of pineapples to the world. An illusory, antipodal line through the earth's center connects Hawai'i, the islands of my physical birth, and Botswana, the island of my intellectual birth on the African continent. Other imaginary lines, the Tropics of Cancer and Capricorn, drift across Botswana and the Hawaiian archipelago, tracing the sun's modulating passages of space / time and the limits of a tropical (and temperate) hermeneutics.

Connecting them all,
the earth's single ocean,
the boundless sea,
moves ceaselessly, in rhythm.

REMEMBRANCE

1. From the text of her "Ohio EPA Superfund Sites" collages on http://masumimuseum.com.

2. *Sights Unseen: The Photographic Constructions of Masumi Hayashi*, May 31–September 14, 2003, Japanese American National Museum, Los Angeles.

INTRODUCTION

1. This history's title, *The Boundless Sea*, is from my father's family name, 沖廣, which translates to "the wide and open sea." Instead, I have chosen to translate the kanji to "the boundless sea." Thanks to my colleagues Hase Naoya and Eun Ja Lee, professors at Kwansei Gakuin University, Japan.

2. In Hawai'i, talk story reveals as much about the speaker as about the subject.

3. A testimonio is a narrative told in the first person to an interlocutor who records, transcribes, and edits the account. The significance of testimonios is further discussed in chapter 7.

4. But not historicism's totalizing, universalizing traditions.

5. See Gayatri Spivak's critique of Kristeva's "pre-semiotic" when, Spivak writes, all is language. Gayatri Chakravorty Spivak, "The Politics of Translation," from her *Outside in the Teaching Machine* (New York: Routledge, 1993), reprinted in

The Translation Studies Reader, ed. Lawrence Venuti, 2nd ed. (New York: Routledge, 2004), 375.

6. Speech is a special type of music, a provocative study holds. In fact, before language there is music, and musical hearing and ability is essential to language acquisition. Anthony Brandt, Molly Gebrian, and L. Robert Slevc, "Music and Early Language Acquisition," *Frontiers in Psychology* 3 (September 2012): 1–17.

7. See, e.g., Nathan Oaklander and Quentin Smith, eds., *The New Theory of Time* (New Haven, CT: Yale University Press, 1994).

8. Elizabeth Grosz, *Time Travels: Feminism, Nature, Power* (Durham, NC: Duke University Press, 2005).

9. As explained by John D. Kelley and Martha Kaplan, *Represented Communities: Fiji and World Decolonization* (Chicago: University of Chicago Press, 2001), 6–7, dialectical history seeks synthesis and a resolution, whereas dialogical history comprises a dense network of relations without a necessary telos.

10. Joan W. Scott, "Experience," in *Feminists Theorize the Political*, ed. Judith Butler and Joan W. Scott (New York: Routledge, 1992), 22–40; Linda Martín Alcoff, "The Problem of Speaking for Others," in *Who Can Speak? Authority and Critical Inquiry*, ed. Judith Roof and Robyn Wiegman (Urbana: University of Illinois Press, 1995), 97–119.

11. I failed to complete that study, but my research and notes for the planned book are at Yale's university archives.

12. After Gaston Bachelard's *The Poetics of Space* (1969), which I discuss in chapter 7.

CHAPTER ONE. BLACK STREAM (OBĀBAN)

1. Geologically, the Ryūkyū chain consists of three arcs composed of different rocks, which connect with Kyūshū and Taiwan. Richard J. Pearson, *Archaeology of the Ryukyu Islands: A Regional Chronology from 3000 B.C. to the Historic Period* (Honolulu: University of Hawai'i Press, 1969), 13.

2. Keaīwa comes from "incomprehensible," referring to the mysterious powers of kahuna (priests) and herbs used in healing, or from "a period of fasting and meditation," which kahuna underwent as part of their training. Elspeth P. Sterling and Catherine C. Summers, eds., *Sites of Oahu* (Honolulu: Bishop Museum Press, 1978), 11–12.

3. This section, "nation / race," is a revised, enlarged version originally published as "Preliminary Thoughts on Migration and the Nation / People," in *Proceedings for the International Symposium: Human Migration and the 21st Century Global Society: Immigration, Language, and Literature*, ed. Nakahodo Masanori, Yamazato Katsunori, and Ishihara Masahide (University of the Ryukyus, March 2009), 79–84.

4. This problem is of course the reason for the "imagined community" of the nation as described by Benedict Anderson in his *Imagined Communities: Reflections on the Origin and Spread of Nationalism* (London: Verso, 1983). See also Étienne Balibar, "The Nation Form: History and Ideology," in *Race, Nation, Class: Ambiguous Identities*, by Étienne Balibar and Immanuel Wallerstein (London: Verso, 1991), on the fictive narrative of nation.

5. As quoted in John W. Dower, *War without Mercy: Race and Power in the Pacific War* (New York: Pantheon Books, 1986), 222.

6. Tessa Morris-Suzuki, "A Descent into the Past: The Frontier in the Construction of Japanese Identity," in *Multicultural Japan: Paleolithic to Postmodern*, ed. Donald Denoon et al. (Cambridge: Cambridge University Press, 1996), 82–88.

7. Morris-Suzuki, "Descent," 83, 85–86.

8. Japonesia also worked against the demands of the post–World War II Ryūkyū independence movement.

9. Hokama Shūzen, "Okinawa in the Matrix of Pacific Ocean Culture," in *Okinawan Diaspora*, ed. Ronald Y. Nakasone (Honolulu: University of Hawai'i Press, 2002), 49. A rejoinder to Shimao's Japonesia is Miki Takeshi's "Okinesia," in his *Okinesia Bunkaron: Seishin no Kyōwakoku o motomete* (Tokyo: Kaifūsha, 1988).

10. See Higuchi Yōichi, "When Society Itself Is the Tyrant," *Japan Quarterly* 35:4 (October–December 1988): 350–56.

11. See, e.g., Hanazaki Kohei, "Ainu Moshir and Yaponesia: Ainu and Okinawan Identities in Contemporary Japan," in Denoon et al., *Multicultural Japan*, 117–31; and Katarina Sjöberg, "Positioning Oneself in the Japanese Nation State: The Hokkaido Ainu Case," in *Transcultural Japan: At the Borderlands of Race, Gender, and Identity*, ed. David Blake Willis and Stephen Murphy-Shigematsu (London: Routledge, 2008), 197–216.

12. Alan S. Christy, "The Making of Imperial Subjects in Okinawa," *positions* 1:3 (Winter 1993): 607–8.

13. Hokama, "Okinawa," 49.

14. Christy, "Making of Imperial Subjects," 623–25.

15. Frantz Fanon, *The Wretched of the Earth*, trans. Constance Farrington (New York: Grove Weidenfield, 1963); Albert Memmi, *The Colonizer and the Colonized* (Boston: Beacon Press, 1967).

16. See, e.g., the second volume of my trilogy, *Pineapple Culture: A History of the Tropical and Temperate Zones* (Berkeley: University of California Press, 2009).

17. Tomiyama Ichirō, "Colonialism and the Sciences of the Tropical Zone: The Academic Analysis of Difference in 'the Island Peoples'," *positions* 3:2 (Fall 1995): 367–91.

18. In retaliation, Okinawans called Japanese "chi ga nai" or people without blood or soul, punning Naichi. Henry Toyama and Ikeda Kiyoshi, "The Okinawan-Naichi Relationship," in *Uchinanchu: A History of Okinawans in Hawaii* (Honolulu: Ethnic Studies Oral History Project, University of Hawai'i, 1981), 130.

19. Cited in Toyama and Ikeda, "Okinawan-Naichi," 128, 129.

20. From an Okinawan folksong, *Jidai nu nagari* (The Flow of Time), cited in Wesley Iwao Ueunten, "Rising Up from a Sea of Discontent: The 1970 Koza Uprising in U.S.-Occupied Okinawa," in *Military Currents: Toward a Decolonized Future in Asia and the Pacific*, ed. Setsu Shigematsu and Keith L. Camacho (Minneapolis: University of Minnesota Press, 2010), 97.

21. Sakihara Mitsugu, "History of Okinawa," in *Uchinanchu*, 6. Cf. Josef Kreiner, "Ryûkyûan History in Comparative Perspective," in *Ryûkyû in World History*, ed. Josef Kreiner (Bonn, Germany: Bier'sche Verlagsanstalt, 2001), 1, 3.

22. On the Southeast Asian trade, see Sakamaki Shunzo, "Ryukyu and Southeast Asia," *Journal of Asian Studies* 23:3 (May 1964): 383–89; Takara Kurayoshi, "The Kingdom of Ryūkyū and Its Overseas Trade," in *Sources of Ryūkyūan History and Culture in European Collections*, Monograph no. 13, ed. Josef Kreiner (Tokyo: Institute of Japanese Studies, 1996), 43–52; Sakihara, "History," 7. See Robert K. Sakai, "The Satsuma-Ryukyu Trade and the Tokugawa Seclusion Policy," *Journal of Asian Studies* 23:3 (May 1964): 391–403, for the trade with Japan.

23. Matsuda Mitsugu, "The Ryukyuan Government Scholarship Students to China, 1392–1868," *Monumenta Nipponica* 21:3 / 4 (1966): 273–304.

24. Patrick Beillevaire, "The Western Discovery of Ryūkyū: From the First Contacts to the Eve of Perry's Expedition," in *Ryūkyū Studies to 1854: Western*

Encounter, part I, vol. 1, ed. Patrick Beillevaire (Richmond, Surrey, UK: Curzon Press, 2000), 3–4.

25. Sakihara, "History," 7. Sakamaki, "Ryukyu and Southeast Asia," 386, cites 62 ships on 48 voyages between Okinawa and Siam during the period 1425 to 1564, and an estimated 150 ships between 1385–1570.

26. Sakamaki, "Ryukyu and Southeast Asia," 387, 388; Matsuda, "Ryukyuan Government," 278.

27. As cited in Sakihara, "History," 7–8. Cf. translation in Pearson, *Archaeology of the Ryukyu Islands*, xiii; Kurayoshi, "Kingdom," 50. See also the song in Matsuda, "Ryukyuan Government," 291.

28. Beillevaire, "Western Discovery," 4–7. For a detailed account of this relationship, see Sakai, "Satsuma-Ryukyu Trade," 391–403.

29. A study called this a "policy of deception." Sakai, "Satsuma-Ryukyu Trade," 391–92.

30. Sakai, "Satsuma-Ryukyu Trade," 392–93; Robert K. Sakai, "The Ryukyu (Liu-Ch'iu) Kings in the Ch'ing Period," in *The Chinese World Order: Traditional China's Foreign Relations*, ed. John King Fairbank (Cambridge, MA: Harvard University Press, 1968), 129–34. For a political history of the Satsuma and Ryūkyū kingdom relationship, see Matsuda Mitsugu, *The Government of the Kingdom of Ryukyu, 1609–1872* (Okinawa: Yui, 2001).

31. Kreiner, "Ryūkyūan History," 13; Ch'en Ta-tuan, "Investiture of Liu-Ch'iu Kings in the Ch'ing Period," in Fairbank, *Chinese World Order*, 159; Sakai, "Satsuma-Ryukyu Trade," 392n7, citing Sakamaki Shunzo's *Ryukyu: A Bibliogaphical Guide to Okinawan Studies* (Honolulu: University of Hawai'i Press, 1963).

32. Ch'en, "Investiture," 160. On Chinese and Japanese influences, see Douglas G. Haring, "Chinese and Japanese Influences," in *Ryukyuan Culture and Society: A Survey*, ed. Allan H. Smith (Honolulu: University of Hawai'i Press, 1964), 39–55; Matsuda, "Ryukyuan Government," 292, 297; Beillevaire, "Western Discovery," 6–7.

33. Ronald Y. Nakasone, "An Impossible Possibility," in Nakasone, *Okinawan Diaspora*, 20.

34. Such as the *Ryūkyū shintōki* (1605) and *Chūzan seikan* (1650), which attributes to the wind the ability to cause pregnancy in women. Sakihara

Mitsugu, *A Brief History of Early Okinawa Based on the Omoro Sōshi* (Tokyo: Honpo Shoseki Press, 1987), 29.

35. Nakasone, "Impossible Possibility," 21; Mabuchi Toichi, "Tales Concerning the Origin of Grains in the Insular Areas of Eastern and Southeastern Asia," *Asian Folklore Studies* 23:1 (1964): 6–18; Sakihara, *Brief History*, 20; Ronald Y. Nakasone, "Agari-umaai: An Okinawan Pilgrimage," in Nakasone, *Okinawan Diaspora*, 144, 147–48; Sakihara, "History of Okinawa," 7–8.

36. As translated in Sakihara, *Brief History*, 15–16.

37. Nakasone, "Agari-umaai," 156.

38. Nakasone, "Impossible Possibility," 6–7. On the study of the *Omoro-sōshi*, see Sakihara, *Brief History*, 219–45; and a review of Sakihara's *Brief History*, Christopher Drake, "A Separate Perspective: Shamanic Songs of the Ryukyu Kingdom," *Harvard Journal of Asiatic Studies* 50:1 (June 1990): 283–333.

39. Sakihara, *Brief History*, 27–32.

40. Sakihara, *Brief History*, 32–33, 38.

41. For my understanding of Oceania, see the first volume of my trilogy, *Island World: A History of Hawaiʻi and the United States* (Berkeley: University of California Press, 2008), 206–11.

42. Bunazi and bunari refer to "sister" on Miyako and Yaeyama islands. Mabuchi, "Spiritual Predominance," 80.

43. As cited in Hokama, "Okinawa," 46; see also G. H. Kerr, [untitled], 99–100, unpubl. manuscript, GHK1J04004, G. H. Kerr Papers, Okinawa Prefectural Archives. For other origin stories of the Oceania type, see G. H. Kerr, "The Eastern Sea Islands," T1–2, Y1–2, unpubl. manuscript, GHK1J04003, G. H. Kerr Papers, Okinawa Prefectural Archives. And on the sister-kami figure as an Oceania type, see Mabuchi Toichi, "Spiritual Predominance of the Sister," in Smith, *Ryukyuan Culture*, 88–89.

44. In 2018, an outstanding Yale undergraduate student of mine, Janis Jin, suggested that I include "song" in the title of this book. I immediately thought of "trance song" as the title but discarded it upon reflection. Not only is it difficult to say, trance songs resonate with contemporary drug cultures.

45. For another version of Miyako's creation, see Mabuchi Toichi, "Toward the Reconstruction of Ryukyuan Cosmology," in *Folk Religion and the Worldview in*

the Southwestern Pacific, ed. Matsumoto Nobuhiro and Mabuchi Toichi (Tokyo: Kokusai, 1968), 119.

46. Chris Drake, "Okinawan Shaman Songs," *Mānoa* 8:1 (Summer 1996): 122–23.

47. For ethnographies of Okinawan sacred women, see Arne Røkkum, *Goddesses, Priestesses, and Sisters: Mind, Gender and Power in the Monarchic Tradition of the Ryukyus* (Oslo, Norway: Scandinavian University Press, 1998). Cf. Susan Sered, *Women of the Sacred Groves: Divine Priestesses of Okinawa* (New York: Oxford University Press, 1999).

48. Monica Wacker, "*Onarigami*—Holy Woman in the Kingdom of Ryūkyū: A Pacific Culture With Chinese Influences," in Kreiner, *Ryûkyû*, 42, 44, 64; William P. Lebra, *Okinawan Religion: Belief, Ritual, and Social Structure* (Honolulu: University of Hawai'i Press, 1966), 21–24, 182–83; Tanaka Masako, "Categories of Okinawan 'Ancestors' and the Kinship System," *Asian Folklore Studies* 36:2 (1977): 47–49.

49. D. C. Holton, "The Meaning of Kami," chap. 1, "Japanese Derivations," *Monumenta Nipponica* 3:1 (January 1940): 1–27; "The Meaning of Kami," chap. 2, "Interpretations by Japanese Writers," *Monumenta Nipponica* 3:2 (July 1940): 392–413; "The Meaning of Kami," chap. 3, "Kami Considered as Mana," *Monumenta Niponica* 4:2 (July 1941): 351–94, especially 352–57.

50. Mabuchi, "Spiritual Predominance," 79–83, 88–89; Lebra, *Okinawan Religion*, 24.

51. Akamine Masanobu, Oral History, Kudaka Island, July 4, 2009; Mabuchi, "Tales," 9–11.

52. Akamine, Oral History.

53. Kerr, "Eastern Sea Islands," T2; Kerr, [untitled], 138.

54. For another version, see Ikema Eizo, *Yonaguni ni Rekishi* (Yonaguni-cho: Ikema Nae, [1959] 1991), 66–72.

55. This account selectively incorporates the versions in Kerr, "Eastern Sea Islands," Y1–Y2; Kerr, [untitled], 178–80; Ikema, *Yonaguni*, 66–72; and as told by Yoneshiro Megumu, Oral History, Yonaguni Island, November 30, 2009.

56. The historian George Kerr observed that many sacred shrines on Okinawa Island face southeast toward Kudaka Island, and on other islands, their shrines are on the southeastern coasts facing the Kūrōshio current. Kerr, "Eastern Sea Islands," 16.

57. Kerr, "Far Eastern Islands," 153. A similar story from Hateruma Island tells of a young woman who paddled to the Philippines nightly to see her lover. Kerr, "Eastern Sea Islands," 17.

58. Kerr, "Far Eastern Islands," 142.

59. Kerr, "Eastern Sea Islands," 17.

60. See, e.g., Josef Kreiner, "Notes on the History of European-Ryūkyūan Contacts," in Kreiner, Sources of Ryūkyūan History, 15–41; Kreiner, "Ryūkyūan History," 1–39.

61. On the Austronesian family and Oceanic languages, see John Lynch, Malcolm Ross, and Terry Crowley, The Oceanic Languages (Richmond, Surrey, UK: Curzon Press, 2002); and on Taiwan as the origin site for Austronesian, Tsang Cheng-hwa, "Recent Discoveries at the Tapenkeng Culture Sites in Taiwan: Implications for the Problem of Austronesian Origins," in The Peopling of East Asia: Putting Together Archaeology, Linguistics and Genetics, ed. Laurent Sagart, Roger Blench, and Alicia Sanchez-Mazas (London: RoutledgeCurzon, 2005), 63–72.

62. Hokama, "Okinawa," 48–49; Sakihara, "History," 4; Christy, "Making of Imperial Subjects," 623, 625–27, 637n49.

63. Richard Pearson, "The Place of Okinawa in Japanese Historical Identity," in Denoon et al., Multicultural Japan, 97, 99, 101.

64. Other suggestions of Okinawa's southern exposure are Ryūkyūan death rituals, which belong to the proto-Malayo-Polynesian cultural area and with Taiwan; the ryūka or five-tone, musical scale, which resembles the widely influential Indonesian gamelan scale; the Okinawan liquor, awamori, which some link with the Thai drink lao-lon; and the South Asian use of banana fibers (bāsho) to weave textiles, bashōfu. Erika Kaneko, "The Death Ritual," in Smith, Ryukyuan Culture, 28; Pearson, Archaeology, 134–38; Hokama, "Okinawa," 46, 50, 51.

65. On the commonalities but also divergences of Jōmon culture in Japan and Okinawa, see Pearson, "Place of Okinawa," 95–116.

66. Michael Pietrusewsky, "The Physical Anthropology of the Pacific, East Asia and Southeast Asia," in Sagart et al., Peopling of East Asia, 201–29, proposes separate origins for Melanesians.

67. Some hypothesize that dispersion of Austronesian speakers from Taiwan and southeast China and not Southeast Asia as the beginnings of Pacific Islanders, including Hawaiians.

68. Katayama Kazumichi, "The Japanese as an Asia-Pacific Population," in Denoon et al., *Multicultural Japan*, 24–27, 28.

69. John C. Maher, "North Kyushu Creole: A Language-Contact Model for the Origins of Japanese," in Denoon et al., *Multicultural Japan*, 31–45.

70. On the social construction of regions and the category "Southeast Asia," see Martin W. Lewis and Kären E. Wigen, *The Myth of Continents: A Critique of Metageography* (Berkeley: University of California Press, 1997), 157–88.

71. The probability remains, nonetheless, that the Jōmon, including those in Okinawa, Japan, Taiwan, the Philippines, and Oceania, spoke languages of the Austronesian family. Katayama, "Japanese," 28.

72. G. H. Kerr, "The Far Islands: Notes on Okinawa and the Southern Ryukyus," 64, 67–68, 116, unpubl. manuscript, GHK1J04002, G. H. Kerr Papers, Okinawa Prefectural Archives.

73. Ishigaki Shigeru, Oral History, Ishigaki City, July 24, 2009. Interviewer: Wesley Ueunten.

74. G. H. Kerr, [untitled manuscript], 132, 136,138.

75. On my understanding of "social formation," see Gary Y. Okihiro and Elda Tsou, "On Social Formation," *Works and Days* 24:1 / 2 (2006): 69–88; Okihiro, *Third World Studies: Theorizing Liberation* (Durham, NC: Duke University Press, 2016).

76. See, e.g., Louis Althusser, *Essays on Ideology* (London: Verso, 1984).

CHAPTER TWO. SELF (OKĀSAN)

NOTE: By "self," I mean the subject-self produced through the process of subjectification.

1. This section draws from my "Self and History," *Rethinking History* 13:1 (March 2009): 5–15.

2. Fanon, *Wretched of the Earth*.

3. C. Wright Mills, *The Sociological Imagination* (New York: Oxford University Press, 1959), 5, 196–97.

4. Gary Y. Okihiro, *Cane Fires: The Anti-Japanese Movement in Hawaii, 1865–1945* (Philadelphia: Temple University Press, 1991), 46.

5. Edward D. Beechert, *Working in Hawaii: A Labor History* (Honolulu: University of Hawai'i Press, 1985), 192.

6. Okihiro, *Cane Fires*, 144.

7. See, e.g., Robert Park, "The Nature of Race Relations," in *Race and Culture* by Robert Ezra Park (Glencoe, IL: Free Press, 1950), 81–116; "Racial Assimilation in Secondary Groups with Particular Reference to the Negro," *American Journal of Sociology* 19:5 (March 1914): 610–11. See also Stanford M. Lyman, "Race Relations as Social Process: Sociology's Resistance to a Civil Rights Orientation," in *Race in America: The Struggle for Equality*, ed. Herbert Hill and James E. Jones, Jr. (Madison: University of Wisconsin Press, 1993), 370–401.

8. See, e.g., Lawrence H. Fuchs, *Hawaii Pono: A Social History* (New York: Harcourt, Brace & World, 1961); Noel J. Kent, *Hawaii: Islands under the Influence* (New York: Monthly Review Press, 1983).

9. See, e.g., Davianna Pomaikaʻi McGregor, *Na Kuaʻaina: Living Hawaiian Culture* (Honolulu: University of Hawaiʻi Press, 2007); Jonathan Kay Kamakawiwoʻole Osorio, *Dismembering Lahui: A History of the Hawaiian Nation to 1887* (Honolulu: University of Hawaiʻi Press, 2002); Noenoe K. Silva, *Aloha Betrayed: Native Hawaiian Resistance to American Colonialism* (Durham, NC: Duke University Press, 2004).

10. Ethnic Studies Oral History Project, *Uchinanchu: A History of Okinawans in Hawaii* (Honolulu: Ethnic Studies Program, University of Hawaii at Manoa, 1981), 358.

11. Mills, *Sociological Imagination*, 3–5, 205, 211, 223, 226.

12. Paulo Freire, *Pedagogy of the Oppressed*, trans. Myra Bergman Ramos (New York: Herder and Herder, 1972), 19–20, 73.

13. As named and described by Carter G. Woodson, *The Mis-education of the Negro* (Washington, DC: Associated, 1933).

14. Memmi, *Colonizer and the Colonized*.

15. Mills, *Sociological Imagination*, 205.

16. Raymond Williams, *Marxism and Literature* (Oxford: Oxford University Press, 1977), 192–98, 199–205, 211–12; Dan P. McAdams, *The Redemptive Self: Stories Americans Live By* (Oxford: Oxford University Press, 2006).

17. In her *My People Shall Live: The Autobiography of a Revolutionary*, ed. George Hajjar (London: Hodder and Stoughton, 1973), 17.

18. Estelle C. Jelinek, *Women's Autobiography: Essays in Criticism* (Bloomington: Indiana University Press, 1980).

19. As pointed out by Sidonie Smith and Julia Watson in their co-edited *De / Colonizing the Subject: The Politics of Gender in Women's Autobiography* (Minneapolis: University of Minnesota Press, 1992).

20. William Zinsser, ed., *Inventing the Truth: The Art and Craft of Memoir* (Boston: Houghton Mifflin, 1987), 56, 111–12.

21. Joan W. Scott, "Experience," in *Feminists Theorize the Political*, ed. Judith Butler and Joan W. Scott (New York: Routledge, 1992), 34. See also "Experience," in Raymond Williams, *Keywords: A Vocabulary of Culture and Society* (1976; rev. ed., New York: Oxford University Press, 1983), 126–29.

22. Portions of the following section were read at my mother's funeral on September 27, 2018, nine days after her 101st birthday.

23. Thomas D. Murphy, *Ambassadors in Arms* (Honolulu: University of Hawai'i Press, 1954), 41.

24. Shamelessly patterned on Toshio Mori's "The Woman Who Makes Swell Doughnuts," in his *Yokohama, California* (1949; reprint, Seattle: University of Washington Press, 1985), 22–25.

25. John E. Reinecke, *Language and Dialect in Hawaii: A Sociolinguistic History to 1935* (Honolulu: University of Hawai'i Press, 1969), 29. Written Hawaiian language, however, was also a means for resistance, especially the vernacular newspapers of the 1860s. See Silva, *Aloha Betrayed*, 54–86.

26. On the complexity of Hawaiian pidgin, see Derek Bickerton, *Roots of Language* (Ann Arbor, MI: Karoma, 1981); Derek Bickerton, "Pidgins and Language Mixture," in *Creole Genesis, Attitudes and Discourse: Studies Celebrating Charlene J. Sato*, ed. John R. Rickford and Suzanne Romaine (Amsterdam: John Benjamins, 1999), 31–43; Sarah Julianne Roberts, "The TMA System of Hawaiian Creole and Diffusion," in Rickford and Romaine, *Creole Genesis*, 45–70.

27. See, e.g., Kent Sakoda and Jeff Siegel, *Pidgin Grammar: An Introduction to the Creole Language of Hawai'i* (Honolulu: Bess Press, 2003).

28. Ngũgĩ wa Thiong'o, *Decolonising the Mind: The Politics of Language in African Literature* (Oxford: James Currey, 1986), 4.

29. Okihiro, *Cane Fires*, 140.

30. For one of the earliest consideration of pidgin as a language, see Elizabeth Ball Carr, *Da Kine Talk: From Pidgin to Standard English in Hawaii* (Honolulu: University of Hawai'i Press, 1972).

31. Aimé Césaire, *Discourse on Colonialism*, trans. Joan Pinkham (New York: Monthly Review Press, [1955] 2000), 43.

32. Adria L. Imada, *Aloha America: Hula Circuits through the U.S. Empire* (Durham, NC: Duke University Press, 2012), 33.

33. Nathaniel B. Emerson, *Pele and Hiiaka: A Myth from Hawaii* (1915; reprint, Honolulu: ʻAi Pōhaku Press, 1993).

34. Pualani Kanakaʻole Kanahele, *Ka Honua Ola: ʻEli ʻeli Kau Mai* (Honolulu: Kamehameha, 2011), 109.

35. Katharine Luomala, *Voices on the Wind* (Honolulu: Bishop Museum Press, 1955), 35.

36. Memmi, *Colonizer and the Colonized*, 91.

37. Fanon, *Wretched of the Earth*, 51, 233.

CHAPTER THREE. NATURALIZATIONS (OTŌSAN)

1. Emerson, *Pele and Hiiaka*, 1–2; trans. by Kanahele, *Ka Honua Ola*, 111. Cf. version used in my *Island World*, 21–22.

2. Emerson, *Pele and Hiiaka*, 92n(d).

3. Kanahele, *Ka Honua Ola*, 55.

4. E.S. Craighill Handy and Elizabeth Green Handy, *Native Planters in Old Hawaii: Their Life, Lore, and Environment*, Bulletin 233 (Honolulu: Bishop Museum Press, 1972), 199–205.

5. Kanahele, *Ka Honua Ola*, 113.

6. Kanahele, *Ka Honua Ola*, 114.

7. Clarence Edward Dutton, *Hawaiian Volcanoes* (1883; reprint, Honolulu: University of Hawaiʻi Press, 2005), 147, 151.

8. Mejiro (white eyes) is native to Japan and East Asia. Its arrival in New York City must have been as a transplant.

9. On the 1790 act and whiteness, see Matthew Frye Jacobson, *Whiteness of a Different Color: European Immigrants and the Alchemy of Race* (Cambridge, MA: Harvard University Press, 1998).

10. U.S. Supreme Court, *Dred Scott v. Sandford*, 60 U.S. 393 (1856).

11. "Women and Naturalization," *Prologue: Quarterly of the National Archives* 30:2 (Summer 1998). In 2015, derivative citizenship is limited to dependent children of parents who naturalize or, under certain circumstances, to foreign-born

children adopted by US citizen parents, as defined by Department of Homeland Security, US Citizenship and Immigration Services, Form N-600, Certificate of Citizenship.

12. Ian Haney López, *White by Law: The Legal Construction of Race* (New York: New York University Press, 2006), 34.

13. This section on my father's military service is a revised version of my *Whispered Silences: Japanese Americans and World War II* (Seattle: University of Washington Press, 1996), 212–15.

14. Okihiro, *Cane Fires*, 249, 250. For a history of the VVV, see Franklin Odo, *No Sword to Bury: Japanese Americans in Hawai'i during World War II* (Philadelphia: Temple University Press, 2004).

15. Okihiro, *Cane Fires*, 251.

16. Okihiro, *Cane Fires*, 255.

17. Chester Tanaka, *Go For Broke: A Pictorial History of the Japanese American 100th Infantry Battalion and the 442d Regimental Combat Team* (Richmond, CA: Go For Broke, 1982), 14.

18. Audrie Girdner and Anne Loftis, *The Great Betrayal: The Evacuation of the Japanese-Americans during World War II* (London: Macmillan, 1969), 331.

19. Martha Beckwith, *Hawaiian Mythology* (Honolulu: University of Hawai'i Press, 1970), 32.

20. Gloria Anzaldúa, *Borderlands: La Frontera: The New Mestiza* (San Francisco: Aunt Lute Books, 1987), 33.

21. Robert Park, "Introduction," in Andrew W. Lind, *An Island Community: Ecological Succession in Hawaii* (Chicago: University of Chicago Press, 1938), xiii.

22. The idea is not original. See, e.g., Brooks Adams, *The Law of Civilization and Decay: An Essay on History* (New York: Macmillan, 1895).

23. Park, "Introduction," xii.

24. From the college alma mater.

25. A. L. Kroeber, *Handbook of the Indians of California*, Smithsonian Institution, Bureau of American Ethnology, Bulletin 78 (Washington, DC: Government Printing Office, 1925), 218.

26. Stephen Powers and John Wesley Powell, *Tribes of California*, Contributions to North American Ethnology, vol. 3, Department of the Interior (Washington, DC: Government Printing Office, 1877), 198.

27. Not to be confused with Frantz Fanon's classic formulation, "Look, a Negro!" *Black Skin, White Masks*, trans. Charles Lam Markmann (New York: Grove Press, 1967), 109, 111–12, 113.

28. "Customs in the Crater," Pacific Union College Student Handbook (rev. 1964–65), 15–16.

29. 2 Corinthians 6:14. The citation concerns yoking with "unbelievers," not (inferior) races.

30. Peggy Pascoe, *What Comes Naturally: Miscegenation Law and the Making of Race in America* (New York: Oxford University Press, 2009), 218.

31. Powers and Powell, *Tribes*, 196, 203.

32. Powers and Powell, *Tribes*, 200.

33. Largely based on interviews with Somersal, researchers published a reference work on the Ashochimi language. Sandra A. Thompson, Joseph Sung-Yul Park, and Charles N. Li, *A Reference Grammar of Wappo* (Berkeley: University of California Press, 2006).

34. Victor Golla, *California Indian Languages* (Berkeley: University of California Press, 2011), 191.

35. Okihiro, *Island World*, 72–82.

36. Okihiro, *Island World*, 82–83.

37. As quoted in Okihiro, *Island World*, 111.

38. Okihiro, *Island World*, 123.

CHAPTER FOUR. EXTINCTIONS

1. Okihiro, *Pineapple Culture*, 32–38.

2. Alexander von Humboldt, *Personal Narrative of Travels in the Equinoctial Regions of America, during the Years 1799-1804*, vol. 1, trans. and ed. Thomasina Ross (London: George Bell and Sons, 1889), xxi.

3. For a history of Humboldt County's anti-Chinese activities during the nineteenth century, see Jean Pfaelzer, *Driven Out: The Forgotten War against Chinese Americans* (Berkeley: University of California Press, 2007), 121–66.

4. Richard Drinnon, *Keeper of Concentration Camps: Dillon S. Myer and American Racism* (Berkeley: University of California Press, 1987).

5. This static rendition of Modoc society misrepresents, of course, its dynamic reality, which eludes me because of my limited historical imagination.

6. For a different origin story, see Rebecca Bales, " 'You Will Be Bravest of All': The Modoc Nation to 1909" (PhD diss., Arizona State University, 2001), 42–44.

7. As cited in Verne F. Ray, *Primitive Pragmatists: The Modoc Indians of Northern California* (Seattle: University of Washington Press, 1963), 21.

8. Ray, *Primitive Pragmatists*, 26.

9. Cited in Bales, " 'You Will Be Bravest'," 48.

10. As recalled by Jefferson C. Davis Riddle, *The Indian History of the Modoc War* (Mechanicsburg, PA: Stackpole Books, 2004), 21.

11. As reported in Bales, " 'You Will Be Bravest'," 179.

12. For a study of the "Ghost Dance," see Cora DuBois, "The 1870 Ghost Dance," *University of California Anthropological Records* 3 (1939): 1–151.

13. On genocide and California Indians, see Benjamin Madley, "California's Yuki Indians: Defining Genocide in Native American History," *Western Historical Quarterly* 39:3 (August 2008): 303–32; Benjamin Logan Madley, "American Genocide: The California Indian Catastrophe, 1846–1873" (PhD diss., History Department, Yale University, May 2009).

14. Arthur Quinn, *Hell with the Fire Out: A History of the Modoc War* (Boston: Faber and Faber, 1997), 39.

15. Quinn, *Hell*, 42.

16. Quoted in Bales, " 'You Will Be Bravest'," 210–11.

17. Riddle, *Indian History*, 69, 72; Bales, " 'You Will Be Bravest'," 228.

18. Bales, " 'You Will Be Bravest'," 228–29.

19. See Erika Lee and Judy Yung, *Angel Island: Immigrant Gateway to America* (New York: Oxford University Press, 2010).

20. Most accounts quote Kintpuash as saying "all ready" or a similar call to arms except Bales, " 'You Will Be Bravest'," 234. See, e.g., Keith A. Murray, *The Modocs and Their War* (Norman: University of Oklahoma Press, 1959), 189; Richard Dillon, *Burnt-Out Fires* (Englewood Cliffs, NJ: Prentice-Hall, 1973), 232.

21. See Okihiro, *Island World*, 25–30.

22. As quoted in Quinn, *Hell*, 72.

23. Quinn, *Hell*, 140; Murray, *Modocs and Their War*, 212.

24. Quinn, *Hell*, 147.

25. Quinn, *Hell*, 162.

26. Cheewa James, *Modoc: The Tribe That Wouldn't Die* (Happy Camp, CA: Naturegraph, 2008), 150.

27. Quinn, *Hell*, 169.

28. Brig. Gen. James T. Kerr, "The Modoc War of 1872–73," in *Proceedings of the Annual Meeting and Dinner of the Order of Indian Wars of the United States*, held January 24, 1931, at the Army and Navy Club, Washington, DC, p. 49.

29. General Sherman to General Schofield, June 3, 1873, House Documents, 43rd Cong., 1st Sess., No. 122, p. 86.

30. As quoted in Quinn, *Hell*, 175–76.

31. For a record of the trial, see "Proceedings of a Military Commission, Fort Klamath, Oregon, For Trial of Modoc Prisoners, July 1873," in War Department, Adjutant General's Office, *Official Copies of Correspondence Relative to the War With Modoc Indians in 1872-73: Prepared under Resolution of the United States House of Representatives, January 7, 1874* (Washington, DC, February 10, 1874).

32. Dillon, *Burnt-Out Fires*, 333–36.

33. Jeremiah Curtin, *Memoirs of Jeremiah Curtin*, ed. Joseph Schafer (Madison: State Historical Society of Wisconsin, 1940), 331, 332.

34. As quoted in Marvin K. Opler, "Japanese Folk Beliefs and Practices, Tule Lake, California," *Journal of American Folklore* 63:250 (October–December 1950): 388–89. Also see my "Religion and Resistance in America's Concentration Camps," *Phylon* 45:3 (September 1984): 220–33.

35. Okihiro, *Cane Fires*, 116–17.

36. See my "Tule Lake under Martial Law: A Study in Japanese Resistance," *Journal of Ethnic Studies* 5:3 (1977): 71–85.

37. "Transcript of the Meeting," November 1, 1943, in Japanese American Research Project, Collection 2010, Research Library, UCLA [henceforth referred to as JARP Collection], Austin Papers, Box 43, Folder 4, Document 3.

38. Drinnon, *Keeper*, 141.

39. Kazue Matsuda, *Poetic Reflections of the Tule Lake Internment Camp, 1944* (n.p., 1987), 15, 23, 26.

40. Drinnon, *Keeper*, 142–43.

41. Another account claims Schaner picked on those two men because they laughed during the roll call. JARP Collection, AP, Folder 8, Document 26.

42. JARP Collection, AP, Folder 8, Document 24.

43. "Stockade Prisoners Rebellion," an investigation by S / Sgt. Sam Yeramian, December 31, 1943, JARP Collection, AP, Folder 7, Document 30.

44. "Stockade Prisoners Rebellion."

45. Interview with Hiroshi Tsuda, January 5, 1944, JARP Collection, AP, Folder 8, Document 8.

46. JARP Collection, AP, Folder 8, Documents 15, 16, 17, 19, 20; "Report of the Informal Interview of the Divisional Responsible Men and the Detained Stockade Internees," January 14, 1944, JARP Collection, AP, Folder 8, Document 26.

47. "Report of Present Condition," Nippon Patriotic Society, JARP Collection, AP, Folder 8, Document 29.

48. Cited and translated in Jeffery F. Burton et al., *Confinement and Ethnicity: An Overview of World War II Japanese American Relocation Sites*, National Park Service, U. S. Department of the Interior, Publications in Anthropology 74 (Tucson, AZ: Western Archeological and Conservation Center, 1999), 300.

49. Burton, *Confinement*, 310.

50. Isaac B. Berkson, *Theories of Americanization* (New York: Teachers College, 1920).

51. Park, "Racial Assimilation in Secondary Groups."

52. As quoted in Okihiro, *Cane Fires*, 143–44.

53. Drinnon, *Keeper*, 50. See also Dillon S. Myer, *Uprooted Americans: The Japanese Americans and the War Relocation Authority during World War II* (Tucson: University of Arizona Press, 1971), 127–43, 286.

54. Drinnon, *Keeper*, 53.

55. Drinnon, *Keeper*, 55. In 1944, the president agreed that placing "one or two families to each county" throughout the United States would help solve the "Japanese problem." Drinnon, *Keeper*, 59.

56. Robert Blauner, *Racial Oppression in America* (New York: Harper & Row, 1972), 67.

57. Frank Miyamoto, "The Structure of Community Relationships," Folder R 20.42, 6–7, Bancroft Library collection of material relating to Japanese American evacuation and resettlement, University of California, Berkeley [henceforth referred to as Bancroft Collection]. See also, "B. B.," "Caucasian Staff at Tule Lake," Folder R 20.15, 8, Bancroft Collection.

58. As quoted in Peter T. Suzuki, "The Ethnolinguistics of Japanese Americans in the Wartime Camps," *Anthropological Linguistics* 18 (December 1976): 422.

59. Tetsuden Kashima, *Buddhism in America* (Westport, CT: Greenwood Press, 1977), 37.

60. G. Gordon Brown, "Final Report on the Gila River Relocation Center as of May 20, 1945," Carr Papers, Box 55, Folder 5, JARP Collection.

61. Lester E. Suzuki, *Ministry in the Assembly and Relocation Centers of World War II* (Berkeley: Yardbird, 1979), 40-41, 345,

62. As quoted by Robert Francis Spencer, "Japanese Buddhism in the United States, 1940-1946: A Study in Acculturation" (PhD diss., University of California, Berkeley, 1946), 172.

63. War Relocation Authority, *WRA, A Story of Human Conservation* (Washington, DC: Government Printing Office, 1946), 95.

64. Opler, "Japanese Folk Beliefs," 385-87.

65. Morris E. Opler and Robert Seido Hashima, "The Rice Goddess and the Fox in Japanese Religion and Folk Practice," *American Anthropologist* 48:1 (January-March 1946): 50.

66. Opler, "Japanese Folk Beliefs," 389-90.

67. Opler and Hashima, "Rice Goddess," 43-50; Opler, "Japanese Folk Beliefs," 391.

68. Marvin K. Opler and F. Obayashi, "Senryu Poetry as Folk and Community Expression," *Journal of American Folklore* 58:227 (January-March 1945): 2.

69. Opler and Obayashi, "Senryu Poetry," 7.

70. Senryu and song lyrics from Opler and Obayashi, "Senryu Poetry," 8-9, 11.

CHAPTER FIVE. THIRD WORLD

1. For a splendid history of this people and region, see Margaret Washington Creel, *"A Peculiar People": Slave Religion and Community-Culture among the Gullahs* (New York: New York University Press, 1988).

2. The following few pages, here revised, appear in my "Self and History," *Rethinking History* 13:1 (March 2009): 9-11.

3. Meena Alexander, *The Shock of Arrival: Reflections on Postcolonial Experience* (Boston: South End Press, 1996).

4. From Freire, *Pedagogy of the Oppressed*.

5. See Tariq Ali and Susan Watkins, *1968: Marching in the Streets* (New York: Free Press, 1998).

6. This section is a revised, edited version of my "Reflections on Viet Nam," in *Tiêp Cân Du'o'ng Dai Văn Hóa My: Contemporary Approaches to American Culture,* ed. Nguyen Lien and Jonathan Auerbach (Hà Nôi: Nhà Xuât Ban Văn Hóa Thông Tin, 2001), 233–46.

7. As quoted in E. Hammer, *The Struggle for Indochina* (Stanford, CA: Stanford University Press, 1954), 102.

8. Excerpted in Rhoads Murphey, *A History of Asia* (New York: HarperCollins, 1996), 395.

9. Robert Buzzanco, *Vietnam and the Transformation of American Life* (Malden, MA: Blackwell, 1999), 144–45, 221.

10. Massimo Teodori, ed., *The New Left: A Documentary History* (Indianapolis: Bobbs-Merrill, 1969), 108; Terry H. Anderson, *The Movement and the Sixties* (New York: Oxford University Press, 1995), 138.

11. Anderson, *Movement,* 146.

12. Teodori, *New Left,* 59.

13. Marilyn B. Young, *The Vietnam Wars, 1945–1990* (New York: HarperCollins, 1991), 197–98.

14. Buzzanco, *Vietnam,* 206.

15. Anderson, *Movement,* 177.

16. Robert R. Moser, *The Winter Soldiers: GI and Veteran Dissent during the Vietnam Era* (New Brunswick, NJ: Rutgers University Press, 1996), 69–70, 71.

17. Stanley Goff and Robert Sanders, *Brothers: Black Soldiers in the Nam* (Novato, CA: Presidio Press, 1982), 1.

18. Young, *Vietnam Wars,* 192, 199.

19. Portions of this section appear in my "Japan, World War II, and Third World Liberation," *Rikkyo American Studies* 31 (March 2009): 77–99.

20. As first published in W. E. Burkhardt Du Bois, "The Freedmen's Bureau," *Atlantic Monthly* 87 (March 1901): 354. See the statement from the first Pan-African Conference in London, 1900, "To the Nations of the World," in *W. E. B. Du Bois: A Reader,* ed. David Levering Lewis (New York: Henry and Holt, 1995), 639. See also W. E. B. Du Bois, *The Souls of Black Folk* (Chicago: A. C. McClurg, 1903), 10; and "The Color Line Belts the World," *Collier's Weekly,* October 20, 1906,

30. Racists used similar language on the problem of the twentieth century. See, e.g., T. Lothrop Stoddard, *The French Revolution in San Domingo* (Boston: Houghton Mifflin, 1914), vii; and his preface in Lothrop Stoddard, *The Rising Tide of Color against White World-Supremacy* (New York: Charles Scribner's Sons, 1920), v–vii.

21. W. E. Burkhardt Du Bois, "The African Roots of War," *Atlantic Monthly* 115 (May 1915): 707–14. For a more contemporary analysis of colonialism and racism, see Robert Miles, *Racism and Migrant Labour: A Critical Text* (London: Routledge and Kegan Paul, 1982); Robert Miles, *Racism* (London: Routledge, 1989).

22. Hubert H. Harrison, *When Africa Awakes: The "Inside Story" of the Stirrings and Strivings of the New Negro in the Western World* (New York: Porro Press, 1920), 5, 6, 96–97.

23. Stoddard, *Rising Tide of Color.*

24. For an account of this conflict and rise and fall of white men, see Marilyn Lake and Henry Reynolds, *Drawing the Global Colour Line: White Men's Countries and the International Challenge of Racial Equality* (Cambridge: Cambridge University Press, 2008).

25. As represented in a commissioned painting, see *Review of Reviews* (London), December 1895, 474–75.

26. Alfred Zimmern, *The Third British Empire* (London: Humphrey Milford, 1926), 82.

27. Gerald Horne, *Race War!: White Supremacy and the Japanese Attack on the British Empire* (New York: New York University Press, 2004), 45.

28. Christopher Thorne, "Racial Aspects of the Far Eastern War of 1941–1945," *Proceedings of the British Academy* (London) 66 (1980): 336. See also Frank Füredi, *The Silent War: Imperialism and the Changing Perception of Race* (London: Pluto Press, 1998), 29–30; Horne, *Race War!*, 251–53.

29. Hugh Tinker, *Race, Conflict and the International Order: From Empire to United Nations* (New York: St. Martin's Press, 1977), 12–14; Füredi, *Silent War*, 2, 27–28, 34.

30. Milton M. Gordon, *Assimilation in American Life: The Role of Race, Religion, and National Origins* (New York: Oxford University Press, 1964), 60–83.

31. Füredi, *Silent War*, 34, 50, 86–87.

32. Park, *Race and Culture*, 82. For a "state of the field" affirmation of Park's views specific to the US South, see Edgar T. Thompson, ed., *Race Relations and the Race Problem: A Definition and Analysis* (Durham, NC: Duke University Press, 1939).

33. See, e.g., Michael Banton, *Race Relations* (New York: Basic Books, 1967); Robert Miles, *Racism after "Race Relations"* (London: Routledge, 1993).

34. Robert E. Park and Ernest W. Burgess, *Introduction to the Science of Sociology* (Chicago: University of Chicago Press, 1926), 578.

35. Thompson, *Race Relations*, vii; Tinker, *Race, Conflict*, 12–14, 42–48; Füredi, *Silent War*, 2, 7.

36. Thorne, "Racial Aspects," 341, 342. See also Christopher Thorne, *The Issue of War: States, Societies, and the Far Eastern Conflict of 1941–1945* (New York: Oxford University Press, 1985), 119–20, 125–31, 135–36; Dower, *War without Mercy*; Füredi, *Silent War*, 18; Yukiko Koshiro, *Trans-Pacific Racisms and the U. S. Occupation of Japan* (New York: Columbia University Press, 1999); Horne, *Race War!*.

37. Thorne, "Racial Aspects," 377.

38. As quoted in Füredi, *Silent War*, 42–43, 44. See also Lake and Reynolds, *Drawing*, 284–309.

39. Thorne, *Issue of War*, 144, 145–46, 148.

40. Akira Iriye, *Power and Culture: The Japanese-American War, 1941–1945* (Cambridge, MA: Harvard University Press, 1981), 97–98, 118–19; Thorne, *Issue of War*, 113, 115.

41. Jawaharlal Nehru, *The Discovery of India* (London: Meridian Books, 1956), 488–89, 492, 495–96, 498–502, 584.

42. Mahatir Mohamad, *A New Deal for Asia* (Tokyo: Tachibana, 1999), 15–17, 68.

43. Horne, *Race War!*, 189. See also Thorne, *Issue of War*, 155, 156.

44. Winston S. Churchill, *The Second World War*, vol. 4, *The Hinge of Fate* (Boston: Houghton Mifflin, 1950), 206.

45. As quoted in Penny M. Von Eschen, *Race against Empire: Black Americans and Anticolonialism, 1937–1957* (Ithaca, NY: Cornell University Press, 1997), 26.

46. As quoted in Horne, *Race War!*, 77, 78. For another overdrawn assessment of a British defeat at the hands of the Japanese, see James Leasor, *Singapore: The Battle That Changed the World* (Garden City, NY: Doubleday, 1968).

47. Thorne, *Issue of War*, 153. See also Horne, *Race War!*, 198, 219, 279, 288–89.

48. As cited in Horne, *Race War!*, 312.

49. Horne, *Race War!*, xiv. See also Tinker, *Race, Conflict*, 42–48.

50. Frank Füredi, *Colonial Wars and the Politics of Third World Nationalism* (London: I. B. Tauris, 1994), 272.

51. Leasor, *Singapore*, 5, 306. See also Thorne, *Issue of War*, 47, 201–3.

52. Füredi, *Silent War*, 1.

53. Quoted in Horne, *Race War!*, 112.

54. David Levering Lewis, *W. E. B. Du Bois: The Fight or Equality and the American Century, 1919–1963* (New York: Henry Holt, 2000), 470.

55. Horne, *Race War!*, 125. See also Marc Gallicchio, *The African American Encounter with Japan and China: Black Internationalism in Asia, 1895–1945* (Chapel Hill: University of North Carolina Press, 2000), 117–21, 204–5.

56. On the global nature of student and social movements of the 1960s, see Alexander Cockburn and Robin Blackburn, eds., *Student Power: Problems, Diagnosis, Action* (Harmondsworth, UK: Penguin Books, 1969); George Katsiaficas, *The Imagination of the New Left: A Global Analysis of 1968* (Boston: South End Press, 1987); Ronald Fraser et al., *1968: A Student Generation in Revolt* (New York: Pantheon Books, 1988).

57. Portions of this chapter's remainder were written for this book, but appeared first in my *Third World Studies*, 15–16.

58. Fanon, *Wretched of the Earth*, 35–36, 311, 315.

59. Fanon, *Wretched of the Earth*, 314.

60. As quoted in George McTurnan Kahin, *The Asian-African Conference, Bandung, Indonesia, April 1955* (Ithaca, NY: Cornell University Press, 1956).

61. The most comprehensive published account of the San Francisco State strike is William H. Orrick, Jr., *Shut It Down! A College in Crisis*, San Francisco State College, October 1968–April 1969, A Staff Report to the National Commission on the Causes and Prevention of Violence (Washington, DC: Government Printing Office, 1969). See also eyewitness accounts by two San Francisco State students, Bill Barlow and Peter Shapiro, a San Francisco State faculty member, Robert Chrisman, and two University of California–Davis sociologists, James McEvoy and Abraham Miller, in *Black Power and Student Rebellion*, ed. James McEvoy and Abraham Miller (Belmont, CA: Wadsworth, 1969), 12–31, 222–32, 277–97.

62. *The Daily Gater* [San Francisco State College], May 22, 1968. The language of this statement draws heavily from the Black Students Union's principles written in late 1966 or early 1967. See Orrick, *Shut It Down!*, 108–9.

63. Memmi, *Colonizer and the Colonized*, 147, 153; Fanon, *Wretched of the Earth*, 246.

64. *The Daily Gater*, May 22, 1969. For the location of the Third World Liberation Front within this context of Third World struggles and not the US civil rights movement, see Jason Michael Ferreira, "All Power to the People: A Comparative History of Third World Radicalism in San Francisco, 1968–1974" (PhD diss., University of California, Berkeley, 2003); Daryl J. Maeda, *Chains of Babylon: The Rise of Asian America* (Minneapolis: University of Minnesota Press, 2009).

65. Joshua Bloom and Waldo E. Martin, Jr., *Black against Empire: The History and Politics of the Black Panther Party* (Berkeley: University of California Press, 2013), 275.

66. On the complexities of the conference and the political stakes for Vietnamese and Third World women in the United States, see Judy Tzu-Chun Wu, *Radicals on the Road: Internationalism, Orientalism, and Feminism during the Vietnam Era* (Ithaca, NY: Cornell University Press, 2013), 219–65.

67. *Asian Women* (Berkeley: n.p., 1971), 79, 80.

68. Fred H. Matthews, *Quest for an American Sociology: Robert E. Park and the Chicago School* (Montreal: McGill-Queen's University Press, 1977), 90–91.

69. Quoted in Winifred Raushenbush, *Robert E. Park: Biography of a Sociologist* (Durham, NC: Duke University Press, 1979), 50. For a review of the Chicago school of sociology, see Andrew Abbott, *Department & Discipline: Chicago Sociology at One Hundred* (Chicago: University of Chicago Press, 1999).

70. See, e.g., William I. Thomas and Florian Znaniecki, *The Polish Peasant in Europe and America: Monograph of an Immigrant Group*, 5 vols. (Chicago: University of Chicago Press, 1918–20); Henry Yu, *Thinking Orientals: Migration, Contact, and Exoticism in Modern America* (New York: Oxford University Press, 2001).

71. Franz Boas, "Introduction," *Handbook of American Indian Languages*, Bulletin 40, Bureau of Ethnology, Smithsonian Institution (Washington, DC: Government Printing Office, 1911), 1–85; George W. Stocking, Jr., *Delimiting Anthropology: Occasional Inquiries and Reflections* (Madison: University of Wisconsin Press, 2001).

72. Stow Persons, *Ethnic Studies at Chicago, 1905-45* (Urbana: University of Illinois Press, 1987), 34-35. Another Midwestern idea was the frontier hypothesis that proposed the American frontier as the leveler of ethnic and class distinctions. See Frederick Jackson Turner, *The Frontier in American History* (New York: Henry Holt, 1920).

73. Likewise, in the 1960s, race riots prompted a study of their causes and remedy. See *Report of the National Advisory Commission on Civil Disorders* (New York: Bantam Books, 1968).

74. Chicago Commission on Race Relations, *The Negro in Chicago: A Study of Race Relations and a Race Riot* (Chicago: University of Chicago Press, 1922).

75. Emory S. Bogardus, "A Race-Relations Cycle," *American Journal of Sociology* 35:4 (January 1930): 612-17; Robert H. Ross and Emory S. Bogardus, "The Second-Generation Race Relations Cycle: A Study in *Issei-Nisei* Relationships," *Sociology and Social Research* 24:4 (March-April 1940): 357-63. See also E. Franklin Frazier's version of Robert Park's cycle in his "Theoretical Structure of Sociology and Sociological Research," *British Journal of Sociology* 4:4 (December 1953): 293-311. Park coined the term "marginal man" in his "Human Migration and the Marginal Man," *American Journal of Sociology* 23:6 (May 1928): 881-93.

76. Robert E. Park, "Introduction," in *The Japanese Invasion: A Study in the Psychology of Inter-Racial Contacts,* by Jesse Frederick Steiner (Chicago: A.C. McClurg, 1917), xvi.

77. See, e.g., Robert E. Park, "The Nature of Race Relations," in Park, *Race and Culture,* 81-116; Park, "Racial Assimilation in Secondary Groups," 610-11. See also Lyman, "Race Relations as Social Process," 370-401.

78. Cf. the resuscitation of ethnicity and assimilation in Richard Alba and Victor Nee, "Rethinking Assimilation Theory for a New Era of Immigration," *International Migration Review* 31:4 (1997): 826-74.

79. Park, "Introduction," in Steiner, *Japanese Invasion,* xiii, xiv.

80. Park, "Introduction," in Steiner, *Japanese Invasion,* xv.

81. Jean-Paul Sartre, "Preface," in Fanon, *Wretched,* 7, 9.

82. Woodson, *Mis-education,* 192.

83. Orrick, *Shut It Down!,* 102.

84. Orrick, *Shut It Down!,* 101.

85. *Daily Gater,* April 16, 1968.

86. *Daily Gater,* April 26, 1968, May 1, 1968, May 16, 1968, May 21, 1968, May 22, 1968.

87. For accounts of the strike, see Orrick, *Shut It Down!,* 37–70; Robert Smith, Richard Axen, and DeVere Pentony, *By Any Means Necessary: The Revolutionary Struggle at San Francisco State* (San Francisco: Jossey-Bass, 1970); Bloom and Martin, Jr., *Black against Empire,* 269–87.

88. As quoted in Bloom and Martin, Jr., *Black against Empire,* 270.

89. Press release from President S. I. Hayakawa, December 6, 1968, San Francisco State University, University Library Archives, College Archives, Box College of Ethnic Studies: Origins—Asian American Studies, Folder College of Ethnic Studies: Origins. The president who settled the strike, Hayakawa distinguished between African and Asian Americans; the latter, he believed, possessed intact cultures and were like Europeans assimilating into the mainstream. Maeda, *Chains of Babylon,* 56–58.

90. *San Francisco State Strike Bulletin,* [n.d.] San Francisco State University, University Library Archives, San Francisco State Strike Collection, Box Third World Liberation Front, Folder 164, Third World Liberation Front. See also, "On Strike, Shut It Down," pamphlet issued by the San Francisco State Strike Committee, [n.d.], San Francisco State University, Labor Archives and Research Center, Box Ephemera Files, LARC, "San Francisco State University—Strike, 1968–1969," Folder San Francisco State University—Strike, 1968.

91. "Demands and Explanations," [n.d.], San Francisco State University, University Library Archives, San Francisco State Strike Collection, Box Third World Liberation Front, Folder 164, Third World Liberation Front.

92. Joint Agreement, March 18, 1969. San Francisco State University. University Library Archives, San Francisco State Strike Collection, Box Third World Liberation Front, Folder 164, Third World Liberation Front.

93. Nancy McDermid, "Strike Settlement," in *Academics on the Line,* ed. Arlene Kaplan Daniels, Rachel Kahn-Hut, et al. (San Francisco: Jossey-Bass, 1970), 229.

94. Orrick, *Shut It Down!,* 78.

95. Private correspondence, October 31, 2011. See also James P. Garrett, "Black / Africana / Pan African Studies: From Radical to Reaction to Reform?—Its Role and Relevance in the Era of Global Capitalism in the New Millennium," *Journal of Pan-African Studies* 1:1 (Fall-Winter 1998–99): 150–79.

96. At the University of California, Berkeley, the Third World Liberation Front demanded a "Third World College," while referring to "Asian Studies, Black Studies, Chicano Studies, Native American Studies" as "ethnic studies programs." Strike Demands, January 1969, Third World Liberation Front, University of California, Berkeley, San Francisco State University, University Library Archives, San Francisco State Strike Collection, Box Third World Liberation Front, Folder 164, Third World Liberation Front.

97. Nathan Hare, "A Conceptual Proposal for a Department of Black Studies," Appendix 4, in Orrick, *Shut It Down!*, 159. See also his account in "A Radical Perspective on Social Science Curricula," in *Black Studies In the University: A Symposium*, ed. Armstead L. Robinson, Craig C. Foster, and Donald H. Ogilvie (New Haven, CT: Yale University Press, 1969), 104–21.

98. Hare, "Conceptual Proposal," 163.

99. See Bloom and Martin, Jr., *Black against Empire*, 271, which describes Hare's "Conceptual Proposal" as having "an anti-imperialist framework."

100. Hare, "Conceptual Proposal," 166.

101. See Dean E. Robinson, *Black Nationalism in American Politics and Thought* (Cambridge: Cambridge University Press, 2001), 104–17, which contends that black nationalism of the 1960s and 1970s adopted the "ethnic paradigm" of the Chicago school of sociology. Cf. Nathan Hare, "The Battle for Black Studies," *Black Scholar* 3:9 (May 1972): 32–47, for his articulation of black education as a means for liberation through the transformation of the black community and the academy.

102. Orrick, *On Strike!*, 116.

103. Smith et al., *By Any Means Necessary*, 140.

104. Frances Beal, "Double Jeopardy: To Be Black and Female," in *Words of Fire: An Anthology of African-American Feminist Thought*, ed. Beverly Guy-Sheftall (New York: New Press, 1995), 146–55.

105. Kimberly Springer, *Living for the Revolution: Black Feminist Organizations, 1968–1980* (Durham, NC: Duke University Press, 2005), 45–49, 185.

106. From an interview in Springer, *Living*, 60.

107. "The Combahee River Collective Statement," in *Home Girls: A Black Feminist Anthology*, ed. Barbara Smith (Latham, NY: Kitchen Table: Women of Color Press, 1983), 26.

108. See, e.g., Kristen Anderson-Bricker, " 'Triple Jeopardy': Black Women and the Growth of Feminist Consciousness in SNCC, 1964-1975," in *Still Lifting, Still Climbing: Contemporary African American Women's Activism*, ed. Kimberly Springer (New York: New York University Press, 1999), 49-69.

109. Kimberlé Crenshaw, "Demarginalizing the Intersection of Race and Sex: A Black Feminist Critique of Antidiscrimination Doctrine, Feminist Theory and Antiracist Politics," *University of Chicago Legal Forum* (1989): 139, 140

110. Patricia Hill Collins, "It's All in the Family: Intersections of Gender, Race, and Nation," *Hypatia* 13:3 (Summer 1998): 62-82; "Gender, Black Feminism, and Black Political Economy," *Annals of the American Academy of Political and Social Science* 568 (2000): 41-53. See also Angela Y. Davis, *Women, Race, and Class* (New York: Random House, 1981); Leith Mullings, *On Our Own Terms: Race, Class, and Gender in the Lives of African American Women* (New York: Routledge, 1997).

111. See, e.g., Cherríe Moraga and Gloria Anzaldúa, eds., *This Bridge Called My Back: Writings by Radical Women of Color* (New York: Kitchen Table: Women of Color Press, 1983); Cherríe Moraga, *Loving in the War Years* (Cambridge, MA: South End Press, 1983); Evelyn Nakano Glenn, "Racial Ethnic Women's Labor: The Intersection of Race, Gender and Class Oppression," *Review of Radical Political Economics* 17:3 (1985): 86-108; Evelyn Nakano Glenn, *Unequal Freedom: How Race and Gender Shaped American Citizenship and Labor* (Cambridge, MA: Harvard University Press, 2002).

112. For the naming and first articulation of "racial formation," see Michael Omi and Howard Winant, *Racial Formation in the United States: From the 1960s to 1980s* (New York: Routledge and Kegan Paul, 1986).

113. Frances Beal, in my telephone conversation with her on November 3, 2017, stressed this important but often overlooked point.

114. See Okihiro and Tsou, "On Social Formation"; Okihiro, *Third World Studies*.

CHAPTER SIX. ANTIPODES

1. For an insightful critique of Sān discourse, particularly ethnographic, and its stakes, see Edwin N. Wilmsen, *Land Filled with Flies: A Political Economy of the Kalahari* (Chicago: University of Chicago Press, 1989), 1-63.

2. "Kgalagadi" not only groups disparate peoples, it designates "servants" and, commonly, animals. Gary Y. Okihiro, *A Social History of the Bakwena and*

Peoples of the Kalahari of Southern Africa, 19th Century (Lewiston, NY: Edwin Mellen Press, 2000), 113–21.

3. David Harvey, *Social Justice and the City* (London: Edward Arnold, 1973), 148–49.

4. This section is a revised version of my "Intellectual Impositions" in Oki-hiro, *Social History*, 148–53.

5. See, e.g., Bronislaw Malinowski, *Argonauts of the Western Pacific* (London: Routledge, 1922); Karl Polanyi, Conrad M. Arensberg, and Harry W. Pearson, eds., *Trade and Market in the Early Empires* (New York: Free Press, 1957); several issues of the *American Anthropologist* in which the debate was carried on; George Dalton, ed., *Tribal and Peasant Economies: Readings in Economic Anthropology* (Garden City, NY: Natural History Press, 1967); George Dalton and Paul Bohannan, *Markets in Africa* (Garden City, NY: Anchor Books, 1965); Marshall Sahlins, *Stone Age Economics* (Chicago: Aldine-Atherton, 1972); A. G. Hopkins, *An Economic History of West Africa* (New York: Columbia University Press, 1973).

6. See, e.g., Raymond Firth, *Primitive Polynesian Economy* (London: Routledge, 1939); Melville J. Herskovits, *Economic Anthropology* (New York: Knopf, 1940); Edward E. LeClair, Jr. and Harold K. Schneider, eds., *Economic Anthropology: Readings in Theory and Analysis* (New York: Holt, Rinehart and Winston, 1968); Polly Hill, *Studies in Rural Capitalism in West Africa* (London: Cambridge University Press, 1970); Harold K. Schneider, *Economic Man: The Anthropology of Economics* (New York: Free Press, 1974).

7. Like Eric R. Wolf, *Sons of the Shaking Earth* (Chicago: University of Chicago Press, 1959); Robert L. Carneiro, "Slash-and-Burn Agriculture: A Closer Look at Its Implications for Settlement Patterns," in *Men and Cultures*, ed. Anthony F. C. Wallace (Philadelphia: University of Pennsylvania Press, 1960); Clifford Geertz, *Agricultural Involution* (Berkeley: University of California Press, 1963); Sherman Roy Krupp, "Equilibrium Theory in Economics and in Functional Analysis as Types of Explanation," in *Functionalism in the Social Sciences*, ed. Don Martindale (Philadelphia: American Academy of Political and Social Science, 1965); Edward Roux, *Grass: A Story of Frankenwald* (Cape Town, South Africa: Oxford University Press, 1969).

8. As in R. F. Salisbury, *From Stone to Steel* (Victoria, Australia: Melbourne University Press, 1962); Dorothy Shineberg, *They Came for Sandalwood* (Victoria, Australia: Melbourne University Press, 1967).

9. See, e.g., the British journal *Economy and Society* during this period; Maurice Bloch, *Marxism and Anthropology: The History of a Relationship* (Oxford: Clarendon Press, 1983); Claude Meillassoux, "From Reproduction to Production: A Marxist Approach to Economic Anthropology," *Economy and Society* 1:1 (February 1972): 93–105; Robert Brenner, "The Origins of Capitalist Development: A Critique of Neo-Smithian Marxism," *New Left Review* 104 (1977): 25–92; Jean Copans and David Seddon, "Marxism and Anthropology: A Preliminary Survey," in *Relations of Production: Marxist Approaches to Economic Anthropology*, ed. David Seddon (London: Frank Cass, 1978), 1–46.

10. Karl Marx, *Pre-Capitalist Economic Formations*, ed. E. J. Hobsbawn (New York: International, 1964); Maurice Godelier, *Rationalité et irrationalité en économie* (Paris: F. Maspero, 1966); Emmanuel Terray, *Marxism and "Primitive" Societies* (New York: Monthly Review Press, 1972); Claude Meillassoux, *Anthropologie economique des Gouro de la Côte d'Ivoire* (Paris: Mouton, 1964); Pierre Philippe Rey, *Colonialisme, neo-colonialisme et transition au capitalism* (Paris: F. Maspero, 1971). See also Catherine Coquery-Vidrovitch, "Recherches sur un mode de production africain," *La Pensee* 144 (1969): 61–78.

11. Colin Bundy, "The Emergence and Decline of a South African Peasantry," *African Affairs* 71:285 (October 1972): 369–88; Robin Palmer and Neil Parsons, eds., *The Roots of Rural Poverty in Central and Southern Africa* (Berkeley: University of California Press, 1977); Colin Bundy, *The Rise and Fall of the South African Peasantry* (Berkeley: University of California Press, 1979); Terence Ranger, "Growing from the Roots: Reflections on Peasant Research in Central and Southern Africa," *Journal of Southern African Studies* 5:1 (October 1978): 99–133; Jack Lewis, "*The Rise and Fall of the South African Peasantry*: A Critique and Reassessment," *Journal of Southern African Studies* 11:1 (October 1984): 1–24.

12. Timothy Keegan, "Trade, Accumulation and Impoverishment: Mercantile Capital and the Economic Transformation of Lesotho and the Conquered Territory, 1870–1920," *Journal of Southern African Studies* 12:2 (April 1986): 196.

13. Leonard Thompson, *African Societies in Southern Africa* (New York: Praeger, 1969); Shula Marks and Anthony Atmore, eds., *Economy and Society in Pre-Industrial South Africa* (London: Longman, 1980); J. B. Peires, *The House of Phalo: A History of the Xhosa People in the Days of Their Independence* (Berkeley: University of California Press, 1982); Peter Delius, *The Land Belongs to Us: The Pedi Polity, the*

Boers and the British in the Nineteenth-Century Transvaal (Berkeley: University of California Press, 1984); William Beinart and Colin Bundy, *Hidden Struggles in Rural South Africa: Politics & Popular Movements in the Transkei & Eastern Cape, 1890-1930* (London: James Currey, 1987); William Beinart, Peter Delius, and Stanley Trapido, eds., *Putting a Plough to the Ground: Accumulation and Dispossession in Rural South Africa, 1850-1930* (Johannesburg: Ravan Press, 1986); and J. B. Peires, *The Dead Will Arise: Nongqawuse and the Great Xhosa Cattle-Killing Movement of 1856-7* (Johannesburg: Ravan Press, 1989).

14. Beinart and Bundy, *Hidden Struggles.*

15. This section is a revised version of my "Bakwena of Molepolole" in Okihiro, *Social History,* 1–25.

16. For instance, I. Schapera, *A Handbook of Tswana Law and Custom* (London: Oxford University Press, 1938).

17. Michel Foucault, *The Foucault Reader,* ed. Paul Rabinow (New York: Pantheon Books, 1984), 76, 77, 81, 82.

18. H/M/105. Kgosing, August 12, 1975. Tumisang Ntloyamodimo, Pepere Gabaraane, and Tsitoeng Mere. These oral histories labeled H / M are in my collection of research notes.

19. H/M/43. Goo-Ra-Tshosa, April 25, 1975. Phutego Mokoka, Magatelo Mokgoko, Ranjahu Kobe, and Nkwane Gaealafshwe.

20. H/M/46. Goo-Ra-Tshosa, April 28, 1975. Phutego Mokoka, Magatelo Mokgoko, Ranjahu Kobe, and Nkwane Gaealafshwe. See Gary Y. Okihiro, "Genealogical Research in Molepolole: A Report on Methodology," *Botswana Notes and Records* 8 (1976): 53–54, for a fuller explanation of the succession and its variant accounts.

21. H/M/102. Kgosing, August 7, 1975. Magatelo Mokgoko, Mapote Keaketswe, Kebelaetse Wamoku, and Koama Motlhale. H/M/123. Chadibe, August 27, 1975. Bale Makepe, Tichara Keabile, Motlhankana Kaang, Mipi Ntsima, and Motai Sekgwa. H/M/125. Ga-Maribana, August 28, 1975. Lekgamelo Sefako, Ramaselesele Difele, Matshego Mojakwate, and Mosarwa Serurubele.

22. A notable twentieth-century assimilation of a large group of immigrants was the Baphalane in 1952–53. See "Bakwena Affairs: Request for Ba-Phalane People to Remove from Vleischfontein (Zeerust Dist.) into Bakwena Reserve," Botswana National Archives (BNA), S. 300/12.

23. For an account of those massive upheavals, see J. D. Omer-Cooper, *The Zulu Aftermath: A Nineteenth-Century Revolution in Bantu Africa* (Evanston, IL: Northwestern University Press, 1966).

24. David Livingstone, for instance, explained some of the motivations for miscounting in a letter to A. Tidman, Kuruman, June 24, 1843, London Missionary Society (Archives of the Council for World Missions), School of Oriental and African Studies, University of London (henceforth LMS-SOAS), Africa, Odds, Box 9, Folder 2A.

25. David Livingstone to A. Tidman, Kuruman, June 24, 1843, LMS-SOAS, Africa, Odds, Box 9, Folder 2A; Gary Y. Okihiro, "Resistance and Accommodation: baKwena-baGasechele, 1842-52," *Botswana Notes and Records* 5 (1973): 111, 116.

26. Okihiro, *Social History,* Appendices B and C.

27. Segakisa's father, Rampena, was a servant of Ngakaemang of the bana ba Motshodi. H/M/53. Difetlhamolelo, June 11, 1975. Letsatsi Mhiko. H/M/127. Goo-Moloi, September 1, 1975. Drake Selwe and Sepotoka Mafuri. H/M/129. Goo-Moloinyana, September 3, 1975. Seforabatho Shatera, Baakane Moloi, and Rakabea Shatera. H/M/149. Difetlhamolelo, September 23, 1975. Kgosinkwe Kgalaeng, Tshweu Kgalaeng, and Pepere Gabaraane.

28. H/M/2. Kgosing, February 13, 1975. Ratlou Ketshabile, Koama Motlhale, Mack K. Sechele II, Pepere Gabaraane, and Kgafela Motswasele.

29. H/M/2. Because Segakisa was old when appointed, his son, Mhiko, replaced him not long after his elevation. H/M/53.

30. H/M/106. Goo-Ra-Tshosa, August 12, 1975. Magatelo Mokgoko, Nkwane Gaealafshwe, Mapote Keaketswe, Samokwati Kgakge, Oatlhotse Kgakge, and Lori Modiakgotla.

31. H/M/122. Goo-Meje, August 27, 1975. Ponatsego Letlamma, Masotho Laolang, Sekaname Setemere, Marumwane Keatlaretsi, and Dorothea Luke.

32. H/M/85. Goo-Ra-Modibedi, July 15, 1975. Sengwato Kobwaatshwene, Mogatsamothosana Modibedi, Okana Modibedi, Magatelo Mokgoko, and Mapote Keaketswe.

33. H/M/56. Goo-Ra-Tshosa, June 19, 1975. Magatelo Mokgoko, Nkwane Gaealafshwe, Mapote Keaketswe, Ratlhaga Kareng, and Kesentswe Kareng. H/M/58. Goo-Kodisa, June 23, 1975. Malanse Bodigelo, Lehubitsa Keetile,

Monametse Gabaki, and Sekee Mogapi. The Babididi were similarly divided into two sections, one kept at Kgosing, the other at Ntlheng-ya Tlhase. H/M/123.

34. See John L. Comaroff and Simon Roberts, *Rules and Processes: The Cultural Logic of Dispute in an African Context* (Chicago: University of Chicago Press, 1981).

35. Like Schapera, *Handbook*. See W. D. Hammond-Tooke, "Descent Groups, Chiefdoms and South African Historiography," *Journal of Southern African Studies* 11:2 (April 1985): 305–19.

36. C. C. Wrigley, "Population in African History," *Journal of African History* 20:1 (1979): 127–31; Georges Dupre and Pierre Philippe Rey, "Reflections on the Relevance of a Theory of the History of Exchange," in *Relations of Production: Marxist Approaches to Economic Anthropology*, ed. David Seddon (London: Frank Cass, 1978), 171–205.

37. H/M/101. Goo-Ra-Tshosa, July 31, 1975. Magatelo Mokgoko, Nkwane Gaealafshwe, Thukhwi Segaetsho, and Keemhitletse Makwati.

38. This section is a revised, condensed version of my "Social Formation" in Okihiro, *Social History*, 86–109.

39. H/M/12. Goo-Ra-Tshosa, February 21, 1975. Thukhwi Segaetsho, Maothwanong Gaealafshwe, Serare Mathong, and Magatelo Mokgoko. H/M/18. Masilwana, March 10, 1975. Kabelo Serole, Keikanetswe Sebolao, Kebopeleng Tshomane, Phutego Kotonyane, Baikalafi Makwatse, and Setlhaku Tawana. H/M/19. Masilwana, March 11, 1975. Kabelo Serole, Kebopeleng Tshomane, Phutego Kotonyane, and Baikalafi Makwatse.

40. David Livingstone to R. Moffat, Kolobeng, August 13, 1847, LMS-SOAS, Africa, Odds, Box 9, Folder 2A; David Livingstone to Benjamin Pyne, Kolobeng, May 28, 1846, LMS-SOAS, Africa, Odds, Box 22; David Livingstone to Agnes Livingstone, Bakwena Country, April 4, 1842, National Library of Scotland (NLS), Ms. 10701; David Livingstone to Mr. Livingston, Kuruman, March 15, 1847, NLS, Ms. 10701.

41. For details on Bakwena agriculture during this period, see William R. Duggan, *An Economic Analysis of Southern African Agriculture* (New York: Praeger, 1986), 69–74.

42. H/M/12; and H/M/28. Kgosing, April 2, 1975. Keakele Sechele II, Nkwane Gaealafshwe, Ditloung Kusi, and Tshitshawenyane Tebele.

43. See David Livingstone, *Missionary Travels and Researches in South Africa* (London: John Murray, 1857), 22.

44. H/M/23. Kgosing, March 20, 1975. Keakele Sechele II, Nkwane Gaealafshwe, Ditloung Kusi, and Tshitshawenyane Tebele.

45. H/M/22. Kgosing, March 19, 1975. Keakele Sechele II, Nkwane Gaealafshwe, Ditloung Kusi, and Tshitshawenyane Tebele. H/M/32. Ga-Morwa, April 11, 1975. Kabelo Kebakae and Gagonthone Kgari.

46. See London Missionary Society, *The Masarwa (Bushmen): Report of an Inquiry* (Lovedale, South Africa: Lovedale Press, 1935), for a discussion on the Bangwato use of Sān labor; and Gaontatlhe Mautle, "Bakgalagadi-Bakwena Relationship: A Case of Slavery, c.1840-c.1920," *Botswana Notes and Records* 18 (1986): 19–31.

47. My women interviewees made this distinction between less ambitious and industrious cultivators. I see both as rational, economic choices. H/M/14. Maunatlala, February 26, 1975. Semetsataola Maselesele, Kokwe Segaetsho, Sepotoka Mafuri, Ramotoko Nonyane, Matome Mpusang, and Moagi Sebomo. H/M/23.

48. H/M/23. See also H/M/11. Goo-Ra-Tshosa, February 20, 1975. Thukhwi Segaetsho, Phutego Mokoka, Maothwanong Gaealafswe, Serare Mathong, and Magatelo Mokgoko.

49. H/M/22; H/M/23.

50. Henry H. Methuen, *Life in the Wilderness* (London: R. Bentley, 1846), 185–86. See also Roualeyn Gordon Cumming, *Five Years of a Hunter's Life in the Far Interior of South Africa*, vol. 1 (London: John Murray, 1850), 232.

51. H/M/20. Masilwana, March 16, 1975. Kabelo Serole, Kebopeleng Tshomane, and Phutego Kotonyane. H/M/28.

52. V. Ellenberger, "Di Robaroba Matlhakola—Tsa Ga Mosodi-a-Mphela," *Transactions of the Royal Society of South Africa* 25 (1937–38): 36, 44; Cumming, *Five Years*, 1:232; Methuen, *Life in the Wilderness*, 142, 145, 182–84; I. Schapera, ed., *Livingstone's Missionary Correspondence, 1841–1856* (Berkeley: University of California Press, 1961), 34–35; David Chamberlin, ed., *Some Letters from Livingstone, 1840–1872* (London: 1940), 41, 81.

53. Livingstone, *Missionary Travels*, 22; Schapera, *Missionary Correspondence*, 127; I. Schapera, ed., *Livingstone's Private Journals, 1851–1853* (Berkeley: University

of California Press, 1960), 304; I. Schapera, ed., *David Livingstone Family Letters, 1841-1848*, vol. 1 (London: Chatto & Windus, 1959), 213–14; I. Schapera, ed., *David Livingstone Family Letters, 1849-1856*, vol. 2 (London: Chatto & Windus, 1959), 25, 28, 49, 60.

54. H/M/28.

55. H/M/27. Kgosing, April 2, 1975. Keakile Sechele II, Nkwane Gaealafshwe, Ditloung Kusi, and Tshitshawenyane Tebele.

56. A sesigo was over two meters high, and had a capacity of over eight hectoliters. Often, the basket was mounted on stones and propped up with supporting stakes. See Robert Moffat, *Apprenticeship at Kuruman*, ed. I. Schapera (London: Chatto & Windus, 1951), 136–37; Robert Moffat, *Missionary Labours and Scenes in Southern Africa* (London: John Snow, 1842), 399; John Barrow, *A Voyage to Cochin-China* (London: T. Cadell & W. Davies, 1806), 392; John Campbell, *Travels in South Africa*, vol. 1 (London: London Missionary Society, 1822), 244.

57. See Duggan, *Southern African Agriculture*, 80–85, for details of women's controls over grains.

58. H/M/22; H/M/23.

59. See, e.g., David Livingstone to Mr. Livingston, Kuruman, March 15, 1847, NLS, Ms. 10701.

60. H/B/1. Ga-Basimane, November 8, 1975. Chabai Chuba, Motshipa Keimetswe, Ntlhogo Keborometswe, Dao Keborometswe, Masego Golwelwang, Ranto Thebogo, and Gaogilwe Motshipa. H/B/2. Boatlaname primary school, November 8, 1975. Kwalona Kgotladintsi, Setsowarona Kgotladintsi, Lepodisi Ratlhaga, and Thankwane Rakhama. H/B oral histories are in my research collection.

61. The neighboring Bangwato used ploughs as early as 1878, and a 1911 census revealed 767 ploughs in the Kweneng. Duggan, *Southern African Agriculture*, 103–5.

62. H/M/23.

63. David Livingstone to Janet Livingston, Kolobeng, April 20, 1849, NLS, Ms. 10701; H. Helmore to J. J. Freeman, Likatlong, October 30, 1851, LMS-SOAS, South Africa, Incoming Letters, Box 27, Folder 1, Jacket B.

64. H/M/3. Kgosing, February 12, 1975. Timpa Mosarwa, Koama Motlhale, Mack K. Sechele II, Pepere Gabaraane, and Kgafela Motswasele. Cf. Duggan, *Southern African Agriculture*, 105.

65. H/M/31. Ga-Morwa, April 10, 1975. Kabelo Kebakae and Gagonthone Kgari.

66. H/M/24. Kgosing, March 21, 1975. Keakele Sechele II, Nkwane Gaealaf-shwe, Ditloung Kusi, and Tshitshawenyane Tebele. H/M/26. Kgosing, March 26, 1975. Keakele Sechele II, Nkwane Gaealafshwe, Ditloung Kusi, and Tshitshawen-yane Tebele.

67. According to European travelers, the Bahurutshe had precedence in first-fruits and the exclusive right to grow tobacco. See, e.g., Moffat, *Apprentice-ship*, 187; William J. Burchell, *Travels in the Interior of Southern Africa*, vol. 2 (London: Longman, Hurst, Rees, Orme, and Brown, 1824), 321; Campbell, *Travels*, 2:216; Percival R. Kirby (ed.), *The Diary of Dr. Andrew Smith*, vols. 1 (Cape Town, 1939), 251, and 2 (Cape Town, 1940), 221–22; Livingstone, *Missionary Travels*, 51; Schapera, *Handbook*, 3–4.

68. H/M/78. Masilwana, July 10, 1975. Motlhatsi Baakang.

69. H/M/9. Goo-Ra-Tshosa, February 19, 1975. Thukhwi Segaetsho, Maothwanong Gaealafshwe, Serare Mathong, Magatelo Mokgoko, and Phutego Mokoka. H/M/11; H/M/23; and H/M/78.

70. H/M/9; H/M/11.

71. H/M/100. Goo-Ra-Tshosa, July 30, 1975. Magatelo Mokgoko, Nkwane Gaealafshwe, Mapote Keaketswe, and Thukhwi Segaetsho.

72. H/M/90. Goo-Ra-Tshosa, July 21, 1975. Magatelo Mokgoko, Nkwane Gae-alafshwe, Mapote Keaketswe, and Keemhitletse Makwati.

73. Schapera, *Handbook*, 128.

74. H/M/69. Goo-Ra-Tshosa, July 2, 1975. Magatelo Mokgoko, Nkwane Gae-alafshwe, Samokwati Kgakge, Thukhwi Segaetsho, and Keemhitletse Makwati.

75. H/M/12.

76. H/M/61. Goo-Ra-Tshosa, June 26, 1975. Magatelo Mokgoko, Nkwane Gaealafshwe, and Mapote Keaketswe. H/M/69.

77. See, e.g., Gofetakgosi's rise in H/M/54. Goo-Ra-Tshosa, June 13, 1975. Samokwati Kgakge and Selebatso G. Masimega. H/M/71. Goo-Ra-Tshosa, July 3, 1975. Magatelo Mokgoko, Nkwane Gaealafshwe, Samokwati Kgakge, Thukhwi Segaetsho, and Mapote Keaketswe. H/M/73. Goo-Ra-Tshosa, July 7, 1975. Magatelo Mokgoko, Nkwane Gaealafshwe, Mapote Keaketswe, Thukhwi Segaet-sho, and Motlhanka Morewang.

78. H/M/70. Goo-Ra-Tshosa, July 2, 1975. Magatelo Mokgoko, Nkwane Gae-alafshwe, Samokwati Kgakge, Thukhwi Segaetsho, Keemhitletse Makwati, and Motlhanka Morewang. H/M/71; H/M/73.

79. H/M/71; H/L/12. Kgesakwe, October 18, 1975. Koepile Sesinye, Kobatile Lentswe, Tinye Baikgati, Mpolaekeswe Banyatsi, and Papadi Sesinye. H/L oral histories are in my research collection.

80. W. H. Surmon to The Resident Commissioner, Gaberones, September 5, 1896, BNA, RC. 4/4; W. H. Surmon to The Resident Commissioner, Gaberone's, August 8, 1901, BNA, RC. 5/5; J. Ellenberger to The Acting Resident Commissioner, Gaberone's, August 31, 1900, BNA, RC. 5/12.

81. See, e.g., Wilmsen, *Land Filled;* Susan G. Wynne, "The Land Boards of Botswana: A Problem in Institutional Design" (PhD diss., Indiana University, 1989).

82. Margaret Kinsman, "Notes on the Southern Tswana Social Formation," in *Africa Seminar: Collected Papers,* no. 2, ed. K. Gottschalk and C. Saunders (Centre for African Studies, University of Cape Town, 1981); Jeff Guy, "Analysing Pre-Capitalist Societies in Southern Africa," *Journal of Southern African Studies* 14:1 (October 1987): 18–37.

83. Belinda Bozzoli, "Marxism, Feminism and South African Studies," *Journal of Southern African Studies* 9:2 (April 1983): 140–71; Margaret Kinsman, " 'Beasts of Burden': The Subordination of Southern Tswana Women, ca.1800–1840," *Journal of Southern African Studies* 10:1 (October 1983): 39–54; Jeff Guy, "Gender Oppression in Southern Africa's Precapitalist Societies," in *Women and Gender in Southern Africa to 1945,* ed. Cherryl Walker (Cape Town, South Africa: David Philip, 1990), 33–47.

84. *Honolulu Star-Bulletin,* November 16, 1998. See also *Honolulu Advertiser,* June 6, 2002.

85. *Honolulu Star-Bulletin,* November 16, 1998.

CHAPTER SEVEN. HISTORY

1. Derek Howse, *Greenwich Time and the Discovery of the Longitude* (Oxford: Oxford University Press, 1980), 127–29, 138–51.

2. A version of this discussion of space / time was published in "Of Space / Time and the Pineapple," *Atlantic Studies* 11:1 (January 2014): 85–102.

3. See the distinction between space and place, movement and pause, by geographer Yi-Fu Tuan in his *Space and Place: The Perspective of Experience* (Minneapolis: University of Minnesota Press, 1977).

4. Brian Greene, *The Fabric of the Cosmos: Space, Time, and the Texture of Reality* (New York: Vintage Books, 2005), ix.

5. Brian Greene, *The Hidden Reality: Parallel Universes and the Deep Laws of the Cosmos* (New York: Vintage Books, 2011), 17.

6. Greene, *Hidden Reality*, 77.

7. Related is the observer effect that holds observations and measurements cannot be made without affecting the system.

8. Cf. W. H. Newton-Smith, *The Structure of Time* (London: Routledge & Kegan Paul, 1980), 241, on the philosophy of time that gestures toward "a positive theory" of time with an understanding of time as indeterminate or a theoretical system "up to underdeterminism."

9. Jean Toomer, *Cane* (1923; reprint, New York: Liveright, 1975), 16.

10. Of course, that biological clock is restricted to humans. Life cycles and evolutionary changes are much more rapid among bacteria and fruit flies, for instance.

11. Judith Halberstam, *In a Queer Time and Place: Transgender Bodies, Subcultural Lives* (New York: New York University Press, 2005), 6.

12. For a more recent example, see Giovanni Arrighi, *The Long Twentieth Century: Money, Power and the Origins of Our Times* (London: Verso, 1994, 2010).

13. Duan Zhongqia, *Marx's Theory of the Social Formation* (Aldershot, UK: Avebury, 1995), 9-10, 11.

14. As quoted in Duan, *Marx's Theory*, 12.

15. K. N. Chaudhuri, *Asia before Europe: Economy and Civilisation of the Indian Ocean from the Rise of Islam to 1750* (Cambridge: Cambridge University Press, 1990), 19-21, 24, 112-13. See Sugata Bose's critique of Chaudhuri in his *A Hundred Horizons: The Indian Ocean in the Age of Global Empire* (Cambridge, MA: Harvard University Press, 2006), 5, 11-12.

16. Claude Lévi-Strauss, *Tristes tropiques*, trans. John and Doreen Weightman (New York: Penguin Books, 1973), 412.

17. Michel Foucault, "Of Other Spaces," trans. Jay Miskowiec, *Diacritics* 16:1 (Spring 1986): 22, 23.

18. Michel Foucault, *Power / Knowledge: Selected Interviews and Other Writings, 1972–1977*, ed. Colin Gordon (New York: Pantheon Books, 1972), 69, 77.

19. Gaston Bachelard, *The Poetics of Space*, trans. Maria Jolas (Boston: Beacon Press, 1969), xv, xvi.

20. Bachelard, *Poetics*, xvii, xviii, xix, xx.

21. Henri Lefebvre, *The Production of Space*, trans. Donald Nicholson-Smith (Malden, MA: Blackwell, 1991).

22. Edward W. Soja, *Postmodern Geographies: The Reassertion of Space in Critical Social Theory* (London: Verso, 1989), 10–11, 15, 18–19, 22–23.

23. Doreen Massey, *For Space* (Los Angeles: Sage, 2005). See also Doreen Massey, "Politics and Space / Time," *New Left Review* 196 (November–December 1992): 65–84; Elizabeth Grosz, *Space, Time, and Perversion: Essays on the Politics of Bodies* (New York: Routledge, 1995).

24. Harvey, *Social Justice*, 10–11, 13, 23–24, 34, 36. For a useful collection of essays on social processes and spatial forms, see Derek Gregory and John Urry, eds., *Social Relations and Spatial Structures* (New York: St. Martin's Press, 1985).

25. Tuan, *Space and Place*, 16–17, 34–38, 120–21.

26. Bose, *Hundred Horizons*, 6, 7. See Barbara Watson Andaya, "Oceans Unbounded: Traversing Asia across 'Area Studies'," *Journal of Asian Studies* 65:4 (November 2006): 669–90, for a similar rearticulation of Asian studies from land-based to ocean-based formations.

27. Antonio Benítez-Rojo, *The Repeating Island: The Caribbean and the Postmodern Perspective*, trans. James Maraniss, 2nd ed. (Durham, NC: Duke University Press, 1996), 2.

28. Clifford Geertz, *Local Knowledge: Further Essays in Interpretive Anthropology* (New York: Basic Books, 1983), 13, 15, 16, 232–34.

29. Mills, *Sociological Imagination*, 145.

30. Aimé Césaire, "Poetry and Knowledge," in *Refusal of the Shadow: Surrealism and the Caribbean*, ed. Michael Richardson, trans. Krzysztof Fijatkowski and Michael Richardson (London: Verso, 1996), 134.

31. See, e.g., the essays in Rob Wilson and Wimal Dissanayake, eds., *Global / Local: Cultural Production and the Transnational Imaginary* (Durham, NC: Duke University Press, 1996).

32. From Rob Wilson and Wimal Dissanayake, "Introduction: Tracking the Global / Local," in Wilson and Dissanayake, *Global / Local*, 2.

33. Lewis and Wigen, *Myth of Continents*.

34. Immanuel Wallerstein, *The Modern World-System* (New York: Academic Press, 1974).

35. See, e.g., Lake and Reynolds, *Drawing the Global Colour Line*.

36. Venuti, *Translation Studies*, 13.

37. Schleiermacher's 1813 lecture, "On the Different Methods of Translating," as translated by Susan Bernofsky, appears in Venuti, *Translation Studies*, 43–63.

38. Jane Bennett, *The Enchantment of Modern Life: Attachments, Crossings, and Ethics* (Princeton, NJ: Princeton University Press, 2001).

39. Walter Benjamin, "The Task of the Translator," from his *Illuminations*, trans. Harry Zohn (1955; reprint, edited and with an introduction by Hannah Arendt, New York: Schocken Books, 1969), 69–82.

40. Gayatri Chakravorty Spivak, "The Politics of Translation," from her *Outside in the Teaching Machine*, reprinted in Venuti, *Translation Studies*, 369.

41. Venuti, *Translation Studies*, 20.

42. Leila Khaled, *My People Shall Live: The Autobiography of a Revolutionary*, ed. George Hajjar (London: Hodder and Stoughton, 1973), 10, 150.

43. John Beverley, "The Margin at the Center: On *Testimonio* (Testimonial Narrative)," in *De / Colonizing the Subject: The Politics of Gender in Women's Autobiography*, ed. Sidonie Smith and Julia Watson (Minneapolis: University of Minnesota Press, 1992), 91–114, contends that testimonios are testimony in the juridical sense and not oral histories, which are "documents." I disagree with that distinction.

44. Georg Gugelberger and Michael Kearney, "Voices for the Voiceless: Testimonial Literature in Latin America," *Latin American Perspectives* 18:3 (Summer 1991): 4, 9.

45. Lynda Marín, "Speaking Out Together: Testimonials of Latin American Women," *Latin American Perspectives* 18:3 (Summer 1991): 51–68. Perhaps the best-known testimonio is Rigoberta Menchú, *I, Rigoberta Menchú: An Indian Woman in Guatemala*, ed. Elisabeth Burgos-Debray, trans. Ann Wright (London: Verso, 1984).

Notes

46. Domitila Barrios de Chungara with Moema Viezzer, *Let Me Speak! Testimony of Domitila, a Woman of the Bolivian Mines*, trans. Victoria Ortiz (New York: Monthly Review Press, 1978), 15.

47. Williams, *Marxism and Literature*, 193–94.

48. Julia Watson and Sidonie Smith, "De / Colonization and the Politics of Discourse in Women's Autobiographical Practices," in Smith and Watson, *De / Colonizing the Subject*, xvii.

49. From H/M/1. February 12, 1975, Kgosing, Molepolole. Timpa Mosarwa. Interviewer: Gary Y. Okihiro. Translator: Selebatso G. Masimega.

50. From Gayatri Chakravorty Spivak, "Can the Subaltern Speak?" in *Marxism and the Interpretation of Culture*, ed. Cary Nelson and Lawrence Grossberg (London: Macmillan, 1988). Cf. Linda Martín Alcoff, "The Problem of Speaking for Others," in *Who Can Speak? Authority and Critical Identity*, ed. Judith Butler and Robyn Wiegman (Urbana: University of Illinois Press, 1995), 97–119.

51. For an explication of oral history as a conversation, see my "Oral History and the Writing of Ethnic History: A Reconnaissance into Method and Theory," *Oral History Review* 9 (1981): 27–46.

52. This composite account is taken from Kerr, "Eastern Sea Islands," Y1–Y2; Kerr, [untitled], 178–80; Ikema, *Yonaguni*, 66–72; and as told by Yoneshiro Megumu, Yonaguni Island, November 30, 2009. Cf. the version by Ikema, *Yonaguni*, 66–72.

53. E-mail, Yamazato Katsunori to Gary Y. Okihiro, July 23, 2010.

54. Translation from English into Japanese by Yamazato Katsunori, and edited (underlines in text) by Yoneshiro Megumu. Reproduction by Takai Shiho.

55. See, e.g., Héctor Lindo-Fuentes, Erik Ching, and Rafael A. Lara-Martínez, *Remembering a Massacre in El Salvador: The Insurrection of 1932, Roque Dalton, and the Politics of Historical Memory* (Albuquerque: University of New Mexico Press, 2007); Jeffrey L. Gould and Aldo A. Lauria-Santiago, *To Rise in Darkness: Revolution, Repression, and Memory in El Salvador, 1920–1932* (Durham, NC: Duke University Press, 2008).

PRIMARY DOCUMENTS

Botswana National Archives.

The Daily Gater [San Francisco State College].

Honolulu Star-Bulletin.

National Library of Scotland, Edinburgh.

Okinawa Prefectural Archives.

Oral History. Okinawa, 2009.

Oral History Research Notes. Botswana, 1975.

San Francisco State University. Labor Archives and Research Center.

San Francisco State University. University Library Archives. College Archives.

University of California, Berkeley. Bancroft Library. Japanese American Evacuation and Resettlement.

University of California, Los Angeles. Research Library. Japanese American Research Project.

University of London. London Missionary Society (Archives of the Council for World Missions). School of Oriental and African Studies.

US House Documents. 43rd Congress, 1st Session. No. 122.

US War Department. Adjutant General's Office. *Official Copies of Correspondence Relative to the War with Modoc Indians in 1872-73: Prepared under Resolution of the United States House of Representatives, January 7, 1874.* Washington, DC.

SECONDARY WORKS

Abbott, Andrew. *Department & Discipline: Chicago Sociology at One Hundred*. Chicago: University of Chicago Press, 1999.

Adams, Brooks. *The Law of Civilization and Decay: An Essay on History*. New York: Macmillan, 1895.

Alba, Richard, and Victor Nee. "Rethinking Assimilation Theory for a New Era of Immigration." *International Migration Review* 31:4 (1997): 826–74.

Alcoff, Linda Martín. "The Problem of Speaking for Others." In *Who Can Speak? Authority and Critical Identity*, edited by Judith Butler and Robyn Wiegman. Urbana: University of Illinois Press, 1995.

Alexander, Meena. *The Shock of Arrival: Reflections on Postcolonial Experience*. Boston: South End Press, 1996.

Ali, Tariq, and Susan Watkins. *1968: Marching in the Streets*. New York: Free Press, 1998.

Althusser, Louis. *Essays on Ideology*. London: Verso, 1984.

Andaya, Barbara Watson. "Oceans Unbounded: Traversing Asia across 'Area Studies'." *Journal of Asian Studies* 65:4 (November 2006): 669–90.

Anderson, Benedict. *Imagined Communities: Reflections on the Origin and Spread of Nationalism*. London: Verso, 1983.

Anderson, Terry H. *The Movement and the Sixties*. New York: Oxford University Press, 1995.

Anderson-Bricker, Kristen. "'Triple Jeopardy': Black Women and the Growth of Feminist Consciousness in SNCC, 1964–1975." In *Still Lifting, Still Climbing: Contemporary African American Women's Activism*, edited by Kimberly Springer. New York: New York University Press, 1999.

Anzaldúa, Gloria. *Borderlands: La Frontera: The New Mestiza*. San Francisco: Aunt Lute Books, 1987.

Arrighi, Giovanni. *The Long Twentieth Century: Money, Power and the Origins of Our Times*. London: Verso, 1994, 2010.

Asian Women. Berkeley: n.p., 1971.

Bachelard, Gaston. *The Poetics of Space*. Translated by Maria Jolas. Boston: Beacon Press, 1969.

Bales, Rebecca. "'You Will Be Bravest of All': The Modoc Nation to 1909." PhD diss., Arizona State University, 2001.

Balibar, Étienne. "The Nation Form: History and Ideology." In *Race, Nation, Class: Ambiguous Identities*, by Étienne Balibar and Immanuel Wallerstein. London: Verso, 1991.

Banton, Michael. *Race Relations*. New York: Basic Books, 1967.

Barrow, John. *A Voyage to Cochin-China*. London: T. Cadell & W. Davies, 1806.

Beale, Frances. "Double Jeopardy: To Be Black and Female." In *Words of Fire: An Anthology of African-American Feminist Thought*, edited by Beverly Guy-Sheftall. New York: New Press, 1995.

Beckwith, Martha. *Hawaiian Mythology*. Honolulu: University of Hawai'i Press, 1970.

Beechert, Edward D. *Working in Hawaii: A Labor History*. Honolulu: University of Hawai'i Press, 1985.

Beillevaire, Patrick. "The Western Discovery of Ryūkyū: From the First Contacts to the Eve of Perry's Expedition." In *Ryūkyū Studies to 1854: Western Encounter*, part I, vol. 1, edited by Patrick Beillevaire. Richmond, Surrey, UK: Curzon Press, 2000.

Beinart, William, and Colin Bundy. *Hidden Struggles in Rural South Africa: Politics & Popular Movements in the Transkei & Eastern Cape, 1890–1930*. London: James Currey, 1987.

Beinert, William, Peter Delius, and Stanley Trapido, eds. *Putting a Plough to the Ground: Accumulation and Dispossession in Rural South Africa, 1850–1930*. Johannesburg: Ravan Press, 1986.

Benítez-Rojo, Antonio. *The Repeating Island: The Caribbean and the Postmodern Perspective*. Translated by James Maraniss. Durham, NC: Duke University Press, 1996.

Benjamin, Walter. *Illuminations*. Translated by Harry Zohn. Edited by Hannah Arendt. New York: Schocken Books, [1955] 1969.

Bennett, Jane. *The Enchantment of Modern Life: Attachments, Crossings, and Ethics*. Princeton, NJ: Princeton University Press, 2001.

Berkson, Isaac B. *Theories of Americanization*. New York: Teachers College, 1920.

Beverley, John. "The Margin at the Center: On *Testimonio* (Testimonial Narrative)." In *De/Colonizing the Subject: The Politics of Gender in Women's Autobiography*, edited by Sidonie Smith and Julia Watson. Minneapolis: University of Minnesota Press, 1992.

Bickerton, Derek. "Pidgins and Language Mixture." In *Creole Genesis, Attitudes and Discourse: Studies Celebrating Charlene J. Sato*, edited by John R. Rickford and Suzanne Romaine. Amsterdam: John Benjamins, 1999.

———. *Roots of Language*. Ann Arbor, MI: Karoma, 1981.

Blauner, Robert. *Racial Oppression in America*. New York: Harper & Row, 1972.

Bloch, Maurice. *Marxism and Anthropology: The History of a Relationship*. Oxford: Clarendon Press, 1983.

Bloom, Joshua, and Waldo E. Martin, Jr. *Black against Empire: The History and Politics of the Black Panther Party*. Berkeley: University of California Press, 2013.

Boas, Franz. "Introduction." In *Handbook of American Indian Languages*. Bulletin 40. Bureau of Ethnology, Smithsonian Institution. Washington, DC: Government Printing Office, 1911.

Bogardus, Emory S. "A Race-Relations Cycle." *American Journal of Sociology* 35:4 (January 1930): 612–17.

Bose, Sugata. *A Hundred Horizons: The Indian Ocean in the Age of Global Empire*. Cambridge, MA: Harvard University Press, 2006.

Bozzoli, Belinda. "Marxism, Feminism and South African Studies." *Journal of Southern African Studies* 9:2 (April 1983): 140–71.

Brandt, Anthony, Molly Gebrian, and L. Robert Slevc. "Music and Early Language Acquisition." *Frontiers in Psychology* 3 (September 2012): 1–17.

Brenner, Robert. "The Origins of Capitalist Development: A Critique of Neo-Smithian Marxism." *New Left Review* 104 (1977): 25–92.

Bundy, Colin. "The Emergence and Decline of a South African Peasantry." *African Affairs* 71:285 (October 1972): 369–88.

———. *The Rise and Fall of the South African Peasantry*. Berkeley: University of California Press, 1979.

Burchell, William J. *Travels in the Interior of Southern Africa*. Vol. 2. London: Longman, Hurst, Rees, Orme, and Brown, 1824.

Burton, Jeffery F. et al. *Confinement and Ethnicity: An Overview of World War II Japanese American Relocation Sites*. National Park Service. U.S. Department of the Interior. Publications in Anthropology 74. Tucson, AZ: Western Archeological and Conservation Center, 1999.

Buzzanco, Robert. *Vietnam and the Transformation of American Life*. Malden, MA: Blackwell, 1999.

Campbell, John. *Travels in South Africa*. Vols. 1 and 2. London: London Missionary Society, 1822.

Carneiro, Robert L. "Slash-and-Burn Agriculture: A Closer Look at Its Implications for Settlement Patterns." In *Men and Cultures*, edited by Anthony F.C. Wallace. Philadelphia: University of Pennsylvania Press, 1960.

Carr, Elizabeth Ball. *Da Kine Talk: From Pidgin to Standard English in Hawaii*. Honolulu: University of Hawai'i Press, 1972.

Césaire, Aimé. *Discourse on Colonialism*. Translated by Joan Pinkham. New York: Monthly Review Press [1955] 2000.

———. "Poetry and Knowledge." In *Refusal of the Shadow: Surrealism and the Caribbean*, edited by Michael Richardson. Translated by Krzysztof Fijatkowski and Michael Richardson. London: Verso, 1996.

Chamberlin, David, ed.. *Some Letters from Livingstone, 1840–1872*. London: 1940.

Chaudhuri, K.N. *Asia before Europe: Economy and Civilisation of the Indian Ocean from the Rise of Islam to 1750*. Cambridge: Cambridge University Press, 1990.

Ch'en, Ta-tuan. "Investiture of Liu-Ch'iu Kings in the Ch'ing Period." In *The Chinese World Order: Traditional China's Foreign Relations*, edited by John King Fairbank. Cambridge, MA: Harvard University Press, 1968.

Chicago Commission on Race Relations. *The Negro in Chicago: A Study of Race Relations and a Race Riot*. Chicago: University of Chicago Press, 1922.

Christy, Alan S. "The Making of Imperial Subjects in Okinawa." *positions* 1:3 (Winter 1993): 607–39.

Churchill, Winston S. *The Second World War*. Vol. 4, *The Hinge of Fate*. Boston: Houghton Mifflin, 1950.

Cockburn, Alexander, and Robin Blackburn, eds. *Student Power: Problems, Diagnosis, Action*. Harmondsworth, UK: Penguin Books, 1969.

Collins, Patricia Hill. "Gender, Black Feminism, and Black Political Economy." *Annals of the American Academy of Political and Social Science* 568 (2000): 41–53.

———. "It's All in the Family: Intersections of Gender, Race, and Nation." *Hypatia* 13:3 (Summer 1998): 62–82.

Comaroff, John L., and Simon Roberts, *Rules and Processes: The Cultural Logic of Dispute in an African Context*. Chicago: University of Chicago Press, 1981.

"The Combahee River Collective Statement." In *Home Girls: A Black Feminist Anthology*, edited by Barbara Smith. Latham, NY: Kitchen Table: Women of Color Press, 1983.

Copans, Jean, and David Seddon. "Marxism and Anthropology: A Preliminary Survey." In *Relations of Production: Marxist Approaches to Economic Anthropology*, edited by David Seddon. London: Frank Cass, 1978.

Coquery-Vidrovitch, Catherine. "Recherches sur un mode de production africain." *La Pensee* 144 (1969): 61–78.

Creel, Margaret Washington. *"A Peculiar People": Slave Religion and Community-Culture among the Gullahs*. New York: New York University Press, 1988.

Crenshaw, Kimberlé. "Demarginalizing the Intersection of Race and Sex: A Black Feminist Critique of Antidiscrimination Doctrine, Feminist Theory and Antiracist Politics." *University of Chicago Legal Forum* (1989): 139–67.

Cumming, Roualeyn Gordon. *Five Years of a Hunter's Life in the Far Interior of South Africa*. Vol. 1. London: John Murray, 1850.

Curtin, Jeremiah. *Memoirs of Jeremiah Curtin*. Edited by Joseph Schafer. Madison: State Historical Society of Wisconsin, 1940.

"Customs in the Crater." Pacific Union College Student Handbook. Rev. 1964–65.

Dalton, George, ed. *Tribal and Peasant Economies: Readings in Economic Anthropology*. Garden City, NY: Natural History Press, 1967.

——— and Paul Bohannan. *Markets in Africa*. Garden City, NY: Anchor Books, 1965.

Davis, Angela Y. *Women, Race, and Class*. New York: Random House, 1981.

Delius, Peter. *The Land Belongs to Us: The Pedi Polity, the Boers and the British in the Nineteenth-Century Transvaal*. Berkeley: University of California Press, 1984.

Dillon, Richard. *Burnt-Out Fires*. Englewood Cliffs, NJ: Prentice-Hall, 1973.

Domitila, Barrios de Chungara with Moema Viezzer. *Let Me Speak! Testimony of Domitila, a Woman of the Bolivian Mines*. Translated by Victoria Ortiz. New York: Monthly Review Press, 1978.

Dower, John W. *War without Mercy: Race and Power in the Pacific War*. New York: Pantheon Books, 1986.

Drake, Christopher. "Okinawan Shaman Songs." *Mānoa* 8:1 (Summer 1996): 122–29.

———. "A Separate Perspective: Shamanic Songs of the Ryukyu Kingdom." *Harvard Journal of Asiatic Studies* 50:1 (June 1990): 283–333.

Drinnon, Richard. *Keeper of Concentration Camps: Dillon S. Myer and American Racism.* Berkeley: University of California Press, 1987.

Duan, Zhongqia. *Marx's Theory of the Social Formation.* Aldershot, UK: Avebury, 1995.

DuBois, Cora. "The 1870 Ghost Dance." *University of California Anthropological Records* 3 (1939): 1–151.

Du Bois, W. E. Burkhardt. "The African Roots of War." *Atlantic Monthly* 115 (May 1915): 707–14.

———. "The Color Line Belts the World." *Collier's Weekly,* October 20, 1906.

———. "The Freedmen's Bureau." *Atlantic Monthly* 87 (March 1901): 354.

———. "To the Nations of the World." In *W. E. B. Du Bois: A Reader,* edited by David Levering Lewis. New York: Henry and Holt, 1995.

———. *The Souls of Black Folk.* Chicago: A. C. McClurg, 1903.

Duggan, William R. *An Economic Analysis of Southern African Agriculture.* New York: Praeger, 1986.

Dupre, Georges, and Pierre Philippe Rey. "Reflections on the Relevance of a Theory of the History of Exchange." In *Relations of Production: Marxist Approaches to Economic Anthropology,* edited by David Seddon. London: Frank Cass, 1978.

Dutton, Clarence Edward. *Hawaiian Volcanoes.* Honolulu: University of Hawai'i Press, [1883] 2005.

Ellenberger, V. "Di Robaroba Matlhakola—Tsa Ga Mosodi-a-Mphela." *Transactions of the Royal Society of South Africa* 25 (1937–38): 1–72.

Emerson, Nathaniel B. *Pele and Hiiaka: A Myth from Hawaii.* Honolulu: 'Ai Pōhaku Press, [1915] 1993.

Ethnic Studies Oral History Project. *Uchinanchu: A History of Okinawans in Hawaii.* Honolulu: Ethnic Studies Program, University of Hawai'i at Mānoa, 1981.

Fanon, Frantz. *Black Skin, White Masks.* Translated by Charles Lam Markmann. New York: Grove Press, 1967.

———. *The Wretched of the Earth.* Translated by Constance Farrington. New York: Grove Weidenfield, 1963.

Ferreira, Jason Michael. "All Power to the People: A Comparative History of Third World Radicalism in San Francisco, 1968–1974." PhD diss., University of California, Berkeley, 2003.

Firth, Raymond. *Primitive Polynesian Economy*. London: Routledge, 1939.

Foucault, Michel. *The Foucault Reader*. Edited by Paul Rabinow. New York: Pantheon Books, 1984.

———. "Of Other Spaces." Translated by Jay Miskowiec. *Diacritics* 16:1 (Spring 1986): 22-27.

———. *Power / Knowledge: Selected Interviews and Other Writings, 1972-1977*. Edited by Colin Gordon. New York: Pantheon Books, 1972.

Fraser, Ronald, et al. *1968: A Student Generation in Revolt*. New York: Pantheon Books, 1988.

Frazier, E. Franklin. "Theoretical Structure of Sociology and Sociological Research." *British Journal of Sociology* 4:4 (December 1953): 293-311.

Freire, Paulo. *Pedagogy of the Oppressed*. Translated by Myra Bergman Ramos. New York: Herder and Herder, 1972.

Fuchs, Lawrence H. *Hawaii Pono: A Social History*. New York: Harcourt, Brace & World, 1961.

Füredi, Frank. *Colonial Wars and the Politics of Third World Nationalism*. London: I. B. Tauris, 1994.

———. *The Silent War: Imperialism and the Changing Perception of Race*. London: Pluto Press, 1998.

Gallicchio, Marc. *The African American Encounter with Japan and China: Black Internationalism in Asia, 1895-1945*. Chapel Hill: University of North Carolina Press, 2000.

Garrett, James P. "Black / Africana / Pan African Studies: From Radical to Reaction to Reform?—Its Role and Relevance in the Era of Global Capitalism in the New Millennium." *Journal of Pan-African Studies* 1:1 (Fall-Winter 1998-99): 150-79.

Geertz, Clifford. *Agricultural Involution*. Berkeley: University of California Press, 1963.

———. *Local Knowledge: Further Essays in Interpretive Anthropology*. New York: Basic Books, 1983.

Girdner, Audrie, and Anne Loftis. *The Great Betrayal: The Evacuation of the Japanese-Americans during World War II*. London: Macmillan, 1969.

Glenn, Evelyn Nakano. "Racial Ethnic Women's Labor: The Intersection of Race, Gender and Class Oppression." *Review of Radical Political Economics* 17:3 (1985): 86-108.

———. *Unequal Freedom: How Race and Gender Shaped American Citizenship and Labor*. Cambridge, MA: Harvard University Press, 2002.

Godelier, Maurice. *Rationalité et irrationalité en économie*. Paris: F. Maspero, 1966.

Goff, Stanley, and Robert Sanders. *Brothers: Black Soldiers in the Nam*. Novato, CA: Presidio Press, 1982.

Golla, Victor. *California Indian Languages*. Berkeley: University of California Press, 2011.

Gordon, Milton M. *Assimilation in American Life: The Role of Race, Religion, and National Origins*. New York: Oxford University Press, 1964.

Gould, Jeffrey L., and Aldo A. Lauria-Santiago. *To Rise in Darkness: Revolution, Repression, and Memory in El Salvador, 1920-1932*. Durham, NC: Duke University Press, 2008.

Greene, Brian. *The Fabric of the Cosmos: Space, Time, and the Texture of Reality*. New York: Vintage Books, 2005.

———. *The Hidden Reality: Parallel Universes and the Deep Laws of the Cosmos*. New York: Vintage Books, 2011.

Gregory, Derek, and John Urry, eds. *Social Relations and Spatial Structures*. New York: St. Martin's Press, 1985.

Grosz, Elizabeth. *Space, Time, and Perversion: Essays on the Politics of Bodies*. New York: Routledge, 1995.

———. *Time Travels: Feminism, Nature, Power*. Durham, NC: Duke University Press, 2005.

Gugelberger, Georg, and Michael Kearney. "Voices for the Voiceless: Testimonial Literature in Latin America." *Latin American Perspectives* 18:3 (Summer 1991): 3-14.

Guy, Jeff. "Analysing Pre-Capitalist Societies in Southern Africa." *Journal of Southern African Studies* 14:1 (October 1987): 18-37.

———. "Gender Oppression in Southern Africa's Precapitalist Societies." In *Women and Gender in Southern Africa to 1945*, edited by Cherryl Walker. Cape Town, South Africa: David Philip, 1990.

Halberstam, Judith. *In a Queer Time and Place: Transgender Bodies, Subcultural Lives*. New York: New York University Press, 2005.

Hammer, E. *The Struggle for Indochina*. Stanford, CA: Stanford University Press, 1954.

Hammond-Tooke, W. D. "Descent Groups, Chiefdoms and South African Histo-riography." *Journal of Southern African Studies* 11:2 (April 1985): 305-19.

Hanazaki, Kohei. "Ainu Moshir and Yaponesia: Ainu and Okinawan Identities in Contemporary Japan." In *Multicultural Japan: Paleolithic to Postmodern*, edited by Donald Denoon et al. Cambridge: Cambridge University Press, 1996.

Handy, E. S. Craighill, and Elizabeth Green Handy. *Native Planters in Old Hawaii: Their Life, Lore, and Environment*. Bulletin 233. Honolulu: Bishop Museum Press, 1972.

Hare, Nathan. "The Battle for Black Studies." *Black Scholar* 3:9 (May 1972): 32-47.

———. "A Conceptual Proposal for a Department of Black Studies." In *Shut It Down! A College in Crisis*. San Francisco State College, October 1968–April 1969. A Staff Report to the National Commission on the Causes and Preven-tion of Violence. William H. Orrick, Jr. Washington, DC: Government Print-ing Office, 1969.

———. "A Radical Perspective on Social Science Curricula." In *Black Studies In the University: A Symposium*, edited by Armstead L. Robinson, Craig C. Foster, and Donald H. Ogilvie, 104-21. New Haven, CT: Yale University Press, 1969.

Haring, Douglas G. "Chinese and Japanese Influences." In *Ryukyuan Culture and Society: A Survey*, edited by Allan H. Smith. Honolulu: University of Hawai'i Press, 1964.

Harrison, Hubert H. *When Africa Awakes: The "Inside Story" of the Stirrings and Striv-ings of the New Negro in the Western World*. New York: Porro Press, 1920.

Harvey, David. *Social Justice and the City*. London: Edward Arnold, 1973.

Herskovits, Melville J. *Economic Anthropology*. New York: Knopf, 1940.

Higuchi, Yōichi. "When Society Itself Is the Tyrant." *Japan Quarterly* 35:4 (Octo-ber–December 1988): 350-56.

Hill, Polly. *Studies in Rural Capitalism in West Africa*. London: Cambridge Univer-sity Press, 1970.

Hokama, Shūzen. "Okinawa in the Matrix of Pacific Ocean Culture." In *Okinawan Diaspora*, edited by Ronald Y. Nakasone. Honolulu: University of Hawai'i Press, 2002.

Holton, D. C. "The Meaning of Kami." *Monumenta Nipponica* 3:1 (January 1940): 1-27; 3:2 (July 1940): 392-413; 4:2 (July 1941): 351-94.

Hopkins, A. G. *An Economic History of West Africa*. New York: Columbia University Press, 1973.

Horne, Gerald. *Race War!: White Supremacy and the Japanese Attack on the British Empire*. New York: New York University Press, 2004.

Howse, Derek. *Greenwich Time and the Discovery of the Longitude*. Oxford: Oxford University Press, 1980.

Humboldt, Alexander von. *Personal Narrative of Travels in the Equinoctial Regions of America, during the Years 1799-1804*. Vol. 1. Translated and edited by Thomasina Ross. London: George Bell and Sons, 1889.

Ikema, Eizo. *Yonaguni ni Rekishi*. Yonaguni-cho: Ikema Nae, [1959] 1991.

Imada, Adria L. *Aloha America: Hula Circuits through the U. S. Empire*. Durham, NC: Duke University Press, 2012.

Iriye, Akira. *Power and Culture: The Japanese-American War, 1941-1945*. Cambridge, MA: Harvard University Press, 1981.

Jacobson, Matthew Frye. *Roots Too: White Ethnic Revival in Post-Civil Rights America*. Cambridge, MA: Harvard University Press, 2006.

———. *Whiteness of a Different Color: European Immigrants and the Alchemy of Race*. Cambridge, MA: Harvard University Press, 1998.

James, Cheewa. *Modoc: The Tribe That Wouldn't Die*. Happy Camp, CA: Naturegraph, 2008.

Jelinek, Estelle C. *Women's Autobiography: Essays in Criticism*. Bloomington: Indiana University Press, 1980.

Kahin, George McTurnan. *The Asian-African Conference, Bandung, Indonesia, April 1955*. Ithaca, NY: Cornell University Press, 1956.

Kanahele, Pualani Kanaka'ole. *Ka Honua Ola: 'Eli'eli Kau Mai*. Honolulu: Kamehameha, 2011.

Kaneko, Erika. "The Death Ritual." In *Ryukyuan Culture and Society: A Survey*, edited by Allan H. Smith. Honolulu: University of Hawai'i Press, 1964.

Kashima, Tetsuden. *Buddhism in America*. Westport, CT: Greenwood Press, 1977.

Katayama, Kazumichi. "The Japanese as an Asia-Pacific Population." In *Multicultural Japan: Paleolithic to Postmodern*, edited by Donald Denoon et al. Cambridge: Cambridge University Press, 1996.

Katsiaficas, George. *The Imagination of the New Left: A Global Analysis of 1968*. Boston: South End Press, 1987.

Keegan, Timothy. "Trade, Accumulation and Impoverishment: Mercantile Capital and the Economic Transformation of Lesotho and the Conquered Territory, 1870–1920." *Journal of Southern African Studies* 12:2 (April 1986): 196–216.

Kent, Noel J. *Hawaii: Islands under the Influence.* New York: Monthly Review Press, 1983.

Kerr, James T. "The Modoc War of 1872–73." In *Proceedings of the Annual Meeting and Dinner of the Order of Indian Wars of the United States.* Washington, DC, January 24, 1931.

Khaled, Leila. *My People Shall Live: The Autobiography of a Revolutionary.* Edited by George Hajjar. London: Hodder and Stoughton, 1973.

Kinsman, Margaret. " 'Beasts of Burden': The Subordination of Southern Tswana Women, ca. 1800–1840." *Journal of Southern African Studies* 10:1 (October 1983): 39–54.

———. "Notes on the Southern Tswana Social Formation." In *Africa Seminar: Collected Papers*, no. 2, edited by K. Gottschalk and C. Saunders. Centre for African Studies. University of Cape Town, 1981.

Kirby, Percival R., ed. *The Diary of Dr. Andrew Smith.* Vols. 1 and 2. Cape Town, 1939, 1940.

Koshiro, Yukiko. *Trans-Pacific Racisms and the U.S. Occupation of Japan.* New York: Columbia University Press, 1999.

Kreiner, Josef. "Notes on the History of European-Ryūkyūan Contacts." In *Sources of Ryūkyūan History and Culture in European Collections.* Monograph no. 13. Edited by Josef Kreiner. Tokyo: Institute of Japanese Studies, 1996.

———. "Ryûkyûan History in Comparative Perspective." In *Ryûkyû in World History*, edited by Josef Kreiner. Bonn, Germany: Bier'sche Verlagsanstalt, 2001.

Kroeber, A. L. *Handbook of the Indians of California.* Smithsonian Institution. Bureau of American Ethnology. Bulletin 78. Washington, DC: Government Printing Office, 1925.

Krupp, Sherman Roy. "Equilibrium Theory in Economics and in Functional Analysis as Types of Explanation." In *Functionalism in the Social Sciences*, edited by Don Martindale. Philadelphia: American Academy of Political and Social Science, 1965.

Lake, Marilyn, and Henry Reynolds. *Drawing the Global Colour Line: White Men's Countries and the International Challenge of Racial Equality*. Cambridge: Cambridge University Press, 2008.

Leasor, James. *Singapore: The Battle That Changed the World*. Garden City, NY: Doubleday, 1968.

Lebra, William P. *Okinawan Religion: Belief, Ritual, and Social Structure*. Honolulu: University of Hawai'i Press, 1966.

LeClair, Edward E., Jr., and Harold K. Schneider, eds. *Economic Anthropology: Readings in Theory and Analysis*. New York: Holt, Rinehart and Winston, 1968.

Lefebvre, Henri. *The Production of Space*. Translated by Donald Nicholson-Smith. Malden, MA: Blackwell, 1991.

Lee, Erika, and Judy Yung. *Angel Island: Immigrant Gateway to America*. New York: Oxford University Press, 2010.

Lévi Strauss, Claude. *Tristes tropiques*. Translated by John and Doreen Weightman. New York: Penguin Books, 1973.

Lewis, David Levering. *W. E. B. Du Bois: The Fight For Equality and the American Century, 1919–1963*. New York: Henry Holt, 2000.

Lewis, Jack. "*The Rise and Fall of the South African Peasantry*: A Critique and Reassessment." *Journal of Southern African Studies* 11:1 (October 1984): 1–24.

Lewis, Martin W., and Kären E. Wigen. *The Myth of Continents: A Critique of Metageography*. Berkeley: University of California Press, 1997.

Lindo-Fuentes, Héctor, Erik Ching, and Rafael A. Lara-Martínez. *Remembering a Massacre in El Salvador: The Insurrection of 1932, Roque Dalton, and the Politics of Historical Memory*. Albuquerque: University of New Mexico Press, 2007.

Livingstone, David. *Missionary Travels and Researches in South Africa*. London: John Murray, 1857.

London Missionary Society. *The Masarwa (Bushmen): Report of an Inquiry*. Lovedale, South Africa: Lovedale Press, 1935.

López, Ian Haney. *White by Law: The Legal Construction of Race*. New York: New York University Press, 2006.

Luomala, Katharine. *Voices on the Wind*. Honolulu: Bishop Museum Press, 1955.

Lyman, Stanford M. "Race Relations as Social Process: Sociology's Resistance to a Civil Rights Orientation." In *Race in America: The Struggle for Equality*, edited by Herbert Hill and James E. Jones, Jr. Madison: University of Wisconsin Press, 1993.

Lynch, John, Malcolm Ross, and Terry Crowley. *The Oceanic Languages*. Richmond, Surrey, UK: Curzon Press, 2002.

Mabuchi, Toichi. "Spiritual Predominance of the Sister." In *Ryukyuan Culture and Society: A Survey*, edited by Allan H. Smith. Honolulu: University of Hawai'i Press, 1964.

———. "Tales Concerning the Origin of Grains in the Insular Areas of Eastern and Southeastern Asia." *Asian Folklore Studies* 23:1 (1964): 6–18.

———. "Toward the Reconstruction of Ryukyuan Cosmology." In *Folk Religion and the Worldview in the Southwestern Pacific*, edited by Matsumoto Nobuhiro and Mabuchi Toichi. Tokyo: Kokusai, 1968.

Madley, Benjamin Logan. "American Genocide: The California Indian Catastrophe, 1846–1873." PhD diss., Yale University, May 2009.

———. "California's Yuki Indians: Defining Genocide in Native American History." *Western Historical Quarterly* 39:3 (August 2008): 303–32.

Maeda, Daryl J. *Chains of Babylon: The Rise of Asian America*. Minneapolis: University of Minnesota Press, 2009.

Maher, John C. "North Kyushu Creole: A Language-Contact Model for the Origins of Japanese." In *Multicultural Japan: Paleolithic to Postmodern*, edited by Donald Denoon et al. Cambridge: Cambridge University Press, 1996.

Malinowski, Bronislaw. *Argonauts of the Western Pacific*. London: Routledge, 1922.

Marín, Lynda. "Speaking Out Together: Testimonials of Latin American Women." *Latin American Perspectives* 18:3 (Summer 1991): 51–68.

Marks, Shula, and Anthony Atmore, eds. *Economy and Society in Pre-Industrial South Africa*. London: Longman, 1980.

Marx, Karl. *Pre-Capitalist Economic Formations*. Edited by E. J. Hobsbawn. New York: International, 1964.

Massey, Doreen. *For Space*. Los Angeles: Sage, 2005.

———. "Politics and Space / Time." *New Left Review* 196 (November–December 1992): 65–84.

Matsuda, Kazue. *Poetic Reflections of the Tule Lake Internment Camp, 1944*. n.p., 1987.

Matsuda, Mitsugu. *The Government of the Kingdom of Ryukyu, 1609-1872*. Okinawa: Yui, 2001.

———. "The Ryukyuan Government Scholarship Students to China, 1392-1868." *Monumenta Nipponica* 21:3 / 4 (1966): 273-304.

Matthews, Fred H. *Quest for an American Sociology: Robert E. Park and the Chicago School*. Montreal: McGill-Queen's University Press, 1977.

Mautle, Gaontatlhe. "Bakgalagadi-Bakwena Relationship: A Case of Slavery, c. 1840-c. 1920." *Botswana Notes and Records* 18 (1986): 19-31.

McAdams, Dan P. *The Redemptive Self: Stories Americans Live By*. Oxford: Oxford University Press, 2006.

McDermid, Nancy. "Strike Settlement." In *Academics on the Line*, edited by Arlene Kaplan Daniels, Rachel Kahn-Hut, et al. San Francisco: Jossey-Bass, 1970.

McEvoy, James, and Abraham Miller, eds. *Black Power and Student Rebellion*. Belmont, CA: Wadsworth, 1969.

McGregor, Davianna Pomaikaʻi. *Na Kuaʻaina: Living Hawaiian Culture*. Honolulu: University of Hawaiʻi Press, 2007.

Meillassoux, Claude. *Anthropologie economique des Gouro de la Côte d'Ivoire*. Paris: Mouton, 1964.

———. "From Reproduction to Production: A Marxist Approach to Economic Anthropology." *Economy and Society* 1:1 (February 1972): 93-105.

Memmi, Albert. *The Colonizer and the Colonized*. Boston: Beacon Press, 1967.

Menchú, Rigoberta. *I, Rigoberta Menchú: An Indian Woman in Guatemala*. Edited by Elisabeth Burgos-Debray. Translated by Ann Wright. London: Verso, 1984.

Methuen, Henry H. *Life in the Wilderness*. London: R. Bentley, 1846.

Miki, Takeshi. *Okinesia Bunkaron: Seishin no Kyōwakoku o motomete*. Tokyo: Kaifūsha, 1988.

Miles, Robert. *Racism*. London: Routledge, 1989.

———. *Racism after "Race Relations."* London: Routledge, 1993.

———. *Racism and Migrant Labour: A Critical Text*. London: Routledge and Kegan Paul, 1982.

Mills, C. Wright. *The Sociological Imagination*. New York: Oxford University Press, 1959.

Moffat, Robert. *Apprenticeship at Kuruman*. Edited by I. Schapera. London: Chatto & Windus, 1951.

———. *Missionary Labours and Scenes in Southern Africa*. London: John Snow, 1842.

Mohamad, Mahatir. *A New Deal for Asia*. Tokyo: Tachibana, 1999.

Moraga, Cherríe. *Loving in the War Years*. Cambridge, MA: South End Press, 1983.

——— and Gloria Anzaldúa. eds. *This Bridge Called My Back: Writings by Radical Women of Color*. New York: Kitchen Table: Women of Color Press, 1983.

Mori, Toshio. *Yokohama, California*. Seattle: University of Washington Press, [1949] 1985.

Morris-Suzuki, Tessa. "A Descent into the Past: The Frontier in the Construction of Japanese Identity." In *Multicultural Japan: Paleolithic to Postmodern*, edited by Donald Denoon et al. Cambridge: Cambridge University Press, 1996.

Moser, Robert R. *The Winter Soldiers: GI and Veteran Dissent during the Vietnam Era*. New Brunswick, NJ: Rutgers University Press, 1996.

Mullings, Leith. *On Our Own Terms: Race, Class, and Gender in the Lives of African American Women*. New York: Routledge, 1997.

Murphey, Rhoads. *A History of Asia*. New York: HarperCollins, 1996.

Murphy, Thomas D. *Ambassadors in Arms*. Honolulu: University of Hawai'i Press, 1954.

Murray, Keith A. *The Modocs and Their War*. Norman: University of Oklahoma Press, 1959.

Myer, Dillon S. *Uprooted Americans: The Japanese Americans and the War Relocation Authority during World War II*. Tucson: University of Arizona Press, 1971.

Nakasone, Ronald Y. "Agari-umaai: An Okinawan Pilgrimage." In *Okinawan Diaspora*, edited by Ronald Y. Nakasone. Honolulu: University of Hawai'i Press, 2002.

———. "An Impossible Possibility." In *Okinawan Diaspora*, edited by Ronald Y. Nakasone. Honolulu: University of Hawai'i Press, 2002.

Nehru, Jawaharlal. *The Discovery of India*. London: Meridian Books, 1956.

Newton-Smith, W. H. *The Structure of Time*. London: Routledge & Kegan Paul, 1980.

Ngũgĩ wa Thiong'o. *Decolonising the Mind: The Politics of Language in African Literature*. Oxford: James Currey, 1986.

Oaklander, Nathan, and Quentin Smith, eds. *The New Theory of Time*. New Haven, CT: Yale University Press, 1994.

Odo, Franklin. *No Sword to Bury: Japanese Americans in Hawai'i during World War II.* Philadelphia: Temple University Press, 2004.

Okihiro, Gary Y. *Cane Fires: The Anti-Japanese Movement in Hawaii, 1865–1945.* Philadelphia: Temple University Press, 1991.

——. "Genealogical Research in Molepolole: A Report on Methodology." *Botswana Notes and Records* 8 (1976): 47–62.

——. *Island World: A History of Hawai'i and the United States.* Berkeley: University of California Press, 2008.

——. "Japan, World War II, and Third World Liberation." *Rikkyo American Studies* 31 (March 2009): 77–99.

——. "Of Space / Time and the Pineapple." *Atlantic Studies* 11:1 (January 2014): 85–102.

——. "Oral History and the Writing of Ethnic History: A Reconnaissance into Method and Theory." *Oral History Review* 9 (1981): 27–46.

——. *Pineapple Culture: A History of the Tropical and Temperate Zones.* Berkeley: University of California Press, 2009.

——. "Preliminary Thoughts on Migration and the Nation / People." In *Proceedings for the International Symposium: Human Migration and the 21st Century Global Society—Immigration, Language, and Literature,* edited by Nakahodo Masanori, Yamazato Katsunori, and Ishihara Masahide. University of the Ryukyus, March 2009.

——. "Reflections on Viet Nam." In *Tiêp Cân Du'o'ng Dai Văn Hóa My: Contemporary Approaches to American Culture,* edited by Nguyen Lien and Jonathan Auerbach. Hà Nôi: Nhà Xuât Ban Văn Hóa Thông Tin, 2001.

——. "Religion and Resistance in America's Concentration Camps," *Phylon* 45:3 (September 1984): 220–33.

——. "Resistance and Accommodation: baKwena-baGasechele, 1842–52." *Botswana Notes and Records* 5 (1973): 104–16.

——. "Self and History." *Rethinking History* 13:1 (March 2009): 5–15.

——. *A Social History of the Bakwena and Peoples of the Kalahari of Southern Africa, 19th Century.* Lewiston, NY: Edwin Mellen Press, 2000.

——. *Third World Studies: Theorizing Liberation.* Durham, NC: Duke University Press, 2016.

——. "Tule Lake under Martial Law: A Study in Japanese Resistance." *Journal of Ethnic Studies* 5:3 (1977): 71–85.

———. *Whispered Silences: Japanese Americans and World War II*. Seattle: University of Washington Press, 1996.

Okihiro, Gary Y., and Elda Tsou. "On Social Formation." *Works and Days* 24:1 / 2 (2006): 69–88.

Omer-Cooper, J. D. *The Zulu Aftermath: A Nineteenth-Century Revolution in Bantu Africa*. Evanston, IL: Northwestern University Press, 1966.

Omi, Michael, and Howard Winant. *Racial Formation in the United States: From the 1960s to 1980s*. New York: Routledge and Kegan Paul, 1986.

Opler, Marvin K. "Japanese Folk Beliefs and Practices, Tule Lake, California." *Journal of American Folklore* 63:250 (October–December 1950): 385–97.

——— and F. Obayashi. "Senryu Poetry as Folk and Community Expression." *Journal of American Folklore* 58:227 (January–March 1945): 1–11.

Opler, Morris E., and Robert Seido Hashima. "The Rice Goddess and the Fox in Japanese Religion and Folk Practice." *American Anthropologist* 48:1 (January–March 1946): 43–53.

Orrick, William H., Jr. *Shut It Down! A College in Crisis*. San Francisco State College, October 1968–April 1969. A Staff Report to the National Commission on the Causes and Prevention of Violence. Washington, DC: Government Printing Office, 1969.

Osorio, Jonathan Kay Kamakawiwoʻole. *Dismembering Lahui: A History of the Hawaiian Nation to 1887*. Honolulu: University of Hawaiʻi Press, 2002.

Palmer, Robin, and Neil Parsons, eds. *The Roots of Rural Poverty in Central and Southern Africa*. Berkeley: University of California Press, 1977.

Park, Robert Ezra. "Human Migration and the Marginal Man." *American Journal of Sociology* 23:6 (May 1928): 881–93.

———, "Introduction." In *An Island Community: Ecological Succession in Hawaii*, by Andrew W. Lind. Chicago: University of Chicago Press, 1938.

———. "Introduction." In *The Japanese Invasion: A Study in the Psychology of Inter-Racial Contacts*, by Jesse Frederick Steiner. Chicago: A. C. McClurg, 1917.

———. *Race and Culture*. Glencoe, IL: Free Press, 1950.

———. "Racial Assimilation in Secondary Groups with Particular Reference to the Negro." *American Journal of Sociology* 19:5 (March 1914): 606–23.

Park, Robert E., and Ernest W. Burgess. *Introduction to the Science of Sociology*. Chicago: University of Chicago Press, 1926.

Pascoe, Peggy. *What Comes Naturally: Miscegenation Law and the Making of Race in America*. New York: Oxford University Press, 2009.

Pearson, Richard J. *Archaeology of the Ryukyu Islands: A Regional Chronology from 3000 B.C. to the Historic Period*. Honolulu: University of Hawai'i Press, 1969.

———. "The Place of Okinawa in Japanese Historical Identity." In *Multicultural Japan: Paleolithic to Postmodern*, edited by Donald Denoon et al. Cambridge: Cambridge University Press, 1996.

Peires, J. B. *The Dead Will Arise: Nongqawuse and the Great Xhosa Cattle-Killing Movement of 1856-7*. Johannesburg: Ravan Press, 1989.

———. *The House of Phalo: A History of the Xhosa People in the Days of Their Independence*. Berkeley: University of California Press, 1982.

Persons, Stow. *Ethnic Studies at Chicago, 1905-45*. Urbana: University of Illinois Press, 1987.

Pfaelzer, Jean. *Driven Out: The Forgotten War against Chinese Americans*. Berkeley: University of California Press, 2007.

Pietrusewsky, Michael. "The Physical Anthropology of the Pacific, East Asia and Southeast Asia." In *The Peopling of East Asia: Putting Together Archaeology, Linguistics and Genetics*, edited by Laurent Sagart, Roger Blench, and Alicia Sanchez-Mazas. London: RoutledgeCurzon, 2005.

Polanyi, Karl, Conrad M. Arensberg, and Harry W. Pearson, eds. *Trade and Market in the Early Empires*. New York: Free Press, 1957.

Powers, Stephen, and John Wesley Powell. *Tribes of California*. Contributions to North American Ethnology. Vol. 3. Department of the Interior. Washington, DC: Government Printing Office, 1877.

Quinn, Arthur. *Hell with the Fire Out: A History of the Modoc War*. Boston: Faber and Faber, 1997.

Ranger, Terence. "Growing from the Roots: Reflections on Peasant Research in Central and Southern Africa." *Journal of Southern African Studies* 5:1 (October 1978): 99-133.

Raushenbush, Winifred. *Robert E. Park: Biography of a Sociologist*. Durham, NC: Duke University Press, 1979.

Ray, Verne F. *Primitive Pragmatists: The Modoc Indians of Northern California*. Seattle: University of Washington Press, 1963.

Reinecke, John E. *Language and Dialect in Hawaii: A Sociolinguistic History to 1935*. Honolulu: University of Hawai'i Press, 1969.

Report of the National Advisory Commission on Civil Disorders. New York: Bantam Books, 1968.

Rey, Pierre Philippe. *Colonialisme, neo-colonialisme et transition au capitalism*. Paris: F. Maspero, 1971.

Riddle, Jefferson C. Davis. *The Indian History of the Modoc War*. Mechanicsburg, PA: Stackpole Books, 2004.

Roberts, Sarah Julianne. "The TMA System of Hawaiian Creole and Diffusion." In *Creole Genesis, Attitudes and Discourse: Studies Celebrating Charlene J. Sato*, edited by John R. Rickford and Suzanne Romaine. Amsterdam: John Benjamins, 1999.

Robinson, Dean E. *Black Nationalism in American Politics and Thought*. Cambridge: Cambridge University Press, 2001.

Røkkum, Arne. *Goddesses, Priestesses, and Sisters: Mind, Gender and Power in the Monarchic Tradition of the Ryukyus*. Oslo, Norway: Scandinavian University Press, 1998.

Ross, Robert H., and Emory S. Bogardus. "The Second-Generation Race Relations Cycle: A Study in *Issei-Nisei* Relationships." *Sociology and Social Research* 24:4 (March-April 1940): 357-63.

Roux, Edward. *Grass: A Story of Frankenwald*. Cape Town, South Africa: Oxford University Press, 1969.

Sahlins, Marshall. *Stone Age Economics*. Chicago: Aldine-Atherton, 1972.

Sakai, Robert K. "The Ryukyu (Liu-Ch'iu) Kings in the Ch'ing Period." In *The Chinese World Order: Traditional China's Foreign Relations*, edited by John King Fairbank. Cambridge, MA: Harvard University Press, 1968.

———. "The Satsuma-Ryukyu Trade and the Tokugawa Seclusion Policy." *Journal of Asian Studies* 23:3 (May 1964): 391-403.

Sakamaki, Shunzo. *Ryukyu: A Bibliographical Guide to Okinawan Studies*. Honolulu: University of Hawai'i Press, 1963.

———. "Ryukyu and Southeast Asia." *Journal of Asian Studies* 23:3 (May 1964): 383-89.

Sakihara, Mitsugu. *A Brief History of Early Okinawa Based on the Omoro Sōshi*. Tokyo: Honpo Shoseki Press, 1987.

———. "History of Okinawa." In *Uchinanchu: A History of Okinawans in Hawaii*. Honolulu: Ethnic Studies Oral History Project, University of Hawai'i, 1981.

Sakoda, Kent, and Jeff Siegel. *Pidgin Grammar: An Introduction to the Creole Language of Hawai'i*. Honolulu: Bess Press, 2003.

Salisbury, R. F. *From Stone to Steel*. Victoria, Australia: Melbourne University Press, 1962.

Sartre, Jean-Paul. "Preface." In *The Wretched of the Earth*, by Frantz Fanon. Translated by Constance Farrington. New York: Grove Weidenfield, 1963.

Schapera, I. *A Handbook of Tswana Law and Custom*. London: Oxford University Press, 1938.

———, ed. *David Livingstone Family Letters, 1841–1848*. Vols. 1 and 2. London: Chatto & Windus, 1959.

———, ed. *Livingstone's Missionary Correspondence, 1841–1856*. Berkeley: University of California Press, 1961.

———, ed. *Livingstone's Private Journals, 1851–1853*. Berkeley: University of California Press, 1960.

Schneider, Harold K. *Economic Man: The Anthropology of Economics*. New York: Free Press, 1974.

Scott, Joan W. "Experience." In *Feminists Theorize the Political*, edited by Judith Butler and Joan W. Scott. New York: Routledge, 1992.

Sered, Susan. *Women of the Sacred Groves: Divine Priestesses of Okinawa*. New York: Oxford University Press, 1999.

Shineberg, Dorothy. *They Came for Sandalwood*. Victoria, Australia: Melbourne University Press, 1967.

Silva, Noenoe K. *Aloha Betrayed: Native Hawaiian Resistance to American Colonialism*. Durham, NC: Duke University Press, 2004.

Sjöberg, Katarina. "Positioning Oneself in the Japanese Nation State: The Hokkaido Ainu Case." In *Transcultural Japan: At the Borderlands of Race, Gender, and Identity*, edited by David Blake Willis and Stephen Murphy-Shigematsu. London: Routledge, 2008.

Smith, Robert, Richard Axen, and DeVere Pentony. *By Any Means Necessary: The Revolutionary Struggle at San Francisco State*. San Francisco: Jossey-Bass, 1970.

Smith, Sidonie, and Julia Watson, eds. *De/Colonizing the Subject: The Politics of Gender in Women's Autobiography.* Minneapolis: University of Minnesota Press, 1992.

Soja, Edward W. *Postmodern Geographies: The Reassertion of Space in Critical Social Theory.* London: Verso, 1989.

Spencer, Robert Francis. "Japanese Buddhism in the United States, 1940–1946: A Study in Acculturation." PhD diss., University of California, Berkeley, 1946.

Spivak, Gayatri Chakravorty. "Can the Subaltern Speak?" In *Marxism and the Interpretation of Culture*, edited by Cary Nelson and Lawrence Grossberg. London: Macmillan, 1988.

———. *Outside in the Teaching Machine.* New York: Routledge, 1993.

Springer, Kimberly. *Living for the Revolution: Black Feminist Organizations, 1968–1980.* Durham, NC: Duke University Press, 2005.

Sterling, Elspeth P., and Catherine C. Summers, eds. *Sites of Oahu.* Honolulu: Bishop Museum Press, 1978.

Stocking, George W., Jr. *Delimiting Anthropology: Occasional Inquiries and Reflections.* Madison: University of Wisconsin Press, 2001.

Stoddard, T. Lothrop. *The French Revolution in San Domingo.* Boston: Houghton Mifflin, 1914.

———. *The Rising Tide of Color against White World-Supremacy.* New York: Charles Scribner's Sons, 1920.

Suzuki, Lester E. *Ministry in the Assembly and Relocation Centers of World War II.* Berkeley: Yardbird, 1979.

Suzuki, Peter T. "The Ethnolinguistics of Japanese Americans in the Wartime Camps." *Anthropological Linguistics* 18 (December 1976): 416–27.

Takara, Kurayoshi. "The Kingdom of Ryūkyū and Its Overseas Trade." In *Sources of Ryūkyūan History and Culture in European Collections.* Monograph no. 13. Edited by Josef Kreiner. Tokyo: Institute of Japanese Studies, 1996.

Tanaka, Chester. *Go For Broke: A Pictorial History of the Japanese American 100th Infantry Battalion and the 442d Regimental Combat Team.* Richmond, CA: Go For Broke, 1982.

Tanaka, Masako. "Categories of Okinawan 'Ancestors' and the Kinship System." *Asian Folklore Studies* 36:2 (1977): 31–64.

Teodoro, Massimo, ed. *The New Left: A Documentary History*. Indianapolis: Bobbs-Merrill, 1969.

Terray, Emmanuel. *Marxism and "Primitive" Societies*. New York: Monthly Review Press, 1972.

Thomas, William I., and Florian Znaniecki. *The Polish Peasant in Europe and America: Monograph of an Immigrant Group*. 5 vols. Chicago: University of Chicago Press, 1918-20.

Thompson, Leonard. *African Societies in Southern Africa*. New York: Praeger, 1969.

Thompson, Edgar T., ed. *Race Relations and the Race Problem: A Definition and Analysis*. Durham, NC: Duke University Press, 1939.

Thompson, Sandra A., Joseph Sung-Yul Park, and Charles N. Li. *A Reference Grammar of Wappo*. Berkeley: University of California Press, 2006.

Thorne, Christopher. *The Issue of War: States, Societies, and the Far Eastern Conflict of 1941-1945*. New York: Oxford University Press, 1985.

———. "Racial Aspects of the Far Eastern War of 1941-1945." *Proceedings of the British Academy* (London) 66 (1980).

Tinker, Hugh. *Race, Conflict and the International Order: From Empire to United Nations*. New York: St. Martin's Press, 1977.

Tomiyama, Ichirō. "Colonialism and the Sciences of the Tropical Zone: The Academic Analysis of Difference in 'the Island Peoples'." *positions* 3:2 (Fall 1995): 367-91.

Toomer, Jean. *Cane*. New York: Liveright, [1923] 1975.

Toyama, Henry, and Ikeda Kiyoshi. "The Okinawan-Naichi Relationship." In *Uchinanchu: A History of Okinawans in Hawaii*. Honolulu: Ethnic Studies Oral History Project, University of Hawai'i, 1981.

Tsang, Cheng-hwa. "Recent Discoveries at the Tapenkeng Culture Sites in Taiwan: Implications for the Problem of Austronesian Origins." In *The Peopling of East Asia: Putting Together Archaeology, Linguistics and Genetics*, edited by Laurent Sagart, Roger Blench, and Alicia Sanchez-Mazas. London: Routledge-Curzon, 2005.

Tuan, Yi-Fu. *Space and Place: The Perspective of Experience*. Minneapolis: University of Minnesota Press, 1977.

Turner, Frederick Jackson. *The Frontier in American History*. New York: Henry Holt, 1920.

Ueunten, Wesley Iwao. "Rising Up from a Sea of Discontent: The 1970 Koza Uprising in U.S.-Occupied Okinawa." In *Military Currents: Toward a Decolonized Future in Asia and the Pacific*, edited by Setsu Shigematsu and Keith L. Camacho. Minneapolis: University of Minnesota Press, 2010.

Venuti, Lawrence, ed. *The Translation Studies Reader*. New York: Routledge, 2004.

Von Eschen, Penny M. *Race against Empire: Black Americans and Anticolonialism, 1937-1957*. Ithaca, NY: Cornell University Press, 1997.

Wacker, Monica. "*Onarigami*—Holy Woman in the Kingdom of Ryūkyū: A Pacific Culture with Chinese Influences." In *Ryûkyû in World History*, edited by Josef Kreiner. Bonn, Germany: Bier'sche Verlagsanstalt, 2001.

Wallerstein, Immanuel. *The Modern World-System*. New York: Academic Press, 1974.

War Relocation Authority. *WRA, A Story of Human Conservation*. Washington, DC: Government Printing Office, 1946.

Williams, Raymond. *Keywords: A Vocabulary of Culture and Society*. New York: Oxford University Press, [1976] 1983.

———. *Marxism and Literature*. Oxford: Oxford University Press, 1977.

Wilmsen, Edwin N. *Land Filled with Flies: A Political Economy of the Kalahari*. Chicago: University of Chicago Press, 1989.

Wilson, Rob, and Wimal Dissanayake, eds. *Global/Local: Cultural Production and the Transnational Imaginary*. Durham, NC: Duke University Press, 1996.

Wolf, Eric R. *Sons of the Shaking Earth*. Chicago: University of Chicago Press, 1959.

Woodson, Carter G. *The Mis-education of the Negro*. Washington, DC: Associated, 1933.

Wrigley, C.C. "Population in African History." *Journal of African History* 20:1 (1979): 127-31.

Wu, Judy Tzu-Chun. *Radicals on the Road: Internationalism, Orientalism, and Feminism during the Vietnam Era*. Ithaca, NY: Cornell University Press, 2013.

Wynne, Susan G. "The Land Boards of Botswana: A Problem in Institutional Design." PhD diss., Indiana University, 1989.

Young, Marilyn B. *The Vietnam Wars, 1945-1990*. New York: HarperCollins, 1991.

Yu, Henry. *Thinking Orientals: Migration, Contact, and Exoticism in Modern America*. New York: Oxford University Press, 2001.

Zimmern, Alfred. *The Third British Empire*. London: Humphrey Milford, 1926.

Zinsser, William, ed. *Inventing the Truth: The Art and Craft of Memoir*. Boston: Houghton Mifflin, 1987.

Atlantic Charter, 144–145
Austin, Verne, 116, 119
Austronesian language, 23, 39, 41, 244n67
autobiography, 5

Babolaongwe, 169
Bachelard, Gaston, 207, 208, 213, 234
Bakgalagadi, 179, 185, 187, 189, 193, 199.
    See also Babolaongwe; Bakwatheng;
    Bangaloga; Bashaga
Bakwatheng, 169, 193
Bakwena. See Botswana: history; people
Bandung Conference (1955), 148, 162
Bangaloga, 169
Bao Dai, 134
Barncho, 111
Barrio Cruz Galana, 232, 234
Bashaga, 169
Beal, Frances, 163–164
Beinart, William, 173
Benjamin, Walter, 213
Berlin Conference (1884–1885), 140, 202
Best, Raymond, 115, 116
Bingham, Hiram, 62
biological determinism, 2
Black Jim, 107–108, 111
Black Panther Party, 137, 150, 158
black power, 5
Black Students Union, 157, 158, 159, 160,
    161, 163
Black Women's Alliance, 164
Black Women's Liberation Caucus, 164
Boas, Franz, 152
Bogardus, Emory, 153
Bolivia, 214, 215
Bonewamang, 178
Bose, Sugata, 210, 211
Boston Charley, 111
Botswana: history, 169, 174–200; nation,
    9, 12, 89, 167–171, 173–174, 200, 201,
215, 235, 236; people, 169, 170, 181,
    182, 183, 184, 200, 201
Bozzoli, Belinda, 199
Braudel, Fernand, 205, 206
Brazil, 4, 49
Brown v. Board of Education (1954), 61, 85
Bundy, Colin, 172, 173
Bureau of Indian Affairs, 97, 103
Burns, John, 200

Cable Act (1922), 73
calendar: Chinese, 29; Japanese, 29
Callinago, 233
Camp McCoy, 75, 76
Canby, Edward, 107, 108, 112
Cane Fires (1991), 76, 77
Capitalism, 2, 10, 24, 163
Carmichael, Stokely, 137
Cayuse, 102
Césaire, Aimé, 62, 64
Chaudhuri, K., 206
Cherokee, 105
Cherokee v. Georgia (1831), 106
Chicago race riot (1919), 153
Chicago sociology, 6, 151–155, 157, 160,
    161, 162
Chilula, 93
China: language, 30, 58; nation, 23, 24,
    26, 27, 28, 29, 39, 40, 41, 143; people,
    27, 28, 49, 60, 94–95, 122, 146
Chinen (Kakazu), Kame, 9, 10, 18–21,
    19*fig.*, 21, 24, 26, 42, 53*fig.*, 54, 56–57
Chinese Exclusion Act (1882), 95
Churchill, Winston, 144–145
Chūzan, 27, 41
Cicero, 212
citizens, 11, 12, 72, 73, 74, 81, 113, 123
class: as social formation, 8, 12, 48, 50,
    113, 150, 163–164, 165
Cold War, 74, 135, 140, 159, 210

Geneva Conference (1954), 135
geography: determinism, 2; imperial,
    202; postmodern, 208
"Ghost Dance," 105, 123, 124
Gila River concentration camp, xi, 125
Godelier, Maurice, 170
Gold Rush: California, 102; Modoc
    country, 96
Goo-Ra-Tshosa, 189
Grant, Ulysses, 107
Great East Asia Conference (1943), 143
Greene, Brian, 203
Greenwich Observatory, 202
Grosz, Elizabeth, 4
Guy, Jeff, 199

Haebaru Town Museum, 226
Hajjar, George, 51, 213, 214
Halberstam, Judith / Jack, 204, 205
Hamburg, 104
Haneji, Chōshū, 25
Hare, Nathan, 157, 158, 161, 162
Harrison, Hubert, 140
Harvey, David, 171, 209, 210, 212
Hateruma: island, 41; people, 41–42
Hatoma Island, 38
Hawai'i: island, 63, 81; islands, 12, 21, 26,
    68, 70, 71, 72, 81, 88, 89, 113, 167, 233,
    235, 236; kingdom, 48; language, 57,
    65, 84; martial law, 74–75; people,
    44, 48, 49, 57, 60, 65, 88, 101, 150,
    156; US state, 200, 201
Hayashi, Masumi, xi–xii, xiii*fig.*
Heisenberg, Werner, 203, 211
Henríquez, Marina, 4, 36, 66, 68, 90, 234
Herskovits, Melville, 172
Hi'iaka, 11, 18, 20*fig.*, 62, 63, 64, 66, 67,
    68, 69, 69*fig.*, 70, 90
Hill, Polly, 172
Hilo Boarding School, 88

Hiroshima: atomic bomb, 78; city, 71, 77
historical: formation, 2–4, 7, 12, 212;
    linguistics, 5; materialism, 8
history: as translation, 213, 215; imperial,
    202, 213; periodization, 1, 6
Ho Chi Minh, 134
Hokkaido, 23, 40
Hokuzan, 27, 41
"Hooker Jim," 107
Hooper, Niels, 1
Hooper, William, 48
Hopi, 210
Hōpoe, 63, 64, 66, 68
Hopu, 88
Hudson's Bay Company, 101
Hughes, Henry, 151
Hugo of St. Victor, 10
hula, 62–65, 70
Humboldt, Alexander von, 93
Humboldt State University, 94, 95
Hupa, 93

Ifa, Fuyū, 24, 31, 39
Iheya Island, 33
imperialism: discourse, 1, 2, 6, 11, 42,
    48, 65, 114, 150, 166, 171, 172, 202,
    213, 215, 235; material relations,
    2, 7, 10, 11, 22, 24, 48, 54, 62, 81,
    131, 135, 136, 137, 143, 144, 150,
    158, 163, 166
indeterminancy, xii, 2, 203, 204, 211
India, 144
Indochinese Women's Conference (1971),
    150
Indonesia, 17, 23, 41
Inouye, 120
Institute of Pacific Relations, 142
Institute of Race Relations, 142
Institute of Social and Religious
    Research, 153

International Geographical Congress (1871), 202
International Meridian Conference (1884), 202
intersectionality, 165, 166
Iolani Palace, 200
Iroquois, 101
Ishigaki: island, 41; people, 33, 41–42
Ishikibama, 36, 37, 38
islands: as represented, 1–2, 12, 201, 212, 235, 236
Island World (2008), 1, 10, 88, 101, 109, 204, 212
issei, 18
Itokazu, Kanna, 226, 227, 228*fig.*
Izalco, 232, 234

Jackson, James, 107
Japan: culture, 33, 54; language, 24, 29, 30, 40, 56–57; nation, 4, 22, 24, 25, 26, 29, 30, 40, 42, 52, 54, 55, 74, 113, 141, 142, 143, 145, 146; people, 21, 22, 24, 25, 26, 41, 42, 58, 60, 76, 77, 94, 95, 112–129, 144, 145, 146, 153; religion, 124–128
Japan kanakas, 10, 26, 41, 49. *See also* South Sea
Japonesia, 23, 24
Johannesburg, 167, 168
Johnson, Charles, 152
Johnson, James, 137
Johnson, Lyndon, 135, 136, 200
Johnson-Reed Act (1924), 124
Johnston, J., 205
Jōmon, 40

Ka'ahumanu, 62
Kahuna, 55, 63
Kakazu, Kame, 25, 26, 46, 48, 53*fig.* 54, 56

Kakazu (Okihiro), Shizue, 9, 10, 43, 45, 49, 52, 53*fig.*, 54–56, 60, 79*fig.*, 84
Kalahari Desert, 168, 182, 184, 193, 195, 198, 199
Kalākaua, 65
Ka-moho-ali'i, 66, 67, 69
Kanahele, Pualani Kanaka'ole, 64, 68
Kanaseki, Takeo, 39
Karuk, 93, 100
Kashima, 115
Kaua'i, 63, 67, 81
Kaumuali'i, 88
Kea'au, 21, 66, 67, 68
Keaīwa heiau, 21
Kealeboga, 177, 179, 180, 196, 216, 222, 224
Keegan, Timothy, 173
Kennedy, John, 135
Kgabo (ya molelo), 181
Kgalagadi. *See* Babolaongwe; Bangologa; Bakgwatheng; Bashaga
Kgari, 216, 224
Kgosi Kgari Sechele II Secondary School, 169, 170
Kgosing, 177, 179, 180, 181
Khaled, Leila, 51, 213, 214
Khama, Seretse, 168, 200
Khoikhoi, 142
Kibei, 54
King, Martin Luther, Jr., 131, 133, 136, 138–139
kino lau, 10, 18, 70
Kinsman, Margaret, 199
Kintpuash, 11, 96, 103–104, 105, 106, 107, 108, 110, 111, 129
Klamath: people, 96, 98, 99, 101, 104, 105, 106
Kokugakusha, 24
Korea: nation, 28, 39, 40; people, 24, 58, 73, 227
Kouri: people, 33

oral history, 2, 3, 9, 215. *See also* talk story
"Oriental problem," 6, 152, 154
Orkney Isles, 174
otōsan. *See* Okihiro, Tetsuo
Overland Trail, 102

Pacific Coast Survey of Race Relations
    (1924-1926), 153
Pacific Union College, 82, 83, 84, 85,
    86-87, 88, 90
Paiute, 99, 100, 104, 105
Palmer, Robin, 173
Park, Robert, 81-82, 122, 142, 151-152, 154
Parsons, Neil, 173
Peace Corps, 131, 169, 170
Peires, J., 173
Pele, 18, 62, 63, 64, 66, 67, 68, 69, 69*fig.*,
    78, 79, 81
Penn Center, 131
Perez v. Sharp (1948), 85
phenomenology, 3, 4, 9, 208, 234-235
Philippines: islands, 17, 28, 36, 37, 38, 39,
    40, 41, 42, 143, 226, 227; people, 26,
    41, 60, 114, 153
"picture bride," 18, 71
pidgin English: hapa haole, 58, 84;
    plantation, 56, 58-59, 60, 61-62, 84
pineapple, 43, 44, 48, 233, 236
Pineapple Culture (2009), 1, 93, 212, 233
Pipil, 232, 233
Pit River: people, 99, 100
plantations: paternalism, 46; pedagogy,
    10, 12, 47, 50; sugar, 10, 45, 46,
    48-49, 54. *See also* education; strike
poetics, 2, 3, 13, 62, 64, 127-128, 207-208,
    211, 234, 235
Polanyi, Karl, 171
Portuguese, 28, 49, 58, 59, 60
power: physical, 202-203; social, 1, 2, 3,
    8, 202

production: means and relations of, 7, 8
Pueblo, 210
Puerto Rican. *See* Latinx
Puna, 63, 66, 67*fig.*, 68, 69, 70, 81, 87

quantum mechanics, 203, 204, 211, 235
queer: method, 83; people, 8; time, 204,
    205

race: as people, 21-25, 41; as social
    formation, 2, 8, 12, 48, 113, 163, 164,
    165
race relations, 47-48, 82, 141-142, 143,
    144, 151-155, 156
Ranger, Terence, 7, 173
Rantao Ogle, Teresa, 218
Reagan, Ronald, 136
Reinecke, John, 58
resistance: practice, 47, 50, 58, 123,
    124, 128, 173; theory, 5, 7, 8, 9, 10,
    212
Rey, Pierre, 172, 183
Rhodesia, 167
Riddle, Frank, 107
Rivera, Juan, 94
Robinson, Edwin, 130
Roling, B., 145
Roosevelt, Franklin, 77, 78, 114, 123, 147
Royal Hawaiian Band, 200-201
Russia, 23, 141, 142
Ryūkyūs: islands, 10, 12, 17, 23, 24, 27, 29,
    31, 37, 38, 39, 40-41, 226, 235;
    kingdom, 39; language, 39; world-
    views, 30, 32, 35, 39, 41. *See also*
    Okinawa

Sahlins, Marshall, 171
Samos, David, 137
San, 142, 168, 169, 182, 187, 199
Sanders, Bob, 138

Wartime Civil Control Administration, 115

weavers, 87, 97, 99, 112, 129

Westphalia, Peace of (1648), 175

Whilkut, 93

Wilhelm II, 141

Williams, Barbara, 149–150

Williams, Raymond, 51, 215

Winema, 107, 108

Wiyot, 93

Women: people, 8; self-writing, 2, 51; white, 73. *See also* Third World: women

Woodson, Carter, 7, 156

Worcester v. Georgia (1832), 105

workers, 8, 24, 46, 47, 50, 54, 58

world-system, 48, 54, 163, 212

Wovoka, 105

Wright, Ben, 103

Wrigley, C., 183

Yaeyama: island, 27, 35–36, 38, 40, 41, 42

Yamane, Tokio, 117

Yamashita, Tomoyuki, 143

Yamato: damashii, 120, 124; minzoku, 23, 39; race, 22, 23, 24, 32, 33, 40

Yamazato, Katsunori, 226, 227

Yanagita, Kunio, 39

Yayoi, 40

Yonaguni: island, 37, 226; people, 38, 227, 228, 229, 230

Yoneshiro, Megumu, 226, 227

Yoshiyama, 118

Yurok, 93

Zimmern, Alfred, 141

Founded in 1893,
UNIVERSITY OF CALIFORNIA PRESS
publishes bold, progressive books and journals
on topics in the arts, humanities, social sciences,
and natural sciences—with a focus on social
justice issues—that inspire thought and action
among readers worldwide.

The UC PRESS FOUNDATION
raises funds to uphold the press's vital role
as an independent, nonprofit publisher, and
receives philanthropic support from a wide
range of individuals and institutions—and from
committed readers like you. To learn more, visit
ucpress.edu/supportus.

S